Enforcing International Judgments Domestically

AF715635

Nijhoff Law Specials

VOLUME 113

The titles published in this series are listed at *brill.com/nlsp*

Enforcing International Judgments Domestically

The Case of the Inter-American Court of Human Rights

By

Ayla do Vale Alves and Lucas Lixinski

BRILL | NIJHOFF

LEIDEN | BOSTON

Library of Congress Cataloging-in-Publication Data

Names: Lixinski, Lucas author | Vale Alves, Ayla do author
Title: Enforcing international judgments domestically : the case of the Inter-American Court of Human Rights / author Ayla do Vale Alves & Lucas Lixinski.
Description: Leiden ; Boston : Brill Academic Publishers, Inc, 2025. | Series: Nijhoff Law Specials ; volume 113 | Includes bibliographical references and index.
Identifiers: LCCN 2025032119 | ISBN 9789004738065 hardback | ISBN 9789004741829 epub
Subjects: LCSH: Inter-American Court of Human Rights | International human rights courts | International and municipal law | Jurisdiction (International law) | Conflict of laws--Jurisdiction | Judicial assistance | Human rights--America | Human rights--Latin America
Classification: LCC KDZ579.I5 E57 2025 | DDC 341.4/8--DC23/ENG/20250724
LC record available at https://lccn.loc.gov/2025032119

Typeface for the Latin, Greek, and Cyrillic scripts: "Brill". See and download: brill.com/brill-typeface.

ISSN 0924-4549
ISBN 978-90-04-73806-5 (paperback)
ISBN 978-90-04-74182-9 (e-book)
DOI 10.1163/9789004741829

Copyright 2025 by Ayla do Vale Alves and Lucas Lixinski. Published by Koninklijke Brill BV, Plantijnstraat 2, 2321 JC Leiden, The Netherlands.
Koninklijke Brill BV incorporates the imprints Brill, Brill Nijhoff, Brill Schöningh, Brill Fink, Brill mentis, Brill Wageningen Academic, Vandenhoeck & Ruprecht, Böhlau and V&R unipress.
Koninklijke Brill BV reserves the right to protect this publication against unauthorized use. Requests for re-use and/or translations must be addressed to Koninklijke Brill BV via brill.com or copyright.com.
For more information: info@brill.com.

This book is printed on acid-free paper and produced in a sustainable manner.

Contents

Acknowledgments

This small book has been a labor of love for both of us. We first met through a common acquaintance, Dr. Vassilis Tzevelekos, who is Lucas's long-time friend and collaborator from their time together at the European University Institute. Ayla was one of Vassilis's students at the University of Liverpool, and wanted to pursue a Ph.D. in cultural heritage law. Vassilis recommended Ayla reach out to Lucas, and she eventually did her Ph.D. at UNSW Sydney, under the supervision of Lucas, Associate Professor Noam Peleg, and Professor Fleur Johns. So, to Vassilis for the collegiality and introductions, and to Noam and Fleur for the joint intellectual enterprise, our thanks.

Ayla started working on this project as a Research Assistant to what was meant to be an article. But Lucas felt she brought so much to the table that they ought to write it together. The topic was sufficiently far from Ayla's Ph.D. to make it workable within the constraints of a then live supervisory relationship (so Lucas would not run the risk of plagiarizing Ayla's research, mindful of the difference in power dynamics). What then restarted as a joint article gradually morphed into a joint book.

In preparing and workshopping this manuscript, we benefitted tremendously from the input of multiple audiences. We will not list everyone who gave us input by name, lest we leave people out. We duly acknowledge some particularly insightful and original feedback that led to specific changes to our argument in the book itself. But from an institutional perspective we are thankful to David Kosař and Lucas Carlos Lima for organizing dedicated workshops with their research groups where we could discuss this work. We were lucky to have a glimpse into the very special communities they have created and keep alive. Emerson Gabardo also facilitated opportunities to discuss this work as the writing came to a close. We are deeply thankful to audiences in Belo Horizonte (Brazil), Brno (Czechia), Curitiba (Brazil), San Juan (Puerto Rico), and Wellington (Aotearoa/New Zealand) for their input, and for giving us the opportunity to articulate, often as much to each other as to the audience, (parts of) the book's argument.

CHAPTER 1

Introduction

The influence of international law on domestic law, from a judicial perspective, is normally measured discursively. We focus on concepts like judicial dialogue,[1] how international courts' judgments are cited in domestic high court judgments,[2] and ultimately trace the 'influence' of international courts on how domestic judges reason and interact with other (international) judges.[3] While tracing these discursive impacts is useful from a broader jurisprudential perspective (in that it builds arguments for the overall entrenchment of international law domestically),[4] it misses how the judgments of international courts are enforced domestically.

This gap is particularly apparent in relation to international human rights law. These judgments are more likely to be of interest to domestic judges, given the law-making nature of human rights treaties,[5] and the fact that there is a close relationship between domestic fundamental rights in constitutions and international human rights instruments.[6] But the focus on influence over compliance misses a key part of the work of international human rights law: enforcement. By enforcement we mean the implementation of the specific measures of a judgment, so as to turn the remedies or reparations orders into reality, and thereby finalize the case from a procedural standpoint. The enforcement of these judgments, after all, is where one can see the impact

1 Anne-Marie Slaughter. "Judicial Globalization." *Va. J. Int'l L.* 40 (1999): 1103.

2 Diego García-Sayán, The Inter-American Court and Constitutionalism in Latin America, 89 *Texas Law Review* 1835 (2011).

3 René Urueña, Compliance as Transformation: The Inter-American System of Human Rights and Its Impact(s), in Research Handbook on Compliance in International Human Rights Law 225–247, 225 (Rainer Grote, Mariela Morales Antoniazzi, and Davide Paris eds.) (Elgar 2021) [Urueña, Compliance as transformation] (on how the focus on compliance is 'too narrow a framework').

4 For a collection of essays, see Research Handbook on Compliance in International Human Rights Law (Rainer Grote, Mariela Morales Antoniazzi, and Davide Paris eds.) (Elgar 2021).

5 Catherine Brölmann. "Law-Making Treaties: Form and Function in International Law." *Nordic Journal of International Law* 74, no. 3–4 (2005): 383–403.

6 Antonio Cassese, Modern Constitutions and International Law, 192 Collected Courses of the Hague Academy of International Law (1985); see also Lucas Lixinski, *International Human Rights Law and Municipal Law*, in Max Planck Encyclopedia of Comparative Constitutional Law (Rainer Grote, Frauke Lachenmann and Rüdiger Wolfrum eds.) (Oxford University Press 2019).

© AYLA DO VALE ALVES AND LUCAS LIXINSKI, 2025 | DOI:10.1163/9789004741829_002

that the emancipatory language of human rights pledges to the victims of human rights violations. It is when we shift away from working on the field of the jurisprudential discourse, and get closer to tackling the problem of how human rights narrates and potentially betters human lives (at least for those victims).[7]

The enforcement of international human rights judgments domestically is not without its jurisprudential effects either. Enforcement creates a pathway of engagement with international courts' judgments, and one that can extend beyond judicial dialogue to other branches of government (and, in federal systems, levels of government),[8] thus arguably making the influence of human rights (as interpreted by international courts) more pervasive across the domestic board.[9] But enforcement is usually more focused engagement, which is also more difficult to trace, and thus arguably not as strong as the multiple points of contact among courts in the jurisprudential discourse of judicial dialogue.

At the same time, there is a lot to be said about the strength of these discrete points of enforcement, in relation to the plurality of judicial dialogue. To use a sewing image: mapping the influence of international courts' judgments via citations and dialogue is like a Velcro patch: it gives us multiple small points of connection, which can bind two pieces of fabric fairly successfully. The strength of this type of analysis comes from a large number of (usually discrete) engagements. On the other hand, the focus on enforcement is like a stitch. It is only one point of contact between the two fabrics, but it goes deeper, and thus on its own has a lot more force than a single point of dialogue.

The answer to the entrenchment of international human rights in all likelihood is a combination of both, of course. Much like Velcro can get unstuck with a certain force, so can stitches be ripped with a certain force. But combining the two tracks can make the sewing together of the fabrics of international human rights law's emancipatory language and domestic law's enforcement capabilities much stronger than either can do on its own, even if not particularly pretty sewing. This book is devoted to thinking about stitches.

---

7 David Kennedy, *The Dark Sides of Virtue: Reassessing International Humanitarianism* (Princeton University Press, 2005).

8 Among the countries that accept the Inter-American Court's jurisdiction, Argentina, Brazil, and Mexico are federations.

9 Courtney Hillebrecht, *Domestic Politics on International Human Rights Tribunals: The Problem of Compliance 3* (Cambridge University Press, 2014).

CHAPTER 1

Introduction

The influence of international law on domestic law, from a judicial perspective, is normally measured discursively. We focus on concepts like judicial dialogue,[1] how international courts' judgments are cited in domestic high court judgments,[2] and ultimately trace the 'influence' of international courts on how domestic judges reason and interact with other (international) judges.[3] While tracing these discursive impacts is useful from a broader jurisprudential perspective (in that it builds arguments for the overall entrenchment of international law domestically),[4] it misses how the judgments of international courts are enforced domestically.

This gap is particularly apparent in relation to international human rights law. These judgments are more likely to be of interest to domestic judges, given the law-making nature of human rights treaties,[5] and the fact that there is a close relationship between domestic fundamental rights in constitutions and international human rights instruments.[6] But the focus on influence over compliance misses a key part of the work of international human rights law: enforcement. By enforcement we mean the implementation of the specific measures of a judgment, so as to turn the remedies or reparations orders into reality, and thereby finalize the case from a procedural standpoint. The enforcement of these judgments, after all, is where one can see the impact

1 Anne-Marie Slaughter. "Judicial Globalization." *Va. J. Int'l L.* 40 (1999): 1103.

2 Diego García-Sayán, The Inter-American Court and Constitutionalism in Latin America, 89 *Texas Law Review* 1835 (2011).

3 René Urueña, Compliance as Transformation: The Inter-American System of Human Rights and Its Impact(s), in Research Handbook on Compliance in International Human Rights Law 225–247, 225 (Rainer Grote, Mariela Morales Antoniazzi, and Davide Paris eds.) (Elgar 2021) [Urueña, Compliance as transformation] (on how the focus on compliance is 'too narrow a framework').

4 For a collection of essays, see Research Handbook on Compliance in International Human Rights Law (Rainer Grote, Mariela Morales Antoniazzi, and Davide Paris eds.) (Elgar 2021).

5 Catherine Brölmann. "Law-Making Treaties: Form and Function in International Law." *Nordic Journal of International Law* 74, no. 3–4 (2005): 383–403.

6 Antonio Cassese, Modern Constitutions and International Law, 192 Collected Courses of the Hague Academy of International Law (1985); see also Lucas Lixinski, *International Human Rights Law and Municipal Law*, in Max Planck Encyclopedia of Comparative Constitutional Law (Rainer Grote, Frauke Lachenmann and Rüdiger Wolfrum eds.) (Oxford University Press 2019).

© AYLA DO VALE ALVES AND LUCAS LIXINSKI, 2025 | DOI:10.1163/9789004741829_002

that the emancipatory language of human rights pledges to the victims of human rights violations. It is when we shift away from working on the field of the jurisprudential discourse, and get closer to tackling the problem of how human rights narrates and potentially betters human lives (at least for those victims).[7]

The enforcement of international human rights judgments domestically is not without its jurisprudential effects either. Enforcement creates a pathway of engagement with international courts' judgments, and one that can extend beyond judicial dialogue to other branches of government (and, in federal systems, levels of government),[8] thus arguably making the influence of human rights (as interpreted by international courts) more pervasive across the domestic board.[9] But enforcement is usually more focused engagement, which is also more difficult to trace, and thus arguably not as strong as the multiple points of contact among courts in the jurisprudential discourse of judicial dialogue.

At the same time, there is a lot to be said about the strength of these discrete points of enforcement, in relation to the plurality of judicial dialogue. To use a sewing image: mapping the influence of international courts' judgments via citations and dialogue is like a Velcro patch: it gives us multiple small points of connection, which can bind two pieces of fabric fairly successfully. The strength of this type of analysis comes from a large number of (usually discrete) engagements. On the other hand, the focus on enforcement is like a stitch. It is only one point of contact between the two fabrics, but it goes deeper, and thus on its own has a lot more force than a single point of dialogue.

The answer to the entrenchment of international human rights in all likelihood is a combination of both, of course. Much like Velcro can get unstuck with a certain force, so can stitches be ripped with a certain force. But combining the two tracks can make the sewing together of the fabrics of international human rights law's emancipatory language and domestic law's enforcement capabilities much stronger than either can do on its own, even if not particularly pretty sewing. This book is devoted to thinking about stitches.

---

7 David Kennedy, *The Dark Sides of Virtue: Reassessing International Humanitarianism* (Princeton University Press, 2005).

8 Among the countries that accept the Inter-American Court's jurisdiction, Argentina, Brazil, and Mexico are federations.

9 Courtney Hillebrecht, *Domestic Politics on International Human Rights Tribunals: The Problem of Compliance* 3 (Cambridge University Press, 2014).

Given the paucity of conversations about modalities of enforcement of judgments (and, more specifically, their reparations orders), we seek to map the different modalities of enforcement as an under-examined yet important way to strengthen the connections between domestic and international ordering. We map these modalities across different domestic jurisdictions, which call into question the relationship between international and domestic law, and international law and different branches of government. Mapping these modes gives us room for pause and strategy-building.

In this book, we focus on the domestic enforcement and implementation of judgments of the Inter-American Court of Human Rights (IACtHR). We do so for four reasons: first, the IACtHR has the broadest reparations competence among regional human rights courts,[10] meaning that the modalities of implementation and enforcement are richer and give us more varied analytical pathways to bring forth more creative thinking about the possibilities of implementation and enforcement; second, given the number of countries that have accepted the jurisdiction of the IACtHR,[11] and their significant commonalities of language, we have a more contained universe to pursue a fuller mapping than might be possible in other contexts; third, there is no literature that compares different modes of enforcement across Latin America, with only discrete, single-country studies available;[12] fourth, and in relation

10 Jo M Pasqualucci, *The Practice and Procedure of the Inter-American Court of Human Rights* 190 (2nd edn 2012) 190.

11 United Nations Treaties, American Convention on Human Rights 'Pact of San José, Costa Rica', at https://treaties.un.org/pages/showdetails.aspx?objid=08000002800f10e1.

12 See eg, Laura Clérico and Celeste Novelli, Argentina: Strong Linkage between IHRL and Domestic Law, in Research Handbook on Compliance in International Human Rights Law 248–271 (Rainer Grote, Mariela Morales Antoniazzi, and Davide Paris eds.) (Elgar 2021); Thiago Carvalho Borges, O monitoramento e fiscalização das sentenças da Corte Interamericana de Direitos Humanos e a relação hierárquica entre o Direito internacional e o Direito brasileiro, 19(1) *Brazilian Journal of International Law* 320–335 (2022); Flávia Piovesan and Julia Cortez da Cunha Cruz, A Multi-level Process: Compliance with International Human Rights Law in Brazil, in *Research Handbook on Compliance in International Human Rights Law* 272–288 (Rainer Grote, Mariela Morales Antoniazzi, and Davide Paris eds.) (Elgar 2021); Judith Schönsteiner and Marcela Zúñiga, *Chile: Compliance after 'Kind' Reminders, in Research Handbook on Compliance in International Human Rights Law* 289–312 (Rainer Grote, Mariela Morales Antoniazzi, and Davide Paris eds.) (Elgar 2021); Juana Acosta-López and Giovanny Vega-Barbosa, *Compliance with International Human Rights Obligations in Colombia: Assessing the Normative Evolution and Practical Challenges, in Research Handbook on Compliance in International Human Rights Law* 313–328 (Rainer Grote, Mariela Morales Antoniazzi, and Davide Paris eds.) (Elgar 2021); Maria Valentina de Moraes and Mônia Clarissa Hennig Leal, *Acompanhamento nacional do cumprimento das sentenças proferidas pela Corte Interamericana de*

to the third reason, there is already some literature on the topic in relation to the European Court of Human Rights (ECtHR),[13] to which we will refer comparatively,[14] but which also means there is no need to replicate other work.

The variety of modalities we identify across Latin America indicates a messy pluralism of approaches, which reminds us of the need for technique. Technique can help channel pluralism without erasing its vibrancy; it can identify and leverage the bureaucratic avenues available to enact change on the ground, being mindful of their diversity but making use of power-sharing and power-shaping possibilities common to (most) bureaucracies. In this sense, we rely heavily on conceptual literature both on foreign relations law, and on the uses of private international law (or conflict of laws) techniques to pursue public international law projects. These two bodies of literature, and particularly the latter, prompt us to think more broadly about how to reframe our perception of the work international law does, and give us (often neglected) technical tools to cut through the discourse-building impetus of most of the existing literature on the topic. They also help highlight different branches of government and undo the prevailing monolithic view of the state, as we discuss below.

We argue that, if we are serious about the emancipatory possibilities of international human rights law, including through enforcement of the Inter-American Court's judgments, we need to think of it as facing specific technical hurdles. These include the identification of whether the decision to enforce sits with the judiciary, legislative, or executive branches, with the consequent

Direitos Humanos: um olhar para as experiências estrangeiras, 19(3) *Brazilian Journal of International Law* 356–371 (2022) (comparing Costa Rica, Colombia, Mexico, and Peru); Guillermo E Estrada Adán and Patricia Cruz Marín, *Reparation without Access to Justice: The Incomplete Compliance with the Judgments of the Inter-American Court of Human Rights in Mexico, in Research Handbook on Compliance in International Human Rights Law* 329–345 (Rainer Grote, Mariela Morales Antoniazzi, and Davide Paris eds.) (Elgar 2021); Venezuela: From the Structural Non-compliance with Judgments of the IACtHR to the Denunciation of the ACHR and the OAS Charter (a Pending Matter for a Future Democratic State), in Research Handbook on Compliance in International Human Rights Law 346–360 (Rainer Grote, Mariela Morales Antoniazzi, and Davide Paris eds.) (Elgar 2021).

13 See eg, David Kosař et al., *Domestic Judicial Treatment of European Court of Human Rights Case Law: Beyond Compliance* (Routledge, 2020).

14 For some comparative work, see Armin Von Bogdandy, Eduardo Ferrer Mac-Grego, Mariela Morales Antoniazzi, and Pablo Saavedra Alessandri (eds.) *Cumplimiento e impacto de las sentencias de la Corte Interamericana y el Tribunal Europeo de Derechos Humanos: Transformando realidades* (México: Instituto de Estudios Constitucionales del Estado de Querétaro, 2019).

different mechanisms for allocation of resources and authority. It also means thinking about different levels of authority within a state (local, centralized, etc.). Without technique, we end up mired in a separate debate about the influence of international human rights adjudication that does little to address the inequalities that human rights bodies like the IACtHR seek to address on the ground. At the same time, this discussion highlights the need for international human rights bodies to be more proactive on domestic means of enforcement. We argue, thus, that the IACtHR ought to be more directive of states in enforcement.

A few caveats are due here. We focus our discussion on the role of state actors, because we are more interested in the institutional pathways and tools for implementation and enforcement than in the argumentative moves of non-state actors.[15] Also, on terminology: by 'implementation' and 'enforcement' we mean the activities aimed at giving domestic effect to the judgments and findings of international courts within a legal context. 'Enforcement' is terminology more appropriate in domestic judicial contexts (borrowing from private international law),[16] and 'implementation' applies to all branches of government. We acknowledge there are other usages of the terminology elsewhere in the literature,[17] including uses of these terms to mean non-legal actions in legal scholarship on the topic,[18] thus we thought it was important to clarify how we use them in this text. Likewise, we focus primarily on the national government, given the prevalence of unitary states in the region. We believe that these insights, nonetheless, also apply to thinking about 'vertical' separation of powers arrangements among local and national levels of government. That said, we also make references to federalism throughout.

We contribute to debates on the effectiveness of international law and on the relationships between domestic and international law in at least three ways. First, we add an in-depth, thick description of comparative domestic

15 But see, on non-state actors, Christian M De Vos and Ashrakat Mohammed, A Vibrant Interplay: Tools and Systems for Monitoring Human Rights Implementation, in *Research Handbook on Implementation of Human Rights in Practice* 235–254 (Rachel Murray and Debra Long eds.) (Elgar, 2022).

16 Ralf Michaels, *Recognition and Enforcement of Foreign Judgments, Max Planck Encyclopedia of International Law* (2009) [Michaels, Recognition and Enforcement].

17 Rachel Murray and Debra Long, Introduction to the Research Handbook on Implementation of Human Rights in Practice, in *Research Handbook on Implementation of Human Rights in Practice* 1–15, 2–3 (Rachel Murray and Debra Long eds.) (Elgar, 2022).

18 Andreas von Staden, 'Implementation and Compliance,' in *Research Handbook on Implementation of Human Rights in Practice* 17–35, 31 (Rachel Murray and Debra Long eds.) (Elgar, 2022).

practice across an entire continent that has to date never been attempted. Beyond the direct benefit for readers in the Americas, these comparative insights also yield useful parameters to think through the impact of international courts in a range of domestic and regional settings, by abstracting from specific jurisdictions to instead ask questions that are of use to international institutions. This angle benefits states (as the implementers of those judgments) directly, by offering means to understand their own roles in these processes and facilitate compliance.

Second, from the perspective of international institutions, what we do here has the obvious benefit of potentially facilitating compliance. Higher compliance rates increase the legitimacy and impact of international institutions, and allow them to have the transformational impact they seek to have. More deeply, however, this book can offer international institutions incentives (and guidance) on how to design remedies that can be implemented more effectively. Note here that we are not suggesting that these human rights bodies bow down to state pressure to order less extensive reparations; rather, what we are saying is that these bodies ought to think more proactively, and spell out to the state, how to implement their orders. Understanding the potentials and pitfalls of domestic enforcement allows the Court to be savvier in its design of reparations orders.

Third, no one has to date used scholarship on private international law applied to public international law, or on foreign relations law, to think deeply about the enforcement or effectiveness of international law, or even to think about international human rights law. This book's deployment of those bodies of scholarship adds heft, urgency, and a sophisticated toolkit with which to create pathways for better enforcement of international legal judgments. On the international human rights law side, these bodies of scholarship can sharpen the stakes of the problem of enforcement for the two traditional poles of a human rights claim (states and alleged victims), demystifying their interests and thus offering international human rights courts incentives and a toolkit with which to further their own transformational possibilities, impact, and legitimacy.

To pursue our thesis, the book proceeds as follows: first, we further ground the conversation about implementation and enforcement of international human rights courts' judgments, in reference to the literature to which we alluded above. Next, we build a typology of implementation and enforcement in Latin America, across 18 of the 20 countries that accept the jurisdiction of the IACtHR.[19] After that typology, we return to key issues of the legitimacy of

19 We exclude Suriname and Haiti, due to lack of access to sufficient primary materials.

international courts in domestic contexts, how implementation and enforcement impact strategy-building for human rights advocates, and discuss some possible lessons for our thinking about the relationships between international courts more broadly and domestic jurisdictions, as well as generally the intersections between domestic and international law. Concluding remarks follow, pointing to directions for further research.

CHAPTER 2

Implementation and Enforcement of International (Human Rights) Judgments

When one speaks of implementing and enforcing the judgments of international (human rights) courts domestically, one means specifically the reparations ordered by the judgment in question. Yet those reparations orders are an often-neglected aspect of the puzzle, which, as we suggested above, tends to ignore the impacts of human rights law on specific victims. This chapter discusses the usual focus of our conversations about the interactions between international human rights judgments and domestic institutions, showing that the field's focus tends to be rather one-sided, and more preoccupied with jurisprudential accretion than actual on-the-ground implementation. We in the field focus on softer compliance as a proxy for international (human rights) law's ability to create global ordering.[1] Instead of focusing on reparations, we in the field tend to focus on substantive law outcomes, and neglect the tangible transformative potentials of human rights litigation in favor of discursive effects. In other words, we choose large patches of relatively easier Velcro over the more laborious and less visible work of stitching as a pathway to ensure domestic adherence to international human rights standards. After unpacking this issue, we shift the conversation towards the mandates for reparations in international human rights adjudication, to set up new ways to map the interactions between international human rights judgments and domestic institutions. These new ways, we suggest, necessitate reimagining our analytical toolkits and embracing the techniques of private international law, alongside the growing field of foreign affairs law.

We use these two bodies of scholarship for different yet complementary reasons. First, foreign affairs law helps us demystify the functioning of the state more broadly, and to see it in an international legal context beyond the monolith to which international lawyers have become accustomed (and that some international law demands us to imagine, as we discuss below). Second, foreign affairs law enables us to see politics as a series of politically charged bureaucratic moves, in which state administrators need to create technical

1 Kal Raustiala and Anne-Marie Slaughter, *International Law, International Relations and Compliance, in Handbook of International Relations* 553 (Walter Carlsnaes, Thomas Risse and Beth A Simmons eds.) (Sage, 2002).

© AYLA DO VALE ALVES AND LUCAS LIXINSKI, 2025 | DOI:10.1163/9789004741829_003

pathways to implement a political decision. Third, the conflict of laws scholarship, as we discuss below, allows us to also suspend politics to see international law, particularly through a dispute-centric prism, as a series of technical moves, at least in terms of the register in which legal decision-makers speak them. Fourth, the conflict of laws style is particularly helpful in better understanding the relationships of courts qua courts, because that is the basis of enforcement in private international law. Finally, both bodies of scholarship offer a sophisticated quasi-outsider perspective to the operation of international courts, intersecting domestic and international law with a view of facilitating the impact of international law while aware of the nuances of domestic resistance.

1 Farsightedness in Implementation and Compliance

The question about the implementation and enforcement of international human rights judgments is very different to the questions we normally ask about the influence of international human rights courts in domestic law. The latter largely sidestep the conversation about reparations and focus on substantive law standards modifying the positions of domestic actors (particularly in the judiciary). The focus on substantive law yields greater insights for the development of jurisprudence in certain areas, and to the development of stronger standards for the protection of human rights and litigation for the establishment of violations of human rights.

These insights, however, focus on the declaration of a violation as an end in itself, and focus more on future cases than on the cases already decided. The focus on declaratory judgments seems to respond to the limitations of the European Court of Human Rights (ECtHR) system, which, as we discuss below, has a much narrower mandate for reparations, and considers the finding of a violation a key (and often the only) reparation. Because the ECtHR is the oldest international human rights court with binding jurisdiction, it tends to set the tone for the conversation about other international human rights adjudicatory and quasi-adjudicatory bodies as well. In other words, its narrower reparations competence hinders the conversation about implementation and enforcement across all of international human rights law. In relation to the focus on future cases, it is a worthwhile emphasis from a litigator's perspective (and that of the scholar seeking to aid impending litigation and help not only diagnose the current state of the field, but also shape its future direction), but it again neglects those people and peoples already recognized as victims of human rights violations in favor of a hypothetical (even if unfortunately likely) future victim. This future focus brings an epistemological consequence in that we fail to track (let alone advocate for) human rights law's purported promotion of change and transformation. Instead, we assume that the international court's work is finished the moment the judgment is announced, and the work for human rights lies in the next case, rather than seeing through the present one (a move which is not unlike what we often see in domestic law).[2] This phenomenon may be described as a diagnosis of farsightedness of international human rights law: in aiming to shape the future, we miss out on the detail of what is happening now. And, in focusing on the state of the field, we lose sight of the problem, as David Kennedy famously said.[3]

This farsightedness has a number of consequences, some of which speak directly to the kind of analysis we undertake in the field, therefore having profound epistemic consequences. Notably, international human rights scholars and practitioners alike, when they speak of the influence of international human rights courts on domestic law and institutions, tend to focus on matters of judicial dialogue or softer engagement of different branches of government over strict enforcement.[4] Perhaps frustrated by the apparent lack of compliance with human rights judgments, scholars instead turn to softer mapping of how international human rights judgments are cited domestically as supporting (never controlling or binding) authority to shift domestic legal argumentation.[5] Even scholarship specifically dedicated to the issue of compliance reframes compliance to mean overall influence.[6]

2 Robert Howse and Ruti Teitel, Beyond Compliance: Rethinking Why International Law Really Matters, 1 *Global Policy* 128, 128 (2010).

3 Kennedy, cit.

4 See eg Nicola Wenzel, Under the Watchful eyes of the Federal Constitutional Court: compliance in Germany, in *Research Handbook on Compliance in International Human Rights Law* 75–94 (Rainer Grote, Mariela Morales Antoniazzi, and Davide Paris eds.) (Elgar 2021) (focusing on the judiciary); Christina Binder and Philipp Janig, The ECHR as a Constitutional Rights Catalogue: Compliance in Austria, in *Research Handbook on Compliance in International Human Rights Law* 42–57 (Rainer Grote, Mariela Morales Antoniazzi, and Davide Paris eds.) (Elgar 2021) (focusing on all branches of government).

5 Cf Ausra Padskocimaite, *Assessing Russia's responses to judgments of the European Court of Human Rights: From Compliance to Defiance, in Research Handbook on Compliance in International Human Rights Law* 136–182, 153–154 (Rainer Grote, Mariela Morales Antoniazzi, and Davide Paris eds.) (Elgar 2021) (on how domestic judges, in the even of incompatibility between ECtHR case law and domestic law, simply state the international law to be inapplicable, without any reasons).

6 Giorgio Repetto, Changing Me Softly? Actors, Tools and Techniques of International Human Rights Compliance in Italy, in *Research Handbook on Compliance in International Human Rights Law* 121–135, 128 (Rainer Grote, Mariela Morales Antoniazzi, and Davide Paris eds.)

This scholarship, of course, has much to offer. Through this type of mapping, the influence of a judgment can happen in multiple places at once, across different countries (in the sense that a domestic court can cite jurisprudence of the international court that does not involve that country directly).[7] It can shift the interpretation of domestic law, and offer judges strapped by entrenched domestic politics and legal interpretations sources of authority and legitimacy for more progressive jurisprudence.[8] But it focuses primarily on substantive law and declaratory judgments, largely dismissing the potential of reparations and the tracking of compliance with specific judgments.

The literature on reparations is somewhat complicit with this trend, by being largely descriptive and missing the point that reparations are a key site for the influence of international human rights law, especially broader measures of reparations that change institutions and order guarantees of non-repetition.[9] Further, reparations can be test labs for future substantive law developments, as the IACtHR itself has shown in its development of the recognition of group rights under the American Convention, for instance.[10] At the same time, however, noting and describing that reparations are ordered by the international court, which is where most of the scholarship in the field sits, is not enough. Simply describing reparations replicates the paths of the focus on substantive law: it has an eye on the next case, and prizes declaratory state-

(Elgar 2021). In the specific context of the Inter-American Court, see Viviana Krsticevic and René Urueña, 'Transformative Impact of the Inter-American Human Rights System: A Methodology to Think beyond Compliance', in *The Impact of the Inter-American Human Rights System*, ed. Armin von Bogdandy, Flávia Piovesan, Eduardo Ferrer MacGregor, and Mariela Morales Antoniazzi (Oxford University Press, 2024), 584–602.

7 García-Sayán, cit.

8 Alice Donald, Compliance in the UK in the 'age of subsidiarity', in *Research Handbook on Compliance in International Human Rights Law* 202–223, 220 (Rainer Grote, Mariela Morales Antoniazzi, and Davide Paris eds.) (Elgar 2021); and Davide Paris, *Judicial Compliance in the Regional Human Rights Systems, in Research Handbook on Compliance in International Human Rights Law* 465–484, 465 (Rainer Grote, Mariela Morales Antoniazzi, and Davide Paris eds.) (Elgar 2021).

9 Thomas M Antkowiak, 'Remedial Approaches to Human Rights Violations: The Inter-American Court of Human Rights and Beyond', 46 *Columbia Journal Transnational Law* 351, 372 (2008); Douglass Cassel, 'The Expanding Scope and Impact of Repatriations Awarded by the Inter-American Court of Human Rights', 7 *Revista do Instituto Brasileiro de Direitos Humanos* 91, 99 (2006).

10 See eg Lucas Lixinski, *Rights of Indigenous Peoples – Collective Rights – Recognition of Legal Personality – Right to Communal Property – Conflict between Nature Reserves and Indigenous Land – Free, Prior, and Informed Consultation – Environmental Impact – Restitution and Reparation*, 111(1) *American Journal of International Law* 147–154 (2017).

ments (in this case, of what a reparation ought to be) over actual change on the ground. The influence of reparations lies in their actual enforcement.

This focus on influence and dialogue also misses that it is possibly the lack of focus on compliance that leads to lower compliance. The political will for compliance with international judgments in any context relies heavily on reputational costs.[11] If no one is paying attention to enforcement and compliance beyond general statements about the lack thereof, that is one lever human rights advocates and scholars fail to pull to shift state attitudes. Further, the lack of attention to and critique of the actual tools and pathways available for enforcement and compliance also hinders (or at least fails to aid) their development. Other studies on the time needed for compliance also excuse the (lack of) means for compliance and simply ask for more patience instead, which victims may not be willing or able to grant.[12] In many ways, though, valuable as the focus on overall influence via judicial dialogue is, it is a pathway to further promote transformation via international human rights law that, ironically, gets in the way of more tangible mechanisms to engender that very transformation.

This conversation about what counts as compliance and the influence or enforcement of international human rights judgments is, therefore, mired in obstacles. The focus on substantive law over reparations, and on overall influence over enforcement, create a farsightedness that undermines the emancipatory promise of international human rights law for the victims of rights violations. The promotion of the transformative effects of these judgments is thus predicated on upending the way we read reparations in international human rights law. To reimagine reparations and the role they can play, it is important to pay attention to what reparations mandates exist, and how they are exercised by international human rights institutions themselves. While the primary focus of our inquiry is the Inter-American System, it is also worth mentioning the other regional human rights systems as points of comparison for the transformative stakes of international human rights judgment enforcement.

11 Beth A Simmons, *Mobilizing for Human Rights: International Law in Domestic Politics 118* (Cambridge University Press 2009).

12 Aníbal Pérez-Liñán, Kelly Morrison, and Luis L Schenoni, 'Addressing Conceptual Challenges: Compliance and Impact', in *The Impact of the Inter-American Human Rights System*, ed. Armin von Bogdandy, Flávia Piovesan, Eduardo Ferrer Mac-Gregor, and Mariela Morales Antoniazzi (Oxford University Press, 2024), 564–583.

1.1 *Reparations Mandates*

The IACtHR has the widest and best-established competence for reparations among regional human rights courts. It focuses on the principle of *restitutio in integrum*,[13] or the legal fiction that it is the IACtHR's duty to return victims to the status quo prior to the violation of their rights. Since it is in fact impossible to do so, the IACtHR takes advantage of its broad competence in the American Convention, which says that in the event of a finding of a violation of a right the IACtHR has the power to order 'that the consequences of the measure or situation that constituted the breach of such right or freedom be remedied and that fair compensation be paid to the injured party.'[14] In the IACtHR practice, there is no difference between individualized and systemic reparations, because of the breadth of this mandate. De rigueur, the IACtHR adds a section on 'guarantees of non-repetition' to all its reparations orders, which are orders for the state to transform itself so that similar violations do not occur again in the future. This activity is in marked contrast, for instance, to the European Court of Human Rights, which, until the pilot judgment procedure, only offered individualized reparations orders. The ECtHR, in fact, still treats individualized and systemic reparations as very separate from one another.

Another important piece of the IACtHR's reparations mandate is Article 2 of the American Convention, which determines that states must adjust their legislation to the requirements of the treaty.[15] This provision gives the IACtHR a clear mandate to test and make determinations on the compatibility of domestic law (even constitutions) with the American Convention, and to order states to wholesale change those laws when the IACtHR finds them to have violated human rights. Article 2 is a fairly unique provision to the ACHR compared to other human rights treaties, and bolsters the Court's reparations mandate and practice. It can present a challenge for judiciary-centric enforcement of international court judgments, since it requires parliamentary involvement. Conversely, though, it is a provision that directly involves the legislative branch in the enforcement of an international judgment.

Deploying this mandate, from its very first judgment on reparations, the IACtHR set the tone for a very broad competence grounded on general inter-

13 I/A Court H.R., Case of Velásquez Rodríguez v. Honduras. Reparations and Costs. Judgment of July 21, 1989. Series C No. 7 [Velásquez Rodríguez], para. 26.

14 American Convention on Human Rights, Article 63(1).

15 American Convention on Human Rights, Article 2.

national law,[16] equity,[17] and the American Convention itself.[18] Importantly, the IACtHR also found early on that the American Convention's mandate 'does not refer to or limit the ability to ensure the effectiveness of the means of reparation available under the internal law of the State Party responsible for the violation, so it is not limited by the defects, imperfections or deficiencies of national law, but functions independently of it.'[19]

Note in this quote the reference to the 'defects, imperfections or deficiencies' of domestic law, and how the Court is giving itself carte blanche to ignore domestic law in favor of its idealized version of remedies. This license to operate in disregard of domestic law derives from the IACtHR's inherent mistrust of states upon whom it is passing judgment, at the core of its raison d'être. It also means, however, that the Court from the very beginning opted to be unaware of how its orders were to be implemented, and unconcerned with the state's institutional ability to comply. In the same way that it disregards domestic law, it disregards domestic power- and competence-sharing arrangements, whether driven by federalism or separation of powers. The Court makes itself blind to the state it seeks to transform, becoming a boss that demands results but gives no guidance on means.

Doing so, we suggest, has undermined the IACtHR in the long run, as it created a position in which the Court seeks to oversee compliance with its own judgments, but gives no guidance to the state on what compliance would look like. The IACtHR's ordinary inclusion of a section on modalities of compliance in its judgments does not solve the issue, because it speaks to the specifics of how to pay compensation, for instance, but does not direct the state apparatus by allocating authority for the enforcement of specific orders.

To better understand this stalemate, it might be useful to borrow from a trope in psychology, the bystander effect. The bystander effect, although based on a discredited factual account,[20] still has great purchase in psychology, and suggests that, when there is a situation that requires urgent and immediate action, people are not likely to act unless they are individually

16 Velásquez Rodríguez, cit., para. 25.

17 Id., para. 27.

18 Id., para. 29.

19 Id., para. 30.

20 Manning, Rachel, Mark Levine, and Alan Collins. 'The Kitty Genovese Murder and the Social Psychology of Helping: The Parable of the 38 Witnesses,' *American Psychologist* 62.6 (2007): 555.

directed to do so.[21] In the IACtHR's context, by saying it will disregard domestic law and institutions, the Court renders all state institutions bystanders, none of whom then feel the particular need to take the lead on implementation. What the Court frames as a disregard (and mistrust) of domestic law has the effect of deference to sovereignty (and unproductive deference at that), the opposite of what the IACtHR judges probably intended.

This deference to sovereignty can seem intentional, too, based on the tone (or lack) of guidance on enforcement in reparations orders. A more generic reparations order gives states the leeway to implement those orders however they deem fit. Doing so might give the IACtHR a greater sense of legitimacy. However, as we discuss further in Chapter 4, it is unlikely in our view that the IACtHR cares much for deference to states, or protecting state sovereignty, as a source of legitimacy. Further, international human rights law is founded on the idea of piercing the veil of state sovereignty,[22] particularly from the perspective of an institution as committed to the internationalization of human rights law as the IACtHR. It is thus unlikely that respect for sovereignty is a serious consideration. The very language of 'defects, imperfections or deficiencies' does not signal respect for a country's domestic situation – quite the contrary, arguably.

Since this first judgment on reparations, the IACtHR used its broad mandate in this area to order a wide range of reparations measures. These include: costs; compensation for tangible harm as well as emotional harm; changes to domestic law (including national constitutions);[23] the construction of memorials;[24] the creation of development funds;[25] scholarships in the name of victims;[26] land titling;[27] the publication of parts of its judgments in national

21 Fischer, Peter, et al. 'The Bystander-Effect: A Meta-analytic Review on Bystander Intervention in Dangerous and Non-dangerous Emergencies,' *Psychological Bulletin* 137.4 (2011): 517.

22 For one of the strongest proponents of this idea, who was also Judge and President of the IACtHR for a decade, see Antônio A. Cançado Trindade, *International Law for Humankind: Towards a New Jus Gentium* (Martinus Nijhoff, 2010).

23 I/A Court H.R., Case of 'The Last Temptation of Christ' (Olmedo Bustos et al.) v. Chile. Merits, Reparations and Costs. Judgment of February 5, 2001. Series C No. 73.

24 I/A Court H.R., Case of the Mapiripán Massacre v. Colombia. Merits, Reparations and Costs. Judgment of September 15, 2005. Series C No. 134.

25 I/A Court H.R., Case of the Saramaka People. v. Suriname. Preliminary Objections, Merits, Reparations, and Costs. Judgment of November 28, 2007 Series C No. 172.

26 I/A Court H.R., Case of Myrna Mack Chang v. Guatemala. Merits, Reparations and Costs. Judgment of November 25, 2003. Series C No. 101.

27 I/A Court H.R., Case of the Sawhoyamaxa Indigenous Community v. Paraguay. Merits, Reparations and Costs. Judgment of March 29, 2006. Series C No. 146.

newspapers of wide circulation; the guaranteeing of free basic education across an entire country;[28] awareness-raising campaigns to create a culture of respect towards LGBTIQ+ people,[29] or enhance environmental rights,[30] or on the best interests of the child principle,[31] across the entire public service (among many other areas of human rights law); that people who lost their jobs be reinstated in them;[32] the staying of death sentences;[33] the retraining of police forces;[34] obligations to reopen police investigations and domestic cases (even those that had been declared final by national high courts);[35] the creation of truth commissions;[36] and the obligation to investigate, prosecute, and punish individuals responsible for human rights violations.[37]

Further, the IACtHR does take action to facilitate and monitor the enforcement of its judgments. On the former, in every judgment the IACtHR adds a section on 'Method of Compliance,' 'Terms of Compliance,' or 'Modalities of Compliance.' These sections allow the Court to outline how the state ought to pay the financial compensation owed, set deadlines for some of the other reparations, and to declare that it will oversee compliance with the judgment via periodic report.

The IACtHR then oversees compliance with its own judgments via hearings and binding resolutions assessing compliance, which creates an additional

28 I/A Court H.R., Case of the Girls Yean and Bosico v. Dominican Republic. Preliminary Objections, Merits, Reparations and Costs. Judgment of September 8, 2005. Series C No. 130.

29 I/A Court H.R., Case of Olivera Fuentes v. Peru. Preliminary Objections, Merits, Reparations and Costs. Judgment of February 4, 2023. Series C No. 484.

30 I/A Court H.R., Case of Baraona Bray v. Chile. Preliminary Objections, Merits, Reparations and Costs. Judgment of November 24, 2022. Series C No. 481.

31 I/A Court H.R., Case of Fornerón and daughter v. Argentina. Merits, Reparations and Costs. Judgment of April 27, 2012. Series C No. 242.

32 I/A Court H.R., Case of Atala Riffo and daughters v. Chile. Merits, Reparations and Costs. Judgment of February 24, 2012. Series C No. 239.

33 I/A Court H.R., Case of DaCosta Cadogan v. Barbados. Preliminary Objections, Merits, Reparations, and Costs. Judgment of September 24, 2009. Series C No. 204.

34 I/A Court H.R., Case of González et al. ('Cotton Field') v. Mexico. Preliminary Objection, Merits, Reparations and Costs. Judgment of November 16, 2009. Series C No. 205.

35 I/A Court H.R., Case of Gomes Lund et al. ('Guerrilha do Araguaia') v. Brazil. Preliminary Objections, Merits, Reparations, and Costs. Judgment of November 24, 2010. Series C No. 219.

36 Id.

37 I/A Court H.R., Case of Gonzalez Medina and family v. Dominican Republic. Preliminary Objections, Merits, Reparations and Costs. Judgment of February 27, 2012. Series C No. 240.

mechanism for enforcement.[38] This mechanism was developed by the Court itself over two decades ago, partly in response to its growth in importance. It came as part of a series of reforms to the Court's rules of procedure that also allowed, for instance, for victims to make representations directly to the Court (even if the Commission still needs to bring the case and lead it, as per the terms of the American Convention). These reforms were largely driven by the late Cançado Trindade, then IACtHR President and a towering figure in human rights law in the Americas and worldwide.[39] While the Court developed these mechanisms in response to the lack of action by the Organization of American States (OAS) to leverage its powers (and for member states to put pressure on each other) for human rights compliance, the Court kept requesting that the OAS political organs to be more involved in compliance.[40] There was even a push for a Protocol to the American Convention to, among other things, include a specific provision on implementation of judgments at the domestic level, rendering clear treaty law the argument that lack of compliance is in itself a new violation of the American Convention that could be brought to the Court (a proposition thus far untested in the Court's jurisprudence), particularly as a denial of access to justice.[41]

---

38 On the compliance mechanism overall, see Lucas Lixinski, *Mechanisms of Systemic Change in Regional Human Rights Courts: Swinging the Pendulum between Legitimacy and Impact*, 8(1) *Cambridge International Law Journal* 60–83 (2019) [Lixinski, *Mechanisms*]; and Cecilia M Bailliet, Procedure for monitoring compliance with judgments and other decisions: Inter-American Court of Human Rights (IACtHR), *Max Planck Encyclopedia of International Procedural Law* (2021). On the compliance hearings specifically, see Edward Pérez and Clara Sandoval, Compliance Hearings before the Inter-American Court of Human Rights: Unleashing the Dynamics of Implementation, in *Research Handbook on Implementation of Human Rights in Practice* 1–15, 2–3 (Rachel Murray and Debra Long eds.) (Elgar, 2022). And on how this mechanism can imply a reinterpretation of the judgment in some key aspects, see Lucas Lima, Interpretation of Judgments: Inter-American Court of Human Rights (IACtHR), *Max Planck Encyclopedia of International Procedural Law* (2022).

39 Antônio Augusto Cançado Trindade, *Informe: Bases para um Proyecto de Protocolo de la Convención Americana sobre Derechos Humanos, para Fortalecer su Mecanismo de Protección* (Corte Interamericana de Derechos Humanos, 2001).

40 Consejo Permanente de la Organización de los Estados Americanos, 'Presentación del Presidente de la Corte Interamericana de Derechos Humanos, Juez Antônio A Cançado Trindade, ante el Consejo Permanente de Organización de los Estados Americanos (OEA): '*El Derecho de Acceso a la Justicia Internacional y las Condiciones para su Realización en el Sistema Interamericano de Derechos Humanos*' (Washington, DC, 16 de octubre de 2002)', OAS Doc. OEA/Ser.G CP/doc.3654/02 (17 October 2002), at 14–18.

41 Cançado Trindade, *Informe*, cit., at 48–49.

Periodically, states, the Inter-American Commission on Human Rights (IACHR), and the representatives of victims make submissions to the Court as to the reparations orders with which the state has complied or failed to comply. On rare occasions, the Court will conduct on-site visits to gather compliance information itself.[42] The Court works with the state to advance compliance efforts with outstanding measures, towards an eventual declaration of full compliance. While these are meant to be for each individual judgment, recently the IACtHR has started merging some of these, when they refer to comparable factual backgrounds and are against the same state, to facilitate compliance with systemic change reparations.

The ECtHR's competence, in contrast, primarily focuses on compensation and just satisfaction (the latter being normally just the finding of a violation in the ECtHR's practice).[43] In theory, the ECtHR has the competence for *restitutio in integrum* as well, but the ECtHR seldom deploys this faculty.[44] At times, it is up to the Council of Europe's Committee of Ministers, in overseeing compliance with the judgment (what in the European system is called 'execution'),[45] to flesh out non-compensatory measures to make reparations to a violation of the European Convention.[46] While this task was originally cast as 'purely supervisory,' it has over time become more proactive.[47] Within the ECtHR, it was with the creation of the pilot judgment procedure that the ECtHR moved to ordering reparations of a broader, more systemic nature,[48] but even those seem to be more restricted to changes in domestic law and

42 As described by Krsticevic and Urueña, cit., at 592.

43 European Convention on Human Rights, Article 41.

44 Loukis G. Loucaides, Reparation for Violations of Human Rights under the European Convention and Restitutio in Integrum, E.H.R.L.R. 2008, 2, 182–192.

45 Elisabeth Lambert, Execution of Judgment: European Court of Human Rights (ECtHR), *Max Planck Encyclopedia of International Procedural Law* (2018); and Başak Bağlayan, Communications Concerning Execution: European Court of Human Rights (ECtHR), *Max Planck Encyclopedia of International Procedural Law* (2020).

46 Gisella Gori, 'Compliance', in The Oxford Handbook of International Human Rights Law (Dinah Shelton ed.) (Oxford University Press, 2013) 893–920, at 906–907. For a comparison of the three regional human rights courts on this matter, and also with reference to other international courts, see Loris Marotti, Remedies Against Non-Compliance with International Judgments, *Max Planck Encyclopedia of International Procedural Law* (2021).

47 Raffaela Kunz, Securing the Survival of the System: The Legal and Institutional Architecture to Supervise Compliance with the ECtHR's Judgments, in *Research Handbook on Compliance in International Human Rights Law* 12–41, 15 (Rainer Grote, Mariela Morales Antoniazzi, and Davide Paris eds.) (Elgar 2021).

48 Haider, Dominik, *The Pilot-Judgment Procedure of the European Court of Human Rights*. Martinus Nijhoff Publishers, 2013.

policy only, which is significantly narrower than the range of reparations orders coming from the IACtHR.[49] Compensation in money allows the ECtHR to boast a high rate of compliance and enforcement. It is an illusory good story, though, for two reasons: first, monetary compensation is the easiest form of reparation with which to comply; second, it produces little to no systemic impacts domestically.[50]

The African Court of Human and Peoples' Rights has the broadest competence, by combining elements from both the Inter-American and European Systems (but relying primarily on the former).[51] The Protocol that creates this court authorizes it to 'make appropriate orders to remedy the violation, including the payment of fair compensation or reparation.'[52] The African Court has interpreted this competence to mean *restitutio in integrum*, like in the IACtHR.[53] This competence is being further widened in the practice of the African Court as well,[54] to even include a mechanism akin to pilot judgments,[55] and to offer measures like compensation, new trials,[56] changes to

49 Francesca Capone, *A Reflection on the Transformative Potential of Reparations: The Approach of the Regional Human Rights Courts*, 12 Hum. Rts. & Int'l Legal Discourse 190 (2018).

50 Veronica Fikfak, Compliance and Compensation: Money as a Currency of Human Rights, in *Research Handbook on Implementation of Human Rights in Practice* 98–117 (Rachel Murray and Debra Long eds.) (Elgar, 2022) (also showing that the ECtHR applies a 'discount' in the amount of compensation for repeat violations by states, which further undermines the potential of financial reparations to induce sustained change).

51 Frans Viljoen, Forging a Credible African System of Human Rights Protection by Overcoming State Resistance and Institutional Weakness: Compliance at a Crossroads, in *Research Handbook on Compliance in International Human Rights Law* 362–390, 382 (Rainer Grote, Mariela Morales Antoniazzi, and Davide Paris eds.) (Elgar 2021).

52 Protocol to the African Charter on Human and Peoples' Rights on the Establishment of an African Court on Human and Peoples' Rights, Article 27(1).

53 African Court of Human and Peoples' Rights, Application 028/2020 – Houngue Eric Noudehouenou v. Republic of Benin, Judgments (Merits and reparations), 01 Dec 2022.

54 On general trends in their jurisprudence, see John M Mbaku, The Emerging Jurisprudence of the African Human Rights Court and the Protection of Human Rights in Africa, 56(1) *Vanderbilt Journal of Transnational Law*, 367–434 (2023).

55 Kevin Sánchez Toro. (2021). The Right to Reparations in the Contentious Process before the African Court on Human and Peoples' Rights: A Comparative Analysis on Account of the Revised Rules of Court. *African Human Rights Law Journal*, 21(2), 812–835. https://dx.doi.org/10.17159/1996-2096/2021/v21n2a32

56 African Court of Human and Peoples' Rights, Application 052/2016 – Marthine Christian Msuguri v. United Republic of Tanzania, Judgments (Merits and reparations), 01 Dec 2022.

domestic law,[57] and others. That the African Court addresses 'situations,' and not just cases involving individuals, is also partly responsible for its very broad mandate on reparations.[58]

This wide competence within the African system is mired by non-compliance issues,[59] not unlike what happens in the Americas.[60] The wider the reparations competence, the harder it is to enforce each court's judgments, and ensure compliance. These regional courts are well aware of the relatively low rate of compliance with certain aspects of their judgments (particularly those that go beyond the payment of compensation or basic satisfaction measures like acknowledgments of responsibility and publications of parts of judgments). The IACtHR, in particular, monitors compliance with its own judgments.[61] At the same time, however, and despite their penchant for ordering multiple institutional design measures as forms of reparation,[62] they seem to be disinterested in the specific dynamics of enforcement of judgments, and on making specific orders in that area. The IACtHR seems more interested in preserving its independence or legitimacy, and reinforcing its mistrust of states.

1.2 *Domestic Entrenchment Doctrines*

The IACtHR compensates for this lack of interest in the institutional design of domestic pathways for enforcement in other ways. Specifically, the IACtHR

57 African Court of Human and Peoples' Rights, Application 012/2019 – Ghati Mwita v. United Republic of Tanzania, Judgments (Merits and reparations), 01 Dec 2022.

58 Frans Viljoen, cit., 387.

59 Frans Viljoen, 'Forging a Credible African System of Human Rights Protection by Overcoming State Resistance and Institutional Weakness: Compliance at a Crossroads', in *Research Handbook on Compliance in International Human Rights Law* 362–390 (Rainer Grote, Mariela Morales Antoniazzi, and Davide Paris eds.) (Elgar 2021); Debra Long, 'Compliance with International Human Rights Decisions in Cameroon: Mechanisms in Place but a Lack of Transparency', in *Research Handbook on Compliance in International Human Rights Law* 391–406 (Rainer Grote, Mariela Morales Antoniazzi, and Davide Paris eds.) (Elgar 2021); and Kounkinè Augustin Somé, 'A Pick and Pay Approach: Burkina Faso's Compliance with International Human Rights Law', in *Research Handbook on Compliance in International Human Rights Law* 407–423 (Rainer Grote, Mariela Morales Antoniazzi, and Davide Paris eds.) (Elgar 2021).

60 René Urueña, 'Compliance as transformation: The Inter-American System of Human Rights and Its Impact(s)', in *Research Handbook on Compliance in International Human Rights Law* 225–247 (Rainer Grote, Mariela Morales Antoniazzi, and Davide Paris eds.) (Elgar 2021).

61 Lixinski, 'Mechanisms', cit.

62 David Kosař and Lucas Lixinski, *Domestic Judicial Design by Regional Human Rights courts*, 109(4) *The American Journal of International Law* 713–760 (2015).

has developed the doctrine of *conventionality control*, through which it asserts that domestic authorities, in undertaking their activities that intersect with human rights, must take into account not only the American Convention (which they already needed to do by virtue of Article 2, as indicated above), but also the interpretation of the American Convention by the IACtHR in any cases (whether or not involving the specific country). In other words, the activities of public authorities must be guided by the work and substantive jurisprudence of the IACtHR, even if these same authorities are reluctant to implement reparations measures. Initially, conventionality control was aimed at domestic judicial authorities as key allies of the IACtHR (first generation),[63] but, over time, the IACtHR expanded it to cover all domestic authorities, in any branch or level of government (second generation).[64] This doctrine helps external forces impose themselves and shape domestic foreign relations law,[65] this being an important lever to mobilize different branches of government, which we discuss further below. One of the effects of this doctrine is that, even when it applies to all branches of government, it can still fore-

63 For more in-depth analysis of this notion and its evolution see Ariel A Dulitzky, *El Impacto del Control de Convencionalidad. ¿Un Cambio de Paradigma en el Sistema Interamericano de Derechos Humanos?* in *Tratado de los Derechos Constitucionales* 533 (Julio Cesar Rivera ed. 2014); Christina Binder, *The Prohibition of Amnesties by the Inter-American Court of Human Rights*, 12 *German Law Journal* 1203 (2011); Oswaldo Ruiz-Chiriboga, *The Conventionality Control: Examples of (Un)successful Experiences in Latin America*, 3(1–2) *Inter-American and European Human Rights Journal* 200 (2010); Juana María Ibáñez Rivas, *Control de convencionalidad: precisiones para su aplicación desde la jurisprudencia de la Corte Interamericana de Derechos Humanos*, (2012) *Anuario de Derechos Humanos* 103; Manuel Fernando Quinche Ramírez, *El control de convencionalidad y el sistema colombiano*, (12) *Revista Iberoamericana de Derecho Procesal Constitucional* 163 (2009); and Juan Carlos Hitters, *Control de Constitucionalidad y Control de Convencionalidade. Comparación*, 7(2) *Estudios constitucionales* 109 (2009). For a discussion in the ECtHR context, see Kosař et al., cit., 6–7 and 36–48.

64 I/A Court H.R., Case Gelman v. Uruguay. Merits and Reparations. Judgment of February 24, 2011 Series C No. 221, para. 239; I/A Court H.R., Case of expelled Dominicans and Haitians v. Dominican Republic. Preliminary Objections, Merits, Reparations and Costs. Judgment of August 28, 2014. Series C No. 282, para. 471; and I/A Court H.R., Case of Rochac Hernández et al. v. El Salvador. Merits, Reparations and Costs. Judgment of October 14, 2014. Series C No. 285, para. 213.

65 Duncan B Hollis and Carlos M Vásquez, Treaty Self-Execution as 'Foreign' Foreign Relations Law, in *The Oxford Handbook of Comparative Foreign Relations Law* 467–484, 481 (Curtis A Bradley ed.) (Oxford University Press, 2019).

ground the judiciary at the expense of other branches.[66] This foregrounding of the judiciary as a natural ally helps coordinate one of the possible negative impacts of the broader doctrine of conventionality control, which is the risk of uncoordinated enforcement at the local level.[67]

This doctrine centers the notion of compliance-as-influence. In this sense, it aligns with the scholarship around compliance with international human rights law. The first generation of conventionality control, by focusing on domestic judicial authorities, relied primarily on judicial dialogue as a path for influence. What this later generation does, instead, is to broaden how international human rights law can be influential, mapping in some respects the breadth of the authorities at whom the IACtHR aims reparations orders. Further, the doctrine as currently implemented also fragments the IACtHR's own authority as the final arbiter of the meaning of the American Convention. By giving all domestic authorities the power to implement the Convention as read by the IACtHR, we can create confusion for domestic authorities across different branches, and even more so in federal countries.[68]

Importantly for our purposes, too, the current version of conventionality control displays the IACtHR's preoccupation with all branches of government having a role to play with entrenching international human rights law and IACtHR findings. While the first generation of conventionality control privileged the domestic judiciary as a key site for the entrenchment of international human rights law, the second generation underscores the roles of legislatures (or parliaments) and executives as well. Likewise, it summons all levels of government (from local to national) and tasks them with taking the IACtHR seriously. While the IACtHR seldom deploys this doctrine in the service of enforcement, its evolution confirms that all levels and branches of government are (or at least can be) responsible for the implementation of international human rights law.

2 Branches of Government and Scholarly Toolkits

Judiciary, executive, and legislative authorities have roles to play in implementing international human rights judgments. Different branches will have

66 René Urueña, Domestic Application of International Law in Latin America, in *The Oxford Handbook of Comparative Foreign Relations Law* 565–582, 572 (Curtis A Bradley ed.) (Oxford University Press, 2019).

67 Id., 573.

68 Id., 574; and Clérico and Novelli, cit., 258.

different roles to play for different reparations. For instance, in respect to monetary compensation, it may be that a domestic judge needs to turn the international order into a domestic order against the domestic public authority in the executive, who then disburses the money. Or, in cases involving Article 2 of the American Convention, the foreign ministry as part of the executive may need to ask parliament to adopt certain legislation. But they also operate in very different technical registers, deploy different tools, and have different ways of connecting their legitimacies to international human rights law. On the latter, for the judiciary, international human rights judgments are a source of de-politicized legal authority that can aid courts in sidestepping hermeneutic dependency paths (thus performing an enhancer role). For the executive, international human rights judgments can be read as part of foreign affairs powers, which can often be part of the executive branch's treasured exclusive competences that are not dependent on the authorization of action by parliament, and less likely to be stopped by judiciaries (thus performing a competence carve-out role). For legislatures, international human rights judgments, read as a type of international instrument, are something they implement at the behest of the executive, and in order to guide courts (thus reinforcing a mediator role for parliaments).

On technical registers and tools, judiciaries might be compelled to treat international human rights judgments as another type of foreign judgment that needs to be recognized and enforced; executives may treat them as extensions of binding instruments; and legislatures as invitations, much like treaties themselves, to modify existing domestic legislation and the policies and practices underpinned by legislation. International human rights judgments thus oscillate between extensions of treaties or foreign judicial awards. The classification calls to action different branches of government, as well as different ways of enforcement. These multiple directions and pathways for enforcement, as we indicated above, are not considered in the reparations orders of international human rights courts, and the plurality of different possibilities and practices may in fact contribute to the enforcement of international human rights judgments being so under-studied.

Federalism presents the same dynamics, to the extent it is also a mechanism for distribution of power. International law also sees a monolith when it comes to federalism, with few exceptions in the area of treaty-making. But when it comes to federalism, the risks of overlap of competences are even greater. In some instances, these risks turn into possibilities of defiance of the national level's attempts at compliance with international law; in other instances, sub-national entities have attempted to implement international law in spite of the national level's rejection of international treaties.[69]

We will return to the study and mapping of these categories in the next chapter. Before doing so, however, it is important to further unpack the different registers in which the enforcement of international human rights judgments can operate, depending on the branch of domestic government involved. Being able to understand these registers sets up a broader conversation about how we understand and theorize the compliance with, and influence of, international human rights courts and law more broadly. It also allows us to contribute to thinking about the intersections between domestic and international law, by demystifying the monolithic state that international law assumes.[70] If we are serious about the implementation and enforcement of international law (particularly, but not limited to, judgments, in that judgments are a clearly compliance-directing type of international legal measure), we need to be more mindful of how different states structure themselves.

This mindfulness can foreground descriptive or normative agendas. The descriptive agenda would mean knowing how implementation and enforcement occur is useful because it allows international human rights courts to tailor their reparations orders with a view to indicating the pathways for compliance, and making compliance monitoring more productive (therefore, the IACtHR would be responding to domestic structures). The normative agenda would mean understanding these different pathways, and their positive and negative aspects, with a view to order domestic institutional design choices that are more conducive to implementation and enforcement (therefore, the IACtHR would be creating domestic structures). Either or both types of agenda would be useful.

But enabling these agendas necessitates also understanding more broadly the possible impacts of conflict of laws or private international law techniques (which include, notably, the enforcement of foreign judgments domestically), and of foreign affairs law. These bodies of scholarship promote key points of contact between domestic and international law. They also allow us to unpack

69 For a discussion with examples, see Lucas Lixinski, 'Trialogical Subsidiarity in International and Comparative Law: Engagement with International Treaties by Sub-State Entities as Resistance or Innovation', 55 *The Canadian Yearbook of International Law* (2017), 1–32.

70 Vienna Convention on the Law of Treaties, 1155 U.N.T.S. 331, 8 I.L.M. 679, entered into force Jan. 27, 1980. 'Article 27. Internal law and observance of treaties. A party may not invoke the provisions of its internal law as justification for its failure to perform a treaty'.

the idea of 'political will,' or lack thereof, that is often to blame for lack of compliance and enforcement. By understanding the technical stakes and possibilities, as well as temporarily separating ourselves from the murky politics of international human rights law, we can focus on the technical possibilities and outcomes for compliance and enforcement instead, and then reintroduce the politics through the technique, rather than in its stead. Because there is no other literature that connects these bodies of scholarship to international courts or to international human rights law, it is worth spending some time describing them.

Each of the three branches of government, therefore, deserve some consideration in the role they perform towards implementing or enforcing the judgments of international human rights courts. These roles are varied, at times interdependent. Specific bodies of scholarship can also help shed significant light on the potentials and pitfalls of each of these three branches. This analysis is useful not only as a contribution to these subfields of the literature in itself (since the specific implementation of international courts' judgments often eludes their analysis), but also because it helps us better understand the dynamics at play in different countries in Latin America, which is the topic of the next section.

2.1 *Foreign Relations Law and Demystifying the State*

The body of scholarship that attempts to explain how the domestic branches of government interact with international law is foreign relations law. It is an invented field, which works as an analytical frame.[71] Foreign relations law's key contribution to international law is probably to enhance our understanding of the intersections between international law and domestic law, politics, and institutions.[72] It focuses on how authority is allocated among different governmental actors.[73] It also acknowledges that different states have different strategies for engaging with international law without querying the legitimacy of these approaches in the abstract,[74] which is important to validate the plethora of approaches we discuss in the next chapter in particular. Relatedly, foreign relations law also affects a nation's compliance with international law

71 Karen Knop, Foreign Relations Law: Comparison as Invention, in *The Oxford Handbook of Comparative Foreign Relations Law* 45–61, 45 (Curtis A Bradley ed.) (Oxford University Press, 2019) [Knop, Foreign Relations Law].

72 Curtis A Bradley, What Is Foreign Relations Law?, in *The Oxford Handbook of Comparative Foreign Relations Law* 1–20, 4 (Curtis A Bradley ed.) (Oxford University Press, 2019).

73 Id.

74 Id.

'because different domestic institutions may have differing levels of commitment to (or capacity for) ensuring compliance.'[75] While some have queried whether there is such a thing as foreign relations law in Latin America,[76] its analytical insights and categories are still helpful in making sense of how international human rights courts' judgments can be implemented and enforced.

Foreign relations law also shows us how international law privileges certain domestic arrangements over others, like the presumption of executive control over certain aspects of foreign relations, which can make it harder for other branches of government to control the executive in relation to international law.[77] Executive branches, for instance, can leverage international law to sidestep domestic political constraints,[78] much like legislatures. A risk with foreign relations law is that it can distort the inner workings of international law,[79] by, for instance, allowing for more domestic intrusion in the interpretation of international law. For instance, separation of powers may allow a branch of government to be more deferent to how another branch sees the steps required for implementation and enforcement of an international judgment than to the international court's instructions.[80] Further, a domestic court's refusal to recognize an international judgment on grounds of public policy (*ordre public*, in French, which includes domestic constitutional values)[81] can be read as privileging the domestic over the international, or, alternatively, as starting a more plural conversation in which there is no binary answer.[82] All these tensions multiply in federal contexts.

Foreign relations law relies on the mapping of the different political stakes and institutional interactions within a state. It is premised on the idea of separation of powers, which is an area in which international human rights courts

---

75 Id., 5.

76 Urueña, Domestic Application, cit., 581.

77 Curtis A Bradley, The Dynamic and Sometimes Uneasy Relationship Between Foreign Relations Law and International Law, in *Encounters Between Foreign Relations Law and International Law: Bridges and Boundaries* 343–354, 350 (Helmut Phillip Aust and Thomas Kleinlein eds.) (Cambridge University Press, 2021).

78 Id., 352.

79 Knop, Foreign Relations Law, cit., 54.

80 Id., 56–57.

81 Martin Gebauer and Felix Berner, *Ordre Public* (Public Policy), *Max Planck Encyclopedia of Public International Law* (2019).

82 Knop, Foreign Relations Law, cit., 57–58; and Andrea Bianchi, Jurisdictional Immunities, Constitutional Values, and System Closures, in *The Oxford Handbook of Comparative Foreign Relations Law* 685–700 (Curtis A Bradley ed.) (Oxford University Press, 2019).

have seldom intervened directly,[83] but which, as we suggest above, would be a fruitful area of consideration particularly in dictating reparations. Foreign affairs law helps explain the entrenchment of and resistance to international law more broadly, and particularly in relation to international courts in areas, like Latin America, where constitutional rights adjudication is an important part of public discourse.[84] But foreign affairs scholarship is also largely silent on optimal institutional design, for the most part restricting itself to describing and comparing, rather than forming archetypes of, domestic institutions and their interactions with international law. This feature can be read as a missed opportunity, but it is also appropriate for analytical frames to not form the picture, and instead remain as the frame, as Karen Knop put it.[85] At the same time, its focus on domestic institutions decenters the victims of human rights violations. Foreign affairs scholarship shows us that, despite some blurriness, the executive branch has greater prerogatives when it comes to international law than other branches. It is thus worth considering the specific possibilities of this branch in the abstract first.

The executive branch often comes to mind first because it is the branch of government with the primary (and at times exclusive) prerogative to represent the country in international law matters,[86] at least if viewed from the standpoint of diplomacy and entering into treaties.[87] But the role can also extend to implementing and enforcing international courts' judgments. At least from an ECtHR perspective, the executive plays a central role,[88] and even beyond Europe 'the executive-based model is largely dominant.'[89] Inter-

83 But see David Kosař, Policing Separation of Powers: A New Role for the European Court of Human Rights?, 8(1) *European Constitutional Law Review* (2012).

84 Urueña, Domestic Application, cit.

85 Knop, Foreign Relations Law, cit., 47.

86 Jenny S Martinez, The Constitutional Allocation of Executive and Legislative Power Over Foreign Relations: A Survey, in *The Oxford Handbook of Comparative Foreign Relations Law* 97–114, 100–101 (Curtis A Bradley ed.) (Oxford University Press, 2019) (indicating that in a large number of constitutions foreign affairs power is vested explicitly and exclusively on the executive branch). See also Piovesan and Cruz, cit., 276 ('The executive branch is the main actor responsible for the process of implementing international human rights decisions in Brazil'.).

87 Id. See also Hannah Woolaver, State Engagement with Treaties: Interactions between International and Domestic Law, in *The Oxford Handbook of Comparative Foreign Relations Law* 431–446 (Curtis A Bradley ed.) (Oxford University Press, 2019).

88 Lambert, cit.

89 Rainer Grote, A Dialogue with the Deaf? The Political Branches as Compliance Partners, in *Research Handbook on Compliance in International Human Rights Law* 449–464, 451 (Rainer Grote, Mariela Morales Antoniazzi, and Davide Paris eds.) (Elgar 2021).

national human rights treaties in general can help executives bypass legislative branch stalemates.[90] This central role in implementation and enforcement may partly be a natural consequence of the executive's participation during the life of the case before reparations are ordered. The national executive branch, after all, is the one that represents the state before international organizations, including the state's legal representatives before international courts. Likewise, the executive is also the branch of government in charge of entering into international obligations more generally. The notification of judgments goes to a branch of the executive, too, and they are the ones in charge of presenting formal responses about implementation. The proverbial buck starts and stops with the executive, as far as international law in general, and international human rights courts, are normally concerned.

2.2 *The Conflict of Laws Style and Technical Foregrounding*

On the judiciary, national courts are natural partners of international courts. There is marked contrast here with attitudes towards the executive, who represent the (violating) state before the international human rights court, and of whom therefore the IACtHR is naturally suspicious. Even if courts can sometimes be read as allies of the other branches of government,[91] the literature on judicial dialogue, as we discussed above, documents extensive connections between international and domestic courts. Further, international human rights courts tend to empower domestic courts, partly because doing so also empowers the international court.[92] Courts can operate as gatekeepers instead, too, when they choose not to give effect to international judgments.[93] Conversely, international law can help courts bolster their independence vis-à-vis other stronger branches of government, particularly in Latin America.[94] There is a pendulum effect of domestic courts relying upon or denouncing international human rights courts and embracing or refusing the enforcement of judgments. Rejections are often part of a concerted strategy to avoid enforcing international courts' judgments.[95]

---

90 Simmons, cit., 128.

91 Machiko Kanetake, Cooperation Between Human Rights Bodies and Domestic Courts, *Max Planck Encyclopedia of International Procedural Law* (2021).

92 Kosař and Lixinski, cit.

93 Jasper Krommendijk, Domestic gatekeepers or international enforcers? National courts' engagement with decisions of international human rights courts and treaty bodies, in *Research Handbook on Implementation of Human Rights in Practice* 163–186 (Rachel Murray and Debra Long eds.) (Elgar, 2022).

94 Urueña, Domestic Application, cit., 569.

95 Id., 579–580.

Scholarship that connects public international law (often human rights-based) problems to techniques of conflict of laws or private international law can be particularly useful in understanding the possibilities of domestic courts to enforce the judgments of international human rights courts. After all, international courts' judgments can be read, as we discuss below, as foreign judgments in need of recognition and enforcement. The recognition and enforcement of international judgments is a key activity in private international law, and consists in a domestic court analyzing the validity of a foreign judgment so as to render it enforceable in domestic law.[96] This analysis for the most part does not involve re-arguing the merits of the foreign judgment, or its remedies orders. Rather, the task is one of checking compatibility with the domestic legal order and translation. The only substantive obstacle to domestic recognition and enforcement of a foreign judgment is when the foreign judgment offends the public policy (*ordre public*) of the jurisdiction where recognition and enforcement are sought.[97] Public policy often includes human rights elements, usually drawn from domestic constitutions, but increasingly also from international law instruments. It is therefore unlikely that this substantive window for the recognition and enforcement of foreign judgments be used against declarations of human rights violations and ensuing remedies.

This assumed substantive compatibility, however, is only a very small part of the contribution of scholarship that connects public international law with conflict of laws technique. Calling it a 'style,'[98] the ground-breaking work of Karen Knop, Ralf Michaels, and Annelise Riles shows us ways to reformulate the problem of the effectiveness of international law in domestic courts.[99] It becomes a problem of 'theory through technique,'[100] which is still imbued with the important political work of critical thinking,[101] and thus suitable for

96 Michaels, Recognition and Enforcement, cit.

97 Gebauer and Berner, cit.

98 Karen Knop, Ralf Michaels, and Annelise Riles, From Multiculturalism to Technique: Feminism, Culture, and the Conflict of Laws Style, 64 *Stanford Law Review*, 589–656 (2012) [Knop, Michaels, and Riles, From Multiculturalism to Technique].

99 Karen Knop, Ralf Michaels, and Annelise Riles, International Law in Domestic Courts: A Conflict of Laws Approach, ASIL Proceedings 269–274, 271 (2009) [Knop, Michaels, and Riles, International Law in Domestic Courts].

100 Id., 273.

101 Ralf Michaels, Post-critical Private International Law: From Politics to Technique, in *Private International Law and Global Governance* 54–67 (Horatia Muir Watt and Diego P Fernández Arroyo eds.) (Oxford University Press, 2014) [Michaels, Post-critical Private International Law].

engagement with international human rights law. Conflict of laws technique, as the brief discussion on the process of recognition and enforcement of foreign judgments shows, also creates a presumption in favor of the validity of international human rights courts' judgments and reparations orders,[102] which sidesteps the murkier questions of political domestic resistance in favor of more clear-cut and available remedies for the victims of rights violations. In the long run, this move also entrenches international human rights law more broadly by rendering it presumptively valid and relevant on technical, rather than political, grounds, which have inherent legitimacy. In this way, the presumption does not avoid the problem of validity and enforceability; rather, it gives us the technical tools to be able to address it.[103] It renders the matter of the impact of international human rights courts on domestic law concrete,[104] in a way that broader debates about influence have failed to do. It offers a path to navigate the binary of either blind formalism, or open-ended policy and political commitments,[105] enlivening the possibilities of implementation and enforcement of international human rights courts' judgments for the beneficiaries of those judgments.

Conflict of laws, relatedly, offers the tool of *dépeçage*, or 'slicing,' as a means to further compartmentalize complex legal matters to achieve better implementation and enforcement.[106] This tool is particularly relevant in the context of reparations, making it thus central to our analysis of enforcement of international courts' decisions.[107] In our specific context, it means that judgments are treated as a series of discrete reparations orders over which responsibility must be allocated, 'each of which might fall under different authorities and have different sources of legitimacy.'[108] Because courts are adept at this practice from the perspective of other private international law disputes, they become apt 'project managers' for the implementation and enforcement of international judgments. At the same time, this technique makes enough room for legal pluralism,[109] which is important when translating international courts' views to domestic contexts, particularly in cases involving historically

102 Knop, Michaels, and Riles, International Law in Domestic Courts, cit., 272.
103 Id., 273.
104 Id.
105 Id., 274.
106 Knop, Michaels, and Riles, From Multiculturalism to Technique, cit., 636.
107 Karen Knop and Annelise Riles, Space, Time, and Historical Injustice: A Feminist Conflict-of-Laws Approach to the 'Comfort Women' Agreement, 102 *Cornell Law Review* 853–927, 898 (2017) [Knop and Riles, Space, Time, and Historical Injustice].
108 Id.
109 Knop, Michaels, and Riles, From Multiculturalism to Technique, cit., 642.

disadvantaged groups like Indigenous peoples and Afro-descendant groups,[110] for whom a grounding of rights on the distinctiveness of culture is part of their rights-claiming model,[111] and therefore part of remedies as well. Usefully, private international law can create more openness towards other legal orders to permeate our reading of international human rights law domestically, making it easier for instance to bring Indigenous perspectives to bear on the implementation of reparations in ways that the IACtHR has so far failed to do, and with the potential to overcome the cultural imperialism and colonialism[112] inherent to the imposition of non-Indigenous law on Indigenous peoples.[113]

Private international law is a fertile ground for judicial understandings of foreign relations law.[114] It can turn international law, read through foreign relations law, into 'a sort of legal space of possibility.'[115] Likewise, conflict of laws techniques can allow for the sequencing of different spatio-temporal horizons that can aid in the implementation of reparations in difficult cases like those involving transitional justice,[116] which are important parts of the IACtHR's jurisprudence in relation to Latin America's past of dictatorships and civil wars. Private international law, in other words, can render the emancipatory work of international human rights courts into a more clearly 'enactable form,' and can be more than transformative – it can be world-making.[117]

Scholarship that applies conflict of laws technique to public international law problems, therefore, can be central to our thinking about the implementation and enforcement of international human rights courts' judgments. It allows us to suspend the politics of human rights momentarily and replace it with fictions as placeholders[118] that enable its transformative potential for the actual victims of violations. It is a language that privileges and foregrounds the action of the judicial branch, which, as a natural ally of international human rights courts, can be a useful outcome. It suspends the possible interference of

110 María Julia Ochoa Jiménez, Indigenous Peoples' Normative Orders and Restitution: Latin American Private International Law and Human Rights, 54(2–3) *Legal Pluralism and Critical Social Analysis* 176–192 (2022).

111 A view not without its critics. See eg Beatriz Garcia and Lucas Lixinski, *Beyond Culture: Reimagining the Adjudication of Indigenous Peoples' Rights in International Law*, 15(3) *Intercultural Human Rights Law Review* 127–168 (2020).

112 Karen Knop, Ralf Michaels, and Annelise Riles, Transdisciplinary Conflict of Laws Foreword: Cavers's Double Legacy, 71(1) *Law and Contemporary Problems* 1–17, 12–14 (2008).

113 Ochoa Jiménez, cit., 186.

114 Knop, Foreign Relations Law, cit., 59.

115 Id., 60.

116 Knop and Riles, Space, Time, and Historical Injustice, cit., 854.

117 Id., 926.

118 Michaels, Post-critical Private International Law, cit., 66.

other branches (which it sees as unwelcome because it is political and it enlarges the issue beyond what technical slicing can do via *dépeçage*), while still allowing for some penetration via concepts like *ordre public*. It helps entrench international law domestically because it renders those judgments enforceable, and more connected to the plural realities on the ground via concepts like pluralism and the recognition of culture-based legal orders. It is ambitious in its world-making aspirations, much like the language of emancipation that underpins international human rights courts' projects. And it centers victims by relying on their private rights over the public politics of human rights to promote change. It forces an encounter between domestic and international law that is grounded on the realities of victims, divided into enactable forms, and aimed at dealing with historical injustices in achievable moments, making it a very fertile means of thinking about the possibilities of domestic implementation and enforcement of international human rights courts' judgments.

2.3 *Parliaments and Relative Scholarly Neglect*

When it comes to parliaments, there is no clear body of scholarship that specifically addresses the role of parliaments in international law, beyond some discussion in more general comparative foreign relations law which tells us that in the vast majority of constitutions foreign affairs powers are at least partly distributed between the executive and legislative branches.[119] There is even more limited scholarship on the role of legislatures in implementing the judgments of international human rights courts. That said, it is known that the United Nations (UN) system, for instance, in the context of the Human Rights Council's Universal Periodic Review that scrutinizes the human rights record of states, increasingly relies on parliaments as partners in implementation of its recommendations.[120] To be sure, Article 2 of the American Convention, by ordering that legislation be adopted, relies heavily on parliaments as well, even if parliaments are seldom directly named by the IACtHR (which instead tends to refer to the state as a monolith, as we indicated above). The UN's draft principles on parliaments and human rights[121] emphasizes in particular the

119 Martinez, cit., 114.

120 Brian Chang and Murray Hunt, The Role of Parliaments in Implementing Decisions and Recommendations from Supranational Human Rights Bodies, in *Research Handbook on Implementation of Human Rights in Practice* 140–162, 141 (Rachel Murray and Debra Long eds.) (Elgar, 2022).

121 United Nations Human Rights Council, Contribution of parliaments to the work of the Human Rights Council and its universal periodic review – Report of the Office of the

responsibilities of parliamentary human rights committees, urging them to 'lead the parliamentary oversight of the work of the Government in fulfilling its human rights obligations, as well as political commitments made in international and regional human rights mechanisms.'[122] The reference to 'political' commitments might undermine the idea of parliamentary committees (and, with them, parliaments more broadly) in engaging with judgments of international human rights courts, but the language on 'fulfilling [states'] human rights obligations' more broadly may be read as including judgments, particularly if judgments order the adoption of legislation.[123] There are arguments for parliaments to be more directly involved in the implementation of international human rights judgments, not only in their law-making capacities, but also as fora for internal political pressure and legitimacy,[124] and in overseeing the actions of the executive branch.[125]

Parliaments thus have important potential roles to play in implementing and enforcing international human rights judgments.[126] They can rely not only on their legislative power to enact new legislation to create binding pathways for compliance,[127] but generally parliaments also approve budgets, which includes the disbursement of monies to pay for financial compensation. Further, legislation creates or modifies roles for courts as well, at least in its basic parameters, not to mention parliaments play a role in the appointment of judges for high judicial office. In other words, legislative branches operate as gatekeepers or background operators to the activities of other branches. Parliaments are also traditionally more attuned to domestic politics and popular sentiment, thus operating as barometers of popular will (or lack thereof) towards international organizations. Even non-binding actions of parliaments (like speeches on the floor, non-binding resolutions urging for action to be

United Nations High Commissioner for Human Rights. Annex – Draft Principles on Parliaments and human rights. UN Doc. A/HRC/38/25 (17 May 2018).

122 Id., para. 2(c).

123 Chang and Hunt, cit., 143.

124 Id., 155–156.

125 Kirsten Roberts Lyer (2019) Parliaments as Human Rights Actors: The Potential for International Principles on Parliamentary Human Rights Committees, *Nordic Journal of Human Rights*, 37:3, 195–215, DOI: 10.1080/18918131.2019.1681610.

126 Gerald Staberock, Human Rights, Domestic Implementation, *Max Planck Encyclopedia of Public International Law* (2011).

127 On one instance of a failure to create a binding legislative procedure, see Eszter Polgári and Boldizsár Nagy, The Chances of Observing Human Rights in an Illiberal State: diagnosis of Hungary, in *Research Handbook on Compliance in International Human Rights Law* 95–120, 100 (Rainer Grote, Mariela Morales Antoniazzi, and Davide Paris eds.) (Elgar 2021).

taken in certain domains) can have (admittedly soft) impacts on how international courts' judgments are received domestically, especially in the aftermath of acts of just satisfaction like publication of parts of a judgment in the national press. Legislative branches also have autonomous political levers to play, which are harder to measure and connect causally to compliance, but which play important roles nonetheless. Even if sometimes their role in compliance is at the behest of other branches,[128] parliaments can direct the other two branches, and, coupled with the power to domestically ratify treaties, they have a lot to say about the entrenchment of international law domestically. There is admittedly a disconnect between domestic ratification of a treaty that gives rise to an international court's competence and implementation of a judgment, but legislatures also have the power to enact and withdraw legislation authorizing implementation and enforcement frameworks, should the latter be tied to legislation incorporating the relevant international treaty (which is not always the case). Parliaments can center victims over institutions by being more connected to the political constituencies that are victims of human rights violations, and thus present an important perspective in implementation and enforcement on the side of victims. Thinking about legislatures and their roles in the context of implementation and enforcement is generally useful to unpack the monolithic state from an international court's perspective, and also to present another set of allies that can help backdoor the international court's influence, alongside judiciaries.

There is much to be gained in understanding the different technical considerations and pathways through which the politics of implementing international human rights judgments plays out, therefore, particularly in connection with different branches of government. Now, it is time to discuss what happens on the ground in the Latin American countries that have accepted the contentious jurisdiction of the IACtHR, to see what is available to implement reparations orders, and what these technical pathways reveal about the political stakes and the transformative possibilities of the IACtHR to victims of human rights violations.

---

128 Piovesan and Cruz, cit., 278.

CHAPTER 3

A Typology of Implementation and Enforcement in Latin America

The specific tools and mechanisms available to implement the IACtHR's decisions in Latin American states under the Court's contentious jurisdiction showcase a variety of strategies and technical structures in the different countries. Amidst the diversity of pathways for implementation, however, the analysis below of different techniques for implementation in Latin American countries confirms the trend indicated by foreign affairs scholarship that the executive branch tends to be the one at the forefront of enforcement efforts. This tendency also seems to reflect the effects of the second generation of conventionality control that expands the points of connection between the domestic legal system and international human rights law beyond the judiciary, elevating the roles of the other powers, especially the executive, as the legislative branch remains somewhat underutilized. In fact, as we further demonstrate below, the effects of the second generation may have gone further to also empower the creation of unique enforcement structures meant to be independent from any specific branch while counting on the cooperation of all the state's powers for the domestic protection and promotion of human rights arising from the implementation of IACtHR's decisions.

An appendix to this book offers a fuller descriptive account of our findings per country, with references to primary sources. For now, the table below offers a descriptive summary of the countries we analyzed. The table organizes countries in the Americas who have accepted the IACtHR's jurisdiction around, first, the branch of government that leads implementation. Next, the columns refer to the main axes of our analysis, which we ran through all the countries regardless of which branch led implementation to enable more fruitful comparison. In building this typology, we consider four topics that allow us to explore key aspects of three main areas. These areas are a) the relationship between the IACtHR and the different branches of government in the implementation of the former's judgments, b) modalities of enforcement in the countries under the IACtHR jurisdiction, and c) how that relationship, being actuated through different modes of enforcement, can affect the entrenchment of international human rights in the domestic sphere. The topics we use to identify and analyze these key areas are: a) the centralization of authority in the domestic implementation systems—that is, whether the

© AYLA DO VALE ALVES AND LUCAS LIXINSKI, 2025 | DOI:10.1163/9789004741829_004

domestic system is centralized (meaning, the authority to engage and manage the implementation system lies with one central branch/authority), or diffuse (that authority is shared among the branches); b) the clarity of the rules of the domestic implementation system, through which we assess whether the law(s) guiding the domestic implementation system is/are clear and detailed in informing the role of each authority and the processes available to enforce an IACtHR decision; c) dependence on shifts in local politics, where we consider the role of local politics in the domestic implementation system, in how the branches respond to the system's norms and to each other in implementation processes; and d) legitimacy of each branch/authority considering their pathways of communication with the IACtHR, in which we assess the possible pathways of interaction between the IACtHR and each branch, and the effects of these pathways on the work of these two actors, as well as on victims (of human rights violations judged by the IACtHR) and on the type of entrenchment of international human rights domestically.

In the following sections, we consider the technical pathways for implementation in most Latin American countries under the IACtHR's contentious jurisdiction to identify their different political strategies and stakes, and assess their concrete effects for victims of human rights violations on the ground. We start with an analysis of the executive branch as the primary authority in implementation, as this model seems currently to be prevalent among Latin American countries. Yet, recent changes in the rules regulating enforcement in some of the countries analyzed, such as Brazil and Guatemala, indicate the mutability of the implementation structures, which may also already reveal elements of the political dimensions of such structures as dependent on shifting governmental priorities and interests. We then investigate the states that center enforcement on the judicial branch, and finally, those that have relied mostly on the legislative for enforcement, or, more indirectly, for the creation of an independent entity administratively disconnected from any of the state powers and aimed only at elevating human rights domestically, including through the implementation of IACtHR's decisions.

This analysis tells us that Latin American jurisdictions privilege Velcro over stitches to bind international and domestic law together, perhaps unsurprisingly. This preference for a Velcro type of implementation reflects states' general concern to protect their sovereignty by not yielding too much power to the IACtHR through unhindered and consistent compliance with the Court's judgments. Instead, states focus on avenues that show the influence of such judgments domestically, but short of enforcement. A Velcro type of implementation also reflects a frequent messiness and lack of clarity in the rules establishing or regulating the authorities, mechanisms and processes for

TABLE 3.1 Summary of domestic enforcement frameworks

	Centralized v diffuse authority	Clarity of rules	Dependency on shifts in local politics	Pathways of connection to IACtHR
		EXECUTIVE-LED		
Argentina	Executive-Centralized; Ministries and Temporary Enforcement Units[a]	Direct, but unclear, overlapping rules	Likely high dependency	Clear pathways only if temporary unit created – enables legitimacy
Bolivia	Executive-Centralized; President and General Prosecutor's Office[b]	Limited clarity and only for pecuniary remedies	Likely high dependency – executive holds much power	Executive's attributions from constitution – pathways unclear
Chile	Executive-led, diffuse[c]	Lack of clarity – superficial; other branches; role unclear	Possibly low dependency – judiciary role in conventionality control	Clear pathways, mainly with judiciary

a Ley 27431, 2 Jan 2018, Art. 108; Decreto Nº 167/18; Decisión Administrativa N° 70 del 10 de febrero de 2020.

b Constitution of Bolivia, Art. 172(13).

c Decreto con Fuerza de Ley N. 3 – Fija el Texto Refundido, Coordinado Y Sistematizado de la Ley Orgánica Del Ministerio de Justicia y Derechos Humanos Ministerio de Justicia y Derechos Humanos – 2 de Diciembre de 2016, Art. 2(d).

TABLE 3.1 Summary of domestic enforcement frameworks (*cont.*)

	Centralized v diffuse authority	Clarity of rules	Dependency on shifts in local politics	Pathways of connection to IACtHR
Colombia	Executive-centralized articulation; Workgroups of the Ministry of Foreign Affairs[d]	Somewhat clear rules[e]	Likely high dependency – unclear overlapping attributions	Executive too power; internal validation of decision – hinders connection
Costa Rica	Executive-led, possibly diffuse[f]	Clear rules on interbranch dynamics[g]	Likely low dependency – interbranch dynamics clear	Clear pathway through executive – enables legitimacy[h]
Ecuador	Executive-led – Diffuse; Secretariat of Human Rights[i]	Some unclear rules – gaps, contradictory rules	Possibly lower dependency[j]	Clear pathway – specific entity for implementation[k]

d Resolución 9709, 5 December 2017, Diario Oficial No. 50.444 de 11 de diciembre de 2017, Arts. 38, 39, 41.
e Resolución 9709, 5 December 2017, Diario Oficial No. 50.444 de 11 de diciembre de 2017, Arts. 38, 39, 41.
f Decreto Presidencial 36776-RE, 9 de agosto de 2011, Art. 6 Annex.
g Decreto Presidencial 36776-RE, 9 de agosto de 2011, Art. 6 Annex
h Decreto Presidencial 36776-RE, 9 de agosto de 2011, Art. 2 Annex.
i Decreto Ejecutivo 560, 14 november 2018, Art. 2(a); Decreto Ejecutivo 1317, 2008
j Constitución de la República del Ecuador, Art. 93; see also Ley Organica de Garantias Jurisdiccionales y Control Constitucional 2009 (última modificación – 2020), Art. 52, Art. 93.
k Decreto Ejecutivo 560, 14 november 2018, Art. 2(a); Decreto Ejecutivo 1317, 2008.

TABLE 3.1 Summary of domestic enforcement frameworks (*cont.*)

	Centralized v diffuse authority	Clarity of rules	Dependency on shifts in local politics	Pathways of connection to IACtHR
Honduras	Executive-led, mostly centralized; Interinstitutional Workgroup on Human Rights	Clear rules only regarding human rights defenders[l]	Possibly high dependency – roles of other branches unclear	Seemingly direct pathways for executive – enables legitimacy
Mexico	Executive-led; diffuse; Unit for Human Rights Defence[m]	Mostly clear rules.	Possibly low dependency – judiciary possibly willing to intervene if needed	Clear pathway through specific entity – enables legitimacy
Nicaragua	Executive - mostly centralized[n]	Lack of clarity - gaps	Likely lower dependency – Executive works with independent organ	Unclear rules or may hinder connection and legitimacy
Panama	Executive - mostly centralized	Lack of clarity - general rules[o]	Likely high dependency[p]	Unclear pathways; unclear possible role for judiciary

l Ley de Protección para las y los Defensores de Derechos Humanos, Periodistas, Comunicadores Sociales y Operadores de Justicia – 15 mayo 2015; Decreto No. 34–2015; ACUERDO EJECUTIVO No.059–2016, Art. 59.

m Reglamento Interior de la Secretaría de Gobernación, 31/05/2019, Arts. 43, 45, 51; Ley Orgánica de la Administración Pública Federal, Artículo 27.

n Decreto Ejecutivo N° 19–2009, Art. 27(5).

o Decreto Ejecutivo No. 367, 17 de Agosto de 2018, Art. 80(f).

p Decreto Ejecutivo No. 367, 17 de Agosto de 2018, Art. 80(f).

TABLE 3.1 Summary of domestic enforcement frameworks (*cont.*)

	Centralized v diffuse authority	Clarity of rules	Dependency on shifts in local politics	Pathways of connection to IACtHR
Paraguay	Executive-led – diffuse; Interinstitutional Executive Commission[q]	Clear rules[r]	Likely low dependency – possible branches' involvement clear	Executive decrees enables clear pathways; joint branch efforts
		JUDICIARY-LED		
Brazil	Executive-led – centralized; other branches engage as needed; Ministry of Human Rights and Citizenship;[s] Scholarly view – judiciary-led-centralized[t]	Clear rules - executive-led,[u] or judiciary-led[v]	Likely lower dependency; executive leads but other branches may be engaged; same in judiciary-led model	Specific entity with clear connection; Approaching IACtHR judgments as foreign creates connection but can hinder legitimacy

q Decreto N° 4367 – 2015, Art. 8.
r Decreto N° 4367 – 2015, Arts. 3–5.
s Decreto No 11.341, 1 January 2023, Annex I, Art. 6.
t Código de Processo Civil (2015), Art. 960.
u Decree Nº 11.341, 1 January 2023; Portaria Nº 412, DE 19 DE JULHO DE 2023.
v Código de Processo Civil (2015), Art. 960.

TABLE 3.1 Summary of domestic enforcement frameworks (*cont.*)

	Centralized v diffuse authority	Clarity of rules	Dependency on shifts in local politics	Pathways of connection to IACtHR
Dominican Republic	Judiciary – Centralized[w]	Lack of clarity	High dependency	IHRL and domestic HR connected – enables legitimacy[x]
Peru	Judiciary-led – Diffuse[y]	Clear rules[z]	Likely lower dependency	Executive interference diminishes judiciary's connection
LEGISLATIVE-LED (OR INDEPENDENT ENTITY CREATED/HARBORED BY THE LEGISLATIVE)				
Barbados	Likely legislative-led – centralized; [insufficient sources]	Lack of clarity – insufficient sources	Unclear dependency	Unclear pathways

w Republica Dominicana, Ley No. 137–11, 11/Jun/2011, Considerando 13°.

x Constitución de la República Dominicana – 2015, aart 74(3). Ley No. 137–11 – 'Ley Orgánica del Tribunal Constitucional y de los procedimientos constitucionales' – 11 Junio 2011, Art. 7(13).

y Peru, Código Procesal Constitucional, Artículo 115; Ley N° 27775, Art. 2.

z Peru, Ley N° 27775.

TABLE 3.1 Summary of domestic enforcement frameworks (*cont.*)

	Centralized v diffuse authority	**Clarity of rules**	**Dependency on shifts in local politics**	**Pathways of connection to IACtHR**
El Salvador	Independent organ (created by legislative) – diffuse[aa]	Clear rules	Likely lower dependency – autonomous leading organ	Open and direct connection – more legitimacy
Guatemala	Legislative – highly diffuse	Lack of clarity; branches' attributions unclear	Likely high dependency	No explicit pathways; hinders legitimacy
Uruguay	Independent organ (created/ harboured by legislative) – diffuse; National Human Rights Institute[ab]	Somewhat clear rules – attributions articulated, but leading authorities shift in practice	Possibly lower dependency	Direct pathways enable legitimacy

aa Ley De La Procuraduria Para La Defensa De Los Derechos Humanos, Art. 2.
ab Ley N° 18446 – 2008.

actual enforcement in several Latin American countries. Velcro is more likely here because, where these elements in the implementation process are unclear, idleness and inaction might follow suit as different authorities that might be capable of advancing implementation are not sure whether they have those prerogatives under the law or how to use them. Further, frequent political shifts domestically might also help explain a preference for a Velcro-type implementation as branches that should work together toward implementation often diverge politically and such divergences can halt enforcement, leaving only more superficial and sparse possible points of connection available in the entrenchment of IHRL into domestic law through IACtHR judgments. Stitch-type implementation works best, in our view, because it promotes better outcomes for victims, and more fundamentally changes state institutions throughout, beyond the Velcro-type influence that is mostly centered on the judiciary, and assumes (rather than tracks) positive human rights impacts on the broader population.

Our analysis also shows us that there is limited deployment of the possibilities of private international law mechanisms across Latin America, which undercuts the possibilities of enforcement and entrenchment of international human rights law through technique. Instead, the focus on the work of political branches muddies pathways for implementation and enforcement. While this predilection for executive action keeps the politics of international human rights law alive, it does so in ways that privilege state narratives at the exclusion of victims and civil society more broadly.

Before getting into the analysis of these branches and building the typology, the next subsection addresses our methodology for this examination. In working through our methodology, we also tease out some further insights about the potential reach and limits of this book.

1 Methodology

Our analysis of the work and potential of the branches in entrenching IHRL domestically is informed by data collected from 18 states that accept the IACtHR jurisdiction, more specifically considering the implementation system in force in each country at a certain point in time. The collection of the data started from a systematic search in online legislation databases in each of the countries analyzed and in careful literature review on the topic. We also compared our findings against and complemented by documents and reports from the Inter-American System for the Protection of Human Rights

(IASPHR)[1] on domestic implementation mechanisms and monitoring efforts. While we structured all the information collected and categorized aspects of states' implementation systems and their respective legal bases, at times access to databases was limited, the availability of sources was hindered by our need for online access, and sources found sometimes offered ambiguous, superficial, or unclear information.

From the initial research in 2021 to the final stages of writing in late 2024, two revisions updating the data showed that changes can quickly happen in the implementation systems in the countries analyzed (to the example of Brazil and Nicaragua). Therefore, it is important to take this analysis as based on information collected at a certain point in time (and up-to-date as of October 2024), but with the awareness that the local circumstances feeding that information change constantly, as well as the written and unwritten, formal and political rules and structures forming a country's system for implementation of IACtHR judgments. While these changes over time can affect the specific data gathered in relation to the implementation system of one or some countries in this examination, the core arguments in this book remain valid for relying on and reflecting broader aspects in the works of different branches of government and its relationship with international institutions, with each other, and with stakeholders. In other words, our key points and arguments concern and impact domestic implementation and enforcement systems, their usual features and actors, despite changes in particular aspects or the elements in the systems of the countries we analyze. That is because we use the specific data on these local systems to identify larger models of implementation and add more tangible information and concrete experiences to the analysis focused on those models. So, while a country's particular circumstances may change, the analysis of the model that the country contributed to identifying is valid and rich in itself as it will still enable higher-level arguments concerning pathways of entrenchment and implementation between international and domestic law.

Finally, in this analysis, we have to acknowledge that our focus is on the positivist slant to our sources, which tell us what the law is and we take it at face value, but does not necessarily reflect how such laws apply or are implemented in practice. Doing so can lead to some mismatches between law in the books and law in practice that are of significance. To name one example from

---

1 Particularly: Comisión Interamericana de Derechos Humanos ['Inter-American Commission on Human Rights'], *'Mecanismos Nacionales de Implementación de Recomendaciones de Derechos Humanos'* [*'National Mechanisms for the Implementation of Human Rights Recommendations'*], Doc No OEA/Ser.L/V/II.doc.8/23, 26 February 2023.

outside the Americas, in Czechia the Constitution says the duty to implement ECtHR judgments falls on the judiciary, but, in practice, it is the executive that takes the lead.[2] This caveat is an important one considering that the way domestic authorities perceive, follow and apply (or not) the rules of the domestic implementation system for international (human rights courts') decisions may lead to the identification of different models of implementation, in practice, from the ones we compile here. However, there are three responses to this caveat that justify our positivist focus. First, a comprehensive assessment of both the normative and practical aspects of 18 states under the IACtHR jurisdiction is an enormous undertaking that, for its sheer size, is outside the scope of this book. Second, despite not directly addressing the practical workings of the domestic implementation systems, much of our analysis addresses precisely the non-legal elements that can affect how the domestic rules are implemented in practice. For instance, as we address the role of local politics in those domestic systems, we highlight how the national authorities and branches, because of political reasons, can behave in ways that differ from what the domestic norms require; therefore, in some aspects we constantly acknowledge that there can be a significant discrepancy between what the law is or says and how national authorities perceive, approach, or apply it. Third, for the purposes of creating a typology of implementation that serves as basis for wider arguments concerning the entrenchment of international human rights (judgments) into domestic law and the possibilities for technique in this entrenchment, a positivist analysis as we perform here, with its caveat and responses to the caveats, is capable of providing a robust basis from which to develop those wider arguments.

1.1 *Methodological Choices*

We use the same four topics around which we organized the table at the beginning of this chapter in our assessment of each branch of government: executive, judicial and legislative. This consistent reliance on the same four topics allows us to paint a more comprehensive picture of the relationship between the international and the domestic spheres in the context of human rights entrenchment from the former into the latter, while still considering, comparatively, the specificities of each branch in their particular relationship with the IACtHR. Moreover, in our research, we noticed a persistent intersection of these topics in that each of them tends to influence what we understand and find about the other. These are likely not the only relevant topics in

2 For an in-depth study, see David Kosař et al., *Domestic Judicial Treatment of European Court of Human Rights Case Law: Beyond Compliance* (Routledge, 2020).

assessing the entrenchment of IHRL domestically. Yet, in needing to filter the topics we analyze to keep the purpose of this project feasible, we focus on these four topics because they reflect key overarching aspects that are also intertwined, which means that are central to the debate, but also needed to be addressed together lest we leave considerable gaps in the analysis. So, we use these four topics because of their mutual influence and because they take us to a more holistic and comprehensive understanding of the three key focus points we mentioned above: the relationship between the IACtHR and the three branches of government; the modalities of enforcement in the countries analyzed, and how this relationship, through these modalities, impact the entrenchment of international human rights domestically. To further unpack and justify our choice of topics, we will briefly draw the connection between each topic to some of the key points of our broader arguments.

1.2 *On Sewing and Legal Analysis*

We start building a typology of implementation by considering whether the domestic implementation system is embedded in a centralized or diffuse authority. This theme helps address the Velcro v stitches question as a centralized system concentrates implementation attributions under one branch, which may facilitate (in different degrees depending on which is the central branch, and without guaranteeing) a stitch-type connection between the domestic system and the Court. With all or most of the power to engage implementation efforts under one branch, it is more likely that the branch will succeed in reaching enforcement if it can coordinate all the pieces that need to be moved in order to reach that goal, as long as there is political will in that branch to do so. Relatedly, in a centralized system, political influences from different branches upon the central branch may be minimized as the other branches will not have much power over implementation efforts. On the downside, depending on which is the central branch and whether its political will favors implementation, victims in a centralized system will have to deposit all their hopes in that central branch, which can yield bad results where political will is unfavorable, leaving victims helpless. Moreover, a centralized system might lead the central branch to be more concerned about maintaining its power within the branch itself, such that it might also be cautious or even resistant to international law's influence, including as regards conventionality control. However, depending on the prevailing politics in the central branch at a given time, the centralized model might in fact facilitate communication with and monitoring by the IACtHR. In that case, the international influence domestically might be heightened precisely because all the implementation structure is coordinated under one branch, making access to information potentially easier for the IASPHR, and, from the opposite direction, clearing the Court's pathway to influence the work of the branch.

Conversely, in a diffuse system, diverging politics among branches may already hinder enforcement as the joint work and cumulative efforts of all branches might be fundamental to enforce an IACtHR judgment. Further, as the branches would share the power or mechanisms necessary for enforcement in a diffuse system, if diverging politics stop the branches from working together, that strong point of connection of enforcement reflected in the stitch might not be possible as the idleness of one branch would represent a much more significant obstacle compared to a centralized system. Moreover, in a diffuse system, as enforcement efforts are shared among branches and there is no central source of control over such efforts, the sparse implementation structure might generate an uncoordinated implementation structure that could make it too confusing and difficult for international influences to penetrate. Conversely, this same sparseness could leave more room for the influence of international law, even if disparately among branches, also facilitating conventionality control. In that case, victims could also benefit by having more avenues to claim their rights and remedies in a diffuse system since power to protect or implement those as shared. Therefore, if one branch is unwilling to engage the implementation system or fulfil its attributions within that system, victims might still have viable compliance pathways through other branches.

As regards our second topic, the clarity of the rules of the domestic implementation system, we consider clarity as it might reflect on the legitimacy and effectiveness of the system, and may be relevant in privileging technique (through clear, structured, rules, and processes) over shifting political will as the driving force underlying enforcement efforts. That is, the clarity of the rules regulating the domestic implementation system may help reduce the influence of political interests in how the system operates. Assessing clarity of these rules also helps consider how much room is left for procedural challenges and idleness within implementation structures. It also contributes to an assessment of the potential for confusion and inconsistency in the implementation system, which, alongside the role played by political influences, can relate (in an inversely proportional way) to how legitimate and effective the system might be. Analyzing the clarity of the domestic implementation system's rules also helps assessing the type of connection between the international and domestic spheres. Clear rules capable of generating consistency and predictability in the system's functioning would potentially point to stronger connections, facilitating a stitch-type entrenchment instead of softer, Velcro-type links. For the same reason, clarity can help victims understand how their rights are being addressed locally and how the remedies they were awarded may be enforced, enabling them to monitor the implementation process by tracking the corresponding (clear) rules. Further, considering how consistent and predictable an implementation system is through how clear its guiding rules are can also inform how open that system is to international influence. That is, with clarity, an international court might more easily understand how the system works, using this knowledge to find openings for productive engagement. Meanwhile, the lack of clarity might hinder, or be instrumentalized by domestic actors to hinder, the Court's influence locally, as well as victims' effective and informed pressure for compliance.

Another topic we investigate is the role of local politics in the domestic implementation system. Local politics can likely be present in any aspect or stage of implementation of IACtHR domestically, and are often a key driving factor of how that process unfolds. It consequently also relates to the legitimacy and efficacy of the system in its interaction with the rules of implementation. That is, when local politics favor implementation, they might also reinforce and facilitate the enforcement of implementation rules, creating, at least an appearance but also possibly a reality, of an effective and legitimate implementation process. In that way, local politics also affects victims, who may deposit more trust and hope in, and get more in return from, an implementation system that is corroborated by favorable political will. Further, favorable local politics also have a better potential to enable stitches in implementation, as the domestic process and rules might be taken more seriously and be undertook more comprehensively if endorsed by positive political will.

Conversely, when local politics oppose implementation, they are likely to hinder the application of those domestic rules, especially if such rules are unclear, which can affect the efficacy of the implementation system and raise questions on its legitimacy. As follows, victims will also be affected in this case by an inability to rely on the domestic system to implement the remedies awarded by the international court. Similarly, a stitch-type implementation is unlikely as the domestic authorities capable of materializing this stronger point of connection between the national and international spheres will possibly be uninterested in doing so, or hindered by other, politically opposed, authorities or branches.

Moreover, local politics are likely to shift constantly depending on a variety of factors, including changes in government and in regional contexts, which may also generate effects in the processes of domestic implementation of IACtHR rules, and lead to uncertainty and, maybe eventually skepticism, for victims. The form and extent of the reverberations of shifting local politics might also depend on which branch is more affected by these shifts, which highlights the need to study this topic in relation to each of the three branches. Ultimately, understanding the role of local politics is also important because of its direct, two-way, connection with IACtHR judgments. As we said above, local politics are likely to influence the enforcement (or not) of international decisions, but these decisions may also have the power to guide or highlight issues in domestic political discussions. This bidirectional relationship then directly relates to the level of influence that international law might have locally and its potential to shape the domestic sentiment, but also structures and processes, regarding human rights protection nationally.

Finally, we investigate the legitimacy of the authority or branch in the implementation process through the available pathways of communication between the IACtHR and that authority or branch. This analysis helps assess the role and possible importance of that branch in implementation efforts, and complements the examination of international law's influence domestically by looking at the possibilities for the Court to interact or partner with each branch, including to promote conventionality control. In assessing the Court's forms of interaction with each branch, we also consider the branch's legitimacy because where the Court finds a partner in compliance among domestic authorities, the Court might highlight this branch's role in implementation and empower it. This prominent role and empowerment may, in turn, reflect in the branch's legitimacy in the implementation system and even make that branch an ally domestically to defend the Court in local political debates regarding human rights protection, while also using (thus promoting) IACtHR judgments to justify the branch's moves. This analysis, thus, assists in understanding the possible modes of implementation (stitch or Velcro) available depending on with which branch the Court interacts and how the interaction unfolds (if in a one- or two-way relationship). In turn, identifying these pathways of communication and how they affect a certain branch's legitimacy may inform local mobilization for rights and remedies, as victims, stakeholders and activists might know which branch to target in seeking support for their claims. Ultimately, considering pathways of communication between the Court and domestic authorities and how they affect the latter's legitimacy is important in understanding the potential in each branch for productive partnerships with the Court, but also in considering how to maximize the potential for enforcement locally.

These topics, and this methodology, are of course useful for other human rights courts with binding jurisdiction (that is, the African and European courts). But it is worth considering whether the same usefulness transfers to United Nations Treaty Bodies, or other human rights bodies without binding jurisdiction. The key difference here is of course the binding nature of the remedies. While most United Nations Treaty Bodies do make recommendations on reparations, they have no mechanism (or formal legal power) to enforce them. Nonetheless, there are multiple instances of compliance with the findings of these bodies (albeit more susceptible to political winds and shifts than courts with binding jurisdiction), meaning that there is much to be learned about thinking of the work of these bodies in terms of stitches as well, as opposed to the Velcro-type analysis that pervades the available scholarship.

We use these four topics in our analysis as mechanisms through which to identify and examine the roles played by executive, judiciary and legislative. Investigating the branches is essential to our main goal of considering the emancipatory possibilities of human rights law in its entrenchment in domestic law, especially through the enforcement of the Inter-American Court's judgments. The branches reflect the avenues for entrenchment through enforcement, so understanding the potential, strengths, weaknesses, and motivations of each branch in fulfilling that goal is key to mapping out and understanding those emancipatory possibilities. As we indicated above, this type of thinking about distribution and sharing of competences also yields insights for federal power arrangements.

As regards motivations, the implementation of international human rights judgments may represent different motivating forces for each of the three branches. For the executive, implementation may reflect or relate to autonomy, mainly through the exercise of exclusive foreign affair powers that enable the executive to act regardless of the potential role to be played by other branches. The executive may also use implementation (or resistance to it) as a political lever to justify its own human rights policy actions domestically, and to strengthen or weaken (demonstrating opposition in) its relationship with other branches, depending on the other branch's stance on implementation.

For the judiciary, motivation in/for implementation might relate to its traditionally closer relationship with the IACtHR, and whether the national judges want to reciprocate the Court's historic alliance-prone and empowering approach to its relationship with domestic judges or push back. In turn, this decision on whether to reciprocate may depend on the domestic courts' willingness to advance human rights protection domestically through enforcement of IACtHR judgments and/or conventionality control, or if national courts want to reject this external influence or criticize it to justify judicial stances against human rights. Further, domestic courts' motivations in how they engage with the enforcement of IACtHR judgements may be influenced by inter-branch politics. Where the judiciary seeks to counter political resistance from other branches regarding human rights protection domestically,

IACtHR judgments may work as powerful reinforcers of national judges' decisions, adding legitimacy to the latter's work.

Finally, the legislature's relationship with the IACtHR is the least explored or is identified less obviously, including by the Court itself, compared to the other branches. Yet, the legislature does have important motivations in its engagement with the entrenchment of IHRL domestically through the enforcement of IACtHR judgments. In implementing remedies like the adoption of legislation or undertaking legal reform, or in regulating the national implementation system, the legislative branch has the ability to influence or create the law on a certain topic in that country and to dictate, through law-making, the work of other branches in implementation efforts. As the legislature is a highly political branch given its connection to the political will of the people, its motivations in acting for the implementation or not of IACtHR judgements concern its ability and willingness to reflect popular will and, in that way, seeking legitimacy to their actions in the Court's decisions or distancing itself from the Court's external influence. Further, the legislative branch might be motivated by its political relationship with the other branches, basing its work in implementing IACtHR decisions or not on whether it wants to use its position to monitor and pressure compliance efforts by other branches.

From this overview of our main methodological choices, we move to building a typology of implementation. First, we consider the executive branch and its work against the four topics we laid out above.

2 Executive Branch and Foreign Affairs

Generally, for the executive, enforcing international human rights judgments may convey exclusive foreign affairs powers unconditioned by the work of other branches.[3] However, despite particularities, different models and techniques in the implementation system of each state, the executive-led system often places the executive branch as a first enabler of implementation. In this role, the branch functions mostly as the organizer of enforcement, identifying other specific state authorities with competence to carry out certain tasks in such efforts. While this system led by the executive has vast potential to facilitate compliance and pursue the guarantee of victims' rights on the ground as it often reflects the second-generation conventionality control doctrine, it is still not shielded from political inclinations capable of affecting the relevant

3 For a broad exploration, see Sofia Reca Milanta, *La tutela ejecutiva en el Sistema Interamericano de Derechos Humanos. Siguiendo las huellas del cumplimiento* (Tirant lo Blanch, 2024).

authorities' will toward implementation. As follows, we will consider this implementation system through four topics that enable a better understanding of the effects of each model and allow us to explore pathways for more effective implementation, centered on the victim. First, we consider the level of concentration of power in implementation.

2.1 *Centralized v Diffuse Authority*

Under this theme, we assess how centralized is the task of enforcement in each country, whether it is mostly retained by one authority, or more diffuse. This analysis is necessary to assess how each country incorporates the current doctrine of conventionality control that seeks to spread the duty of implementation among different state authorities, and given that there are different models in Latin American states. On the one hand, in models within a federal system, the operationalization of this version of conventionality control can be complicated as the different branches, among different levels of government, can perceive their competence in conflicting ways, creating confusion in implementation. On the other hand, the role of the executive in federal states, when exercising foreign affair powers, can enhance its autonomy, or empower its initiative for action, in relation to other branches, at least compared to the executive's role vis-à-vis a domestic understanding of separation of powers.[4] Ultimately, here, we examine how this apportionment of authority to lead implementation unfolds in countries that privilege the role of the executive branch in implementation. This analysis is important as we consider issues that may arise in how this executive-centered system for implementation relates to the attributions, if any, of other state branches, and even within the executive itself.

Overall, a centralized system may be detached from the current idea of conventionality control, yet a model centered on the executive might facilitate implementation by being fully or mostly managed by a specific and sometimes specialized entity, despite possibly subjecting implementation to shifting political trends.[5] Conversely, a diffuse system seems to present a deeper engagement with conventionality control by enabling the spreading of enforcement efforts across the state's structure, which, in turn, may entail uncoordinated implementation, yet less conditioned to the political will of a specific branch of government.[6]

---

4 See Curtis A Bradley, 'What Is Foreign Relations Law?' in Curtis A Bradley (ed), *The Oxford Handbook of Comparative Foreign Relations Law* (Oxford University Press, 2019) 2, 13.

5 See Bolivia, Constitution of Bolivia, Art. 172(13); and Decreto Supremo No. 29894.

6 See Ecuador, Decreto Ejecutivo 560, and Decreto Ejecutivo 1317, 2008.

In any case, by reflecting the first point of contact with the international court when receiving judgments and its orders, executive-led enforcement efforts can, at least, enable a soft tracking of influence of human rights domestically through the executive's responses, references, debates, or mentions of IACtHR judgments. Yet, as the actual enforcement of IACtHR orders might require more focused engagement, a centralized authority exercising this engagement may more clearly track human rights influence domestically, serving as a better reflection of the stitch where the two points of contact, the centralized authority and the international court, are bonded closer together. Meanwhile, a diffuse enforcement system that may distribute enforcement efforts among competent entities throughout different branches may make the fewer points of connection between the international court and the domestic context in enforcement even more difficult to trace, perhaps better reflecting the Velcro patch (through the multitude of small points). This connection in an executive-led system, however, could reflect a stronger version of the Velcro patch as it originates from one initial strong, or closer, engagement, later diluting into smaller ones as the orders are scattered among other branches for implementation.

Against this backdrop, among the Latin American countries we analyzed, two models emerge amid a plurality of approaches. On the one hand, there is a diffuse system that entitles the executive to articulate implementation by being the initial enabler of it, but in charge of engaging other state authorities in implementing the orders for which they are competent.[7] This diffuse system favors the second generation of conventionality control by more actively engaging all the branches in implementation, but it also creates a risk of uncoordination among branches as regards their roles and prerogatives in implementation efforts, which can halt such efforts. On the other hand, there is a centralized system that centers most of the power to carry out the implementation efforts in one government authority, such as the President.[8] While this system can simplify the coordination of implementation as it falls under the centralized power of one branch that can make all decisions, it can also allow for too much unchecked political influence in implementation dependent on shifting political inclinations of the executive branch.

Showcasing the diffuse system, Ecuador's implementation of IACtHR judgments falls into the competence of the Secretariat of Human Rights[9] (previously the Ministry of Justice and Human Rights), a permanent body within the

7 See Ecuador, Decreto Ejecutivo 560, and Decreto Ejecutivo 1317, 2008.
8 See Bolivia, Constitution of Bolivia, Art. 172(13); and Decreto Supremo No. 29894.
9 Secretaría de Derechos Humanos.

executive branch which has the responsibility to 'coordinate the execution' of any type of IACtHR decisions,[10] either final judgments, provisional measures, advisory opinions, or others.[11] The Secretariat, working in collaboration with the 'General Prosecutor's Office',[12] has the function to 'coordinate with the competent state entity' to take the necessary measures for the full compliance with such obligations, which also entitles the executive to take the leading role in enforcement, but enabling the involvement of any relevant state bodies.[13] However, the Constitution shifts the responsibility from the executive to the judiciary where there is a failure to comply with a IHRL judgment that sets a 'an obligation to do or not to do [that] is clear, express and enforceable.'[14] This action for non-compliance must be presented before the Constitutional Court.[15] Finally, another act may complement this already complex structure by stating that an international decision (not necessarily from a human rights court) that orders material reparation, can be taken to the General Prosecutor's Office,[16] seemingly, for enforcement, not conditioned to a prior failure to comply.

As a possible example of the centralized system, Bolivia, at least as it regards enforcement of reparation orders for material compensation, assigns to the President the duty to '[t]o enforce the decisions of the courts.'[17] The state has itself also reported that the General Prosecutor's Office, in coordination with entities in the executive branch, is the one responsible for coordinating the implementation of IASPHR decisions on a case-by-case basis, including by identifying competent authorities in other branches, and engaging measures

10 Decreto Ejecutivo 560, 14 November 2018, Art. 2(a); Decreto Ejecutivo 1317, 2008.

11 Decreto Ejecutivo 560, 14 November 2018, Art. 2(a).

12 'Procurador General del Estado'; *Reglamento Orgánico Funcional de la Procuraduría General del Estado*, Resolución de la Procuraduría General del Estado 107, Registro Oficial Edición Especial 36, 13 July 2017, Art. 31.

13 Decreto Ejecutivo 1317, 2008, Art. 2(3). See also Comisión Interamericana de Derechos Humanos ['Inter-American Commission on Human Rights'], '*Mecanismos Nacionales de Implementación de Recomendaciones de Derechos Humanos*' ['*National Mechanisms for the Implementation of Human Rights Recommendations*'], Doc No OEA/Ser.L/V/II.doc.8/23, 26 February 2023, para 161.

14 Constitución de la República del Ecuador, Art. 93; see also Asamblea Nacional de la República del Ecuador, Ley Orgánica de Garantías Jurisdiccionales y Control Jurisdiccional, Suplemento del Registro Oficial N° 52, 22 de octubre de 2009, Art. 52.

15 Constitución de la República del Ecuador, Art. 93.

16 Ley Organica de Garantias Jurisdiccionales y Control Constitucional 2009, Art. 68. 'Procuradora o Procurador General'.

17 Constitution of Bolivia, Art. 172(13).

for domestic implementation.[18] Although other branches may have roles to play in implementation[19] (like congress acting when the IACtHR's orders involve legislative change,[20] and the judiciary when the IACtHR's decisions concern national judges),[21] we could not find further sources detailing their roles. Instead, several Supreme Decrees[22] or Acts[23] issued by the President seem to highlight the constitutional provision and indicate the President as the 'entity' responsible for implementation, especially for payment of damages, establishing the specific measures to be taken by different internal organs for compliance with IACtHR's reparation orders that involve some kind of pecuniary remedy.[24]

Considering these two main models, while a centralized system may concentrate the efforts toward enforcement under one authority and facilitate coordination, and possibly communication with and monitoring by the international court, it may more easily subject implementation to varying political

---

18 Comisión Interamericana de Derechos Humanos ['Inter-American Commission on Human Rights'], *'Mecanismos Nacionales de Implementación de Recomendaciones de Derechos Humanos'* [*'National Mechanisms for the Implementation of Human Rights Recommendations'*], Doc No OEA/Ser.L/V/II.doc.8/23, 26 February 2023, para. 139.

19 Ibid, para. 138.

20 Ibid, para. 142.

21 Ibid, para. 143. See also Tribunal Constitucional Plurinacional de Bolivia, *Sentencia Constitucional Plurinacional 0487/2014, Relator Tata Gualberto Cusi Mamani, Acción de Amparo Constitucional Expediente 04751-2013-10-AAC*, 25 February 2014; and Tribunal Constitucional Plurinacional de Bolivia, *Sentencia Constitucional 0110/2010-R, Relator Abigael Burgoa Ordóñez, Acción de Amparo Constitucional Expediente 2006–13381–27-RAC*, 10 de mayo de 2010.

22 DECRETO SUPREMO No 0840 del 06 de Abril de 2011, Establece el mecanismo financiero de pago de las medidas indemnizatorias a los beneficiarios señalados en la Sentencia de 1 de septiembre de 2010, Fondo, Reparaciones y Costas, emitida por la Corte Interamericana de Derechos Humanos en el Caso 'Ibsen Cárdenas e Ibsen Peña Vs. Bolivia; Decreto Supremo N° 27001, 17 de abril de 2003'; 'El presente Decreto Supremo tiene por objeto establecer los mecanismos para el cumplimiento de la Sentencia de Reparaciones dictada por la Corte Interamericana de Derechos Humanos, en fecha 27 de febrero de 2002', Art. 1; DECRETO SUPREMO N° 3260, 26 DE JULIO DE 2017, caso I.V. vs. Bolivia; DECRETO SUPREMO N° 3264, EVO MORALES AYMA, 26/07/2017, caso 'Andrade Salmón vs. Bolivia'; DECRETO SUPREMO N°. 1935, EVO MORALES AYMA, 19 Marzo 2014, CASO FAMILIA PACHECO TINEO VS. ESTADO PLURINACIONAL DE BOLIVIA.

23 LEY N° 971, LEY DE 16 DE AGOSTO DE 2017, related to enforcement of reparations orders in the case of I.V. Vs. Bolivia; LEY N° 091, LEY DE 2 DE MARZO DE 2011, caso Ticona Estrada y Otros Vs. Bolivia; y el caso Ibsen Cárdenas e Ibsen Peña Vs. Bolivia.

24 Comisión Interamericana de Derechos Humanos ['Inter-American Commission on Human Rights'], *'Mecanismos Nacionales de Implementación de Recomendaciones de Derechos Humanos'* [*'National Mechanisms for the Implementation of Human Rights Recommendations'*], Doc No OEA/Ser.L/V/II.doc.8/23, 26 February 2023, para 141.

trends, without a counterbalance or checking from other state authorities. A diffuse system thus might work better by enabling a structuring of the enforcement efforts based on the authorities better placed to perform them, and allowing all the branches to engage in conventionality control through their active role in implementation. Moreover, despite risking uncoordinated implementation, this diffuse model at least creates space for slicing and use of techniques specific to different governmental entities rather than highlighting the role political will may take in enforcement.

Nevertheless, to address the main shortcoming of the diffuse model (the risk of uncoordinated implementation), there must be clear rules establishing specific methods, mechanisms and techniques for enforcement of each type of international decision (final, provisional, recommendation) and the respective competent body to enforce them. That is, such rules should also clearly determine which state branch and organs should be responsible for different types of reparation orders (financial compensation, legislative reform, creation of entities or funds, and others based on existing IACtHR case law), as well as indicate specific alternative pathways in case of failure in compliance.

To help achieve these goals, the IACtHR could then, first, pursue a normative agenda by ordering states to establish clear rules to facilitate the understanding of the domestic implementation system, which would subsequently also facilitate monitoring. Second, this clarity could enable the pursuit of a descriptive agenda by the Court, allowing it to design their reparation orders according to a clear domestic model for implementation, and already indicating the pathways for enforcement, also facilitating monitoring. Considering the importance of clarity of the rules of implementation, we now assess this issue as a separate theme.

2.2 *Clarity of Rules for Implementation*

In this section, we assess the importance of clarity in domestic rules on implementation as a feature that may affect the legitimacy of the enforcement system and the effectiveness of implementation on the ground. Where the executive branch leads compliance efforts, clarity in the rules regulating the domestic implementation system may be particularly relevant as a lever for technique as opposed to creating room (through lack of clarity) for the prevalence of political considerations widely subjecting effective enforcement to political will.

Accordingly, clarity in the domestic implementation norms in an executive-led system may help minimize discretion, grounded on political interests, in the executive's power to engage or lead implementation. Meanwhile, the lack of clarity in such rules may hinder enforcement by generating idleness or procedural obstacles (like cyclical discussions among authorities as to who is competent to do what) in face of uncertainty as to possible pathways and the right entity to pursue them. Lack of clarity can also hamper enforcement by widening confusion and perpetuating inconsistency where obscure rules enable heightened discretion regarding tools for implementation to be employed in each case. In turn, confusion and inconsistency can undermine the legitimacy of the implementation system,[25] weakening its effectiveness in redressing violations in practice, and hindering monitoring by victims and/or the international court.

Moreover, clear rules on implementation can highlight the possible points of connection between the domestic and the international in the entrenchment of human rights locally by creating predictability, through consistency, in how the system is engaged. That is, with clear rules and the prevalence of technique that clarity enables, it may become easier to identify and expect, hence also track, those points of connection in the enforcement of a new judgement, which may go beyond a softer tracking of influence, instead entailing a closer and deeper connection. Lack of clarity, conversely, muddies the identification of a logic in the implementation system, making monitoring difficult, and hindering consistency and predictability. This confusing or blurred model thus obscures the possible points of connection between the IACtHR and domestic compliance, hindering its tracking either through specific enforcement efforts or the Court's broader 'influence' locally.

Considering these different effects of clear or unclear rules against the countries analyzed that centered implementation on the executive, there is one main model, with some divergences among countries, and one exceptional model from Colombia, as regards clarity of rules. For most countries, there is legislation, and often executive decrees, indicating the organ responsible for implementation, but frequently without mentioning the IACtHR directly, instead stating the competence as one to implement international judgements, or international decisions concerning human rights (violations).[26] A few countries within this model provide more detailed norms, such as Paraguay, that identifies the entity competent to implement decisions

25 See section 2.4 in this chapter.

26 Brazil, DECRETO Nº 11.341, DE 1º DE JANEIRO DE 2023, Annex I, Art. 6(I); Panama, Decreto Ejecutivo No. 367 de 17 de Agosto de 2018, Art. 80(f). Mexico, Reglamento Interior de la Secretaría de Gobernación, 31/05/2019, Arts. 45, III.

from the Inter-American System specifically, which already adds to clarity by directly stating which norms concern IACtHR judgements.[27]

Further, Honduras also has specific and detailed rules concerning the implementation of international decisions particularly involving the rights of human rights defenders,[28] but leaving unclear how this particular mechanism relates to the country's wider implementation system (involving other classes of victims). According to the state's submission to the IACHR in the latter's preparation of a report on implementation, Honduras's broader implementation system is predominantly executive-led, although with some participation from other branches in an Interinstitutional Workgroup on Human Rights that reflects the collaborative effort of several state entities toward implementation. However, we could not locate and get access to the document regulating the Workgroup and laying out each branch's attributions, which hinders a closer analysis. In any case, in this general model, beyond Honduras, the rules on implementation usually go only so far as to identify a competent entity and its sub-divisions (with other norms sometimes seeming to overlap and partially contradict these).[29] Yet, such rules mostly do not establish specific courses of action for different types of decisions or reparation orders, or clarify the executive's relationship with other state branches possibly involved (at the behest of the executive) in enforcement,[30] with exceptions like Costa Rica, which does address the relationship among the different branches.[31]

Finally, a model found exceptionally in Colombia counts on Working Groups created within the executive branch, through the Ministry of Foreign

27 Decreto N° 4367–2015 – Por cual se reestructura da Comisión Interinstitucional responsable de la ejecución de la acciones necesarias para el cumplimiento de las sentencias internacionales (CICSI), Arts. 3–5.

28 See Honduras, Ley de Protección para las y los Defensores de Derechos Humanos, Periodistas, Comunicadores Sociales y Operadores de Justicia – 15 mayo 2015 – Decreto No. 34–2015; REGLAMENTO GENERAL DE LA LEY DE PROTECCIÓN PARA LAS Y LOS DEFENSORES DE DERECHOS HUMANOS, PERIODISTAS, COMUNICADORES SOCIALES Y OPERADORES DE JUSTICIA – ACUERDO EJECUTIVO No.059–2016, Art. 59.

29 Decreto Ejecutivo 560, 14 November 2018, Art. 2(a). See Argentina: Ley 27431, Apruébase el Presupuesto General de la Administración Nacional para el Ejercicio 2018, 2 jan 2018, Art. 108; Decreto 50/2019 – DCTO-2019–50-APN-PTE – Estructura organizativa. Anexo II, p 253; and Decisión Administrativa N° 70 del 10 de febrero de 2020.

30 Decreto con Fuerza de Ley N. 3 – FIJA EL TEXTO REFUNDIDO, COORDINADO Y SISTEMATIZADO DE LA LEY ORGÁNICA DEL MINISTERIO DE JUSTICIA Y DERECHOS HUMANOS MINISTERIO DE JUSTICIA Y DERECHOS HUMANOS – 2 de diciembre de 2016, Art. 2(d); Nicaragua, Ley N° 212–1995–Ley de la Procuraduría para la Defensa de los Derechos Humanos, Art. 1.

31 Decreto Presidencial 36776-RE, del 9 de agosto de 2011, Art. 6 Annex.

Affairs, with specific attributions particular to (a) certain international human rights body(ies), and certain types of decision.[32] That is, considering the Inter-American System, a Working Group on compliance with international human rights organs' orders and recommendations handles decisions from the IACHR, and friendly agreements arising from the IASPHR system, for instance,[33] whereas a Working Group on issues of human rights protection manages cautionary and provisional measures from the IACHR and IACtHR.[34] Yet, the normative attributions of these Groups seem to focus on exchanging information, documentation, promotion of enforcement measures, and even representing the state[35] and preparing responses to individual petitions on human rights violations before UN bodies,[36] but the Groups themselves do not seem to possess implementation mechanisms.[37] The detailed rules assigning specific functions to each Working Group and identifying the IASPHR organs directly add clarity to a level of entrenchment of IHRL domestically, but they are limited to informing and 'articulating' internal measures,[38] leaving actual enforcement to each competent national authority, without as much clarity of their attributions at the practical compliance level.

As regards active mechanisms for implementation, Colombia subjects the domestic implementation of international pecuniary orders to validation by a committee of ministries,[39] and establishes rather detailed rules on the proce-

---

32 Resolución 9709, 5 December 2017, Diario Oficial No. 50.444 de 11 de diciembre de 2017, Arts. 38, 39, 41. See also Comisión Interamericana de Derechos Humanos ['Inter-American Commission on Human Rights'], *'Mecanismos Nacionales de Implementación de Recomendaciones de Derechos Humanos'* [*'National Mechanisms for the Implementation of Human Rights Recommendations'*], Doc No OEA/Ser.L/V/II.doc.8/23, 26 February 2023, para 122.

33 Resolución 9709, 5 December 2017, Diario Oficial No. 50.444 de 11 de diciembre de 2017, Art. 41(1).

34 Resolución 9709, 5 December 2017, Diario Oficial No. 50.444 de 11 de diciembre de 2017, Art. 39(1).

35 Resolución 9709, 5 December 2017, Diario Oficial No. 50.444 de 11 de diciembre de 2017, Art. 41(2).

36 Resolución 9709, 5 December 2017, Diario Oficial No. 50.444 de 11 de diciembre de 2017, Art. 39(4).

37 Comisión Interamericana de Derechos Humanos ['Inter-American Commission on Human Rights'], *'Mecanismos Nacionales de Implementación de Recomendaciones de Derechos Humanos'* [*'National Mechanisms for the Implementation of Human Rights Recommendations'*], Doc No OEA/Ser.L/V/II.doc.8/23, 26 February 2023, para 123.

38 Resolución 9709, 5 December 2017, Diario Oficial No. 50.444 de 11 de diciembre de 2017, Art. 41(7).

39 LEY 288 DE 1996, julio 5, 'Por medio de la cual se establecen instrumentos para la indemnización de perjuicio a las víctimas de violaciones de derechos humanos en

dure for execution of the international reparation orders that involve payment of compensation.[40] For other types of orders, an intersectoral committee is in charge of promoting compliance with international human rights obligations,[41] and determining which state entity is responsible for implementing reparation orders in international human rights judgments; although how this last function reconciles with the Working Groups' articulation of implementation is unclear. It then seems that Colombian authorities have placed significant emphasis on the regulation of the entrenchment of IHRL domestically, such that it ends up creating some obscurity due to overlapping norms and a variety of entities with also potentially overlapping attributions. Case law in Colombia, for instance related to the case of *Ituango Massacres v. Colombia*,[42] has confirmed that, in IACtHR decisions that offer other measures beyond compensation in its reparations—such as *restitutio in integrum*, rehabilitation or guarantees of non-repetition—the domestic system offer significant challenges for implementation.[43]

Further, within the broader model, there is Panama offering rather general, abstract, rules, that relate to complying with international obligations more generally,[44] or restricting the human rights department within the Ministry of Foreign Affairs to a mere function of 'incentivizing' compliance with human rights international obligations, instead of setting more precise norms concerning IACtHR decisions specifically. Conversely, Argentina has more direct norms, but still not entirely clear given the seemingly overlapping character of some applicable rules.[45] That is, a 2018 act,[46] complemented by a decree,[47] assign to the executive branch, through ministries, the power to create 'tem-

---

virtud de lo dispuesto por determinados órganos internacionales de Derechos Humanos', Art. 2.

40 LEY 288 DE 1996, julio 5, 'Por medio de la cual se establecen instrumentos para la indemnización de perjuicio a las víctimas de violaciones de derechos humanos en virtud de lo dispuesto por determinados órganos internacionales de Derechos Humanos', Art. 2(2).

41 Decree 1216/2016, Art. 2.1.7.2.3(5).

42 I/A Court H.R., Case of the Ituango Massacres v. Colombia. Preliminary Objection, Merits, Reparations and Costs. Judgment of July 1, 2006. Series C No. 148.

43 Expediente T-2499665, Fecha sentencia 2010–05–11, Sentencia T-367/10.

44 Decreto Ejecutivo No. 367 de 17 de Agosto de 2018, Art. 80(f). Ley organica, Art. 86(c).

45 For an exploration of the Argentinean context, see A. Rousset Siri, *Ejecución de las sentencias de la Corte Interamericana de Derechos Humanos en el ámbito interno de la República Argentina* (Buenos Aires: EDIAR, 2018).

46 Ley 27431, Apruébase el Presupuesto General de la Administración Nacional para el Ejercicio 2018, 2 jan 2018, Art. 108.

47 Decreto Nº 167/18.

porary enforcement units'[48] to manage transitional and exceptional projects, including enforcing IACtHR judgments. Yet, an Administrative Decision of 2020 assigns to the Directorate of International Disputes in the Field of Human Rights,[49] within the Ministry of Foreign Affairs, International Commerce and Worship[50] the responsibility to take actions to advance the domestic implementation of provisional measures, recommendations or full judgments from the IACtHR.[51]

Thus, in relation to the IACtHR judgment on *Indigenous Communities of the Lhaka Honhat (Our Land) Association v. Argentina*,[52] the Ministry of Justice and Human Rights, through a resolution,[53] created a special temporary executory unit to take action toward implementing the decision within its Secretariat of Human Rights, yet this unit must work in coordination with the Directorate. Overall, despite apparently overlapping, but more likely complementary, norms, Argentina centers implementation on the executive power, entitling ministries to create new, temporary organs, entirely targeted at the implementation of IACtHR decisions, but working alongside, and in coordination with, other (permanent) bodies. The state has informed the IACHR that its system aims to deal with each international decision on an ad hoc basis, in a tailored way, with the executive leading the efforts and directing decisions to the respective competent entity, while the Supreme Court and Congress have also played important roles in implementation.[54] This structure, which the IACHR has perceived as lacking a formal implementation mechanism,[55] could favor effective implementation given the executive's flexibility in articulating compliance efforts according to the most appropriate entity to oper-

48 'Unidades ejecutoras temporarias'.

49 'Dirección de Contencioso Internacional en Materia de Derechos Humanos'.

50 'Ministerio de Relaciones Exteriores, Comercio Internacional y Culto'.

51 Decisión Administrativa N° 70 del 10 de febrero de 2020.

52 I/A Court H.R., Case of the Indigenous Communities of the Lhaka Honhat Association (Our Land) v. Argentina. Merits, Reparations and Costs. Judgment of February 6, 2020. Series C No. 400.

53 Resolución 979/2021, RESOL-2021–979-APN-MJ, 20 August 2021.

54 Comisión Interamericana de Derechos Humanos ['Inter-American Commission on Human Rights'], *'Mecanismos Nacionales de Implementación de Recomendaciones de Derechos Humanos'* [*'National Mechanisms for the Implementation of Human Rights Recommendations'*], Doc No OEA/Ser.L/V/II.doc.8/23, 26 February 2023, paras. 131 and 134.

55 Comisión Interamericana de Derechos Humanos ['Inter-American Commission on Human Rights'], *'Mecanismos Nacionales de Implementación de Recomendaciones de Derechos Humanos'* [*'National Mechanisms for the Implementation of Human Rights Recommendations'*], Doc No OEA/Ser.L/V/II.doc.8/23, 26 February 2023, para 132.

ationalize a given order, yet it does not seem to offer an alternative in case the executive fails to articulate its attributions toward implementation.

From these examples, while it may be useful to have flexibility in domestic rules on implementation so that national authorities can adjust to and accommodate new forms of reparations more easily, a flexibility that arises from lack of clarity may be risky, instead of beneficial. Especially in the executive branch, clarity in enforcement norms is important to maintain the technical boundaries or pathways of implementation against the discretion attached to political will. Yet, a system with clear, detailed but still flexible, rules would benefit from being comprehensive by covering specific pathways for implementation of each type of decision, addressing enforcement tools for a variety of possible reparation orders, and being applicable to any type of victim coming before the IACtHR. The norms in such a system should be targeted rather than general; that is, mentioning specifically that they apply to the implementation of IACtHR (or international human rights courts) decisions, rather than general international commitments, which may facilitate the development of the system on the ground through human rights-based rationales.

As follows, clarity of rules can be important for the IACtHR in developing both descriptive and normative agendas. For a descriptive agenda, clarity is fundamental to enable the IACtHR to understand the domestic implementation system when the Court designs its reparation orders, indicating the adequate pathways for enforcement, and being able to monitor compliance effectively. With a normative agenda, in turn, the IACtHR can actively address the lack of clear rules, taking a stronger role in pushing for domestic institutional design choices capable of clarifying the domestic implementation system, making it human-rights-oriented, facilitating and fostering compliance.

While clarity could aid the Court's work in designing its orders as it would be aware of the specific mechanisms and attributions within a country's system for implementation and use this knowledge to tailor its judgment and monitor compliance, there are still other domestic circumstances capable of hindering enforcement. That is, a heightened influence of domestic politics can render even clear rules somewhat impotent, since the lack of political will may overpower the potential of technique afforded by clarity.[56] The next section thus assesses how dependence on shifts in local politics may affect enforcement in executive-led implementation systems.

---

56 See Courtney Hillebrecht, 'The Domestic Mechanisms of Compliance with International Human Rights Law: Case Studies from the Inter-American Human Rights System' (2012) 34(4) *Human Rights Quarterly* 959, 971–72 ('The Domestic Mechanisms of Compliance').

2.3 *Dependence on Shifts in Local Politics*

Extensive literature on this topic has reiterated that domestic politics is a significant, if not predominant, element affecting enforcement of international human rights judgments domestically.[57] One reason for this influence might be because the OAS political organs, unlike their European counterparts, do not engage with monitoring or fostering compliance with the OAS's human rights instruments, and member states will also refrain from pressuring others to comply in fear of retribution when they are the respondent state,[58] leaving compliance susceptible to shifting domestic political winds. That is, this hands-off approach from OAS political bodies makes enforcement especially susceptible to pressure (or lack thereof) from national authorities, institutions, and civil society, despite the role the IASPHR plays in monitoring.

Moreover, the relationship between IACtHR judgments and domestic politics is bidirectional, since not only domestic politics may dictate whether and how a judgment is enforced, but IACtHR judgements can also stir the domestic political debates and mobilization in a certain direction, making this topic doubly relevant.[59] In this two-way relationship, national authorities may approach enforcement as a political tool, depending on their political interests at a given time.[60] For instance, if the executive wants to build an image of respect to human rights and commitment to the IASPHR, compliance can be used to demonstrate this intention; conversely, if the executive wants to undermine the work of the IASPHR, a judgment can be used to criticize the Court's intervention domestically, and strengthen nationalistic discourses.[61] Other branches of government and civil society, however, if opposing the executive, may also use an IACtHR decision to counter the executive, embed their opposition and seek political change.[62] Ultimately, these political instru-

---

57 Jillienne Haglund, 'International Institutional Design and Human Rights: The Case of the Inter-American Human Rights System' (2019) 36(6) *Conflict Management and Peace Science* 608, 608 ('International Institutional Design and Human Rights'); Hillebrecht, 'The Domestic Mechanisms of Compliance', cit., 962.

58 Hillebrecht, 'The Domestic Mechanisms of Compliance', cit., 962.

59 Haglund, cit., 608.

60 See Courtney Hillebrecht, *Domestic Politics and International Human Rights Tribunals: The Problem of Compliance* (Cambridge University Press, 2014) 136.

61 See Rene Uruena, 'Double or Nothing: The Inter-American Court of Human Rights in an Increasingly Adverse Context' (2017) 35(2) *Wisconsin International Law Journal* 398, 417–418 ('Double or Nothing').

62 Hillebrecht, *Domestic Politics and International Human Rights Tribunals: The Problem of Compliance*, cit., 136.

mentalizations of IACtHR decisions, and their consequent effects on enforcement, justify the need to consider this topic closely here.

As follows, although all branches of government may use an IACtHR judgment to advance their political interests, depending on which branch leads the implementation process, the politicization of an IACtHR decision may have different effects on enforcement. For one, in an executive-led system, the government's national agenda for human rights, based on the political inclinations of the leader of the executive branch, could also affect availability of or access to mechanisms and resources for compliance, hence also severely affecting, positively or negatively, efforts for enforcement.[63] In a system reflective of the current generation of conventionality control, the other branches would also have a significant role to play in enforcement[64] and in keeping the executive in check, which will happen if doing so is politically appealing for the other branches. Yet the executive, in a centralized system, may still yield enough power to push (at least some of) their political interests forward through (compliance or non-compliance with) IACtHR judgments despite some resistance from other branches or civil society. Thus, the type of system in place might indeed affect how domestic politics affect enforcement, perhaps especially when such a system is led by and centralized on the executive. Or, as Courtney Hillebrecht has put it, '[…] while international law can be an impetus for action for a range of domestic actors, their relative power affects who can leverage the power of international law.'[65]

For an executive-led implementation system, the role of politics affects both the overall influence of IACtHR decisions nationally and actual enforcement efforts. In that way, the political inclinations of the executive vis-à-vis human rights and international human rights courts can shape the broader national discourse around human rights, creating either supportive or dismissive policies and approaches from the executive towards the domestic impact of IACtHR judgments.[66] The other branches may contest whatever position the executive takes, yet the executive may still ensure its approach dictates at least some of the efforts for the softer tracking of the Court's influence. For instance, the executive's stance on human rights is likely to also dictate whether it will promote or refute rights reforms, engage with or ignore civil

63 See Hillebrecht, 'The Domestic Mechanisms of Compliance', cit., 965.

64 See Ibid.

65 Ibid 966.

66 Ibid 969. Courtney Hillebrecht, 'Human Rights Tribunals and the Challenge of Compliance' in Courtney Hillebrecht (ed), *Domestic Politics and International Human Rights Tribunals: The Problem of Compliance* (Cambridge University Press, 2014) 1, 17.

society mobilization, seek support toward compliance from other branches or rebut their calls for joint action,[67] and call society's attention to human rights issues or minimize or overlook them. Ultimately, the direction the executive takes based on its political interest regarding human rights can enable or hinder the tracking of their influence domestically. In any case, even if contrary views lead to national debate and mobilization that draws attention to an IACtHR decision, it still does not necessarily reflect a stronger enforcement record. Or worse, it can further dim this already soft effort to connect international human rights judgments with domestic effects in practice, and undermine the tracking of influence, which would likely not reflect positively on enforcement.

Connecting the influence of local politics in enforcement with the other themes above, two main models seem to be available: one, in which the executive is indeed leading the implementation effort, but, according to the rules, such an effort is shared with other branches, thus more diffuse, pending a prompt from the executive engaging another branch in implementation. In this model, the role of local politics in enforcement may be somewhat diminished as the other branches would have a clearer and stronger role in compliance efforts, thus theoretically better placed to push the executive towards compliance. Another model may have clear or unclear domestic rules on implementation, but either way it does provide a centralized, executive-led, system that leaves little room for interference and checks from other branches (unless their involvement is clearly prompted by the executive, which, here, becomes more dependent on the executive's political stance). This context could mean more room for political influence since the executive would choose a course of action for implementation based on its political interest, and would remain unchecked, or could ignore any pressure, by other domestic authorities.

While Panama could be an example of the first (diffuse) model, where the influence of local politics can be minimized by the role of other branches, especially the judiciary, it may also, and perhaps more likely, exemplify the centralized, more politically influenced model. That is, the norms establishing responsibility for implementation, coming from executive decrees,[68] are somewhat vague and concern international obligations broadly, rather than human rights judgments, besides not spelling out how this responsibility is shared with other branches. Further, considering the Supreme Court of Justice judgment on a case about the enforcement of the *Baena Ricardo et al.*

67 Hillebrecht, 'The Domestic Mechanisms of Compliance', cit., 969.

68 Decreto Ejecutivo No. 367, Art. 80(f), Departamento de Asesoría legal Internacional.

v. Panama judgment,[69] it appears that the judiciary will not get involved in enforcement if the executive is in the process of implementing the IACtHR judgment.[70] While this decision could indicate the possibility of judicial intervention when the executive fails to comply, it more readily shows that the judiciary will refrain from acting if the executive claims to still be carrying out implementation. This scenario leaves a lot of room for political influence, first, because the prevalence of executive power with no clarity regarding when other branches should get involved gives the executive plenty of room for political maneuvering, and second, because the judiciary withdrew itself from a position to check/get involved with the executive efforts at implementation, which widens the latter's power. Moreover, it is unclear whether this move from the Supreme Court is part of an effort to distance itself from politics by not engaging in the executive's political motivations to pursue compliance or not, or it is, in fact, a political move from the Supreme Court to not oppose the executive because, perhaps, of aligned political inclinations between both branches.

An example of the diffuse model, potentially less inclined to political influence, is Ecuador. It does have an executive-led system, in which the executive is entitled to coordinate implementation,[71] and expressly entails involving any relevant, competent, state bodies in that coordination.[72] This clearer, necessary engagement with other state authorities could also work to validate other branches' checks on the executive if it is leading implementation based on political interests. At the same time, it means that divergent political inclinations between branches could have a stronger role to play, including to the point of halting enforcement measures. Ultimately, however, in Ecuador, the Constitution (reflecting the legislature's role) entitles the Judiciary to act, through an action presented to the Constitutional Court, when the executive fails to implement a clearly enforceable obligation to do or not do.[73] In this case, a more concerted, integrated, action involving the legislature (through the constitution) and the judiciary (through the Constitutional Court) in view

---

69 I/A Court H.R., Case of Baena Ricardo et al. v. Panama. Merits, Reparations and Costs. Judgment of February 2, 2001. Series C No. 72.

70 Corte Suprema de Justicia, Panamá, 18 Octubre 2004 – Supreme Court Judgment regarding the enforcement of the IACtHR decision on Baena Ricardo et al. v. Panama (2001). https://vlex.com.pa/vid/sentencia-tercera-administrativo-laboral-31666740.

71 Decreto Ejecutivo 560, 14 november 2018, Art. 2(a); Decreto Ejecutivo 1317, 2008.

72 Decreto Ejecutivo 1317, 2008, Art. 2(3).

73 Constitución de la República del Ecuador, Art. 93; see also Ley Organica de Garantias Jurisdiccionales y Control Constitucional 2009 (última modificación – 2020), Art. 52, Art. 93.

of the executive's failure to comply, could reflect an attempt, based on technique, to respond to the executive's political inclinations leading to non-compliance.

Considering those examples and the models assessed above, an executive-led, diffuse system with clear rules that enable other branches to be involved in a compliance coalition would possibly represent a better model. This model would not eliminate the role domestic politics play in implementation, but could at least limit the extent to which the executive could lead implementation according to its political inclinations. This limitation is not necessarily positive in a context where the executive favors human rights and other branches counter its approach, yet this model, with clear rules on each branch's role in implementation, is more likely to enable some consistency by limiting the width of changes in compliance efforts based on local political shifts.

These considerations suggest that there is not yet a model capable of eliminating political interests from the domestic implementation of IACtHR judgements. Thus, as we suggested above, a turn to technique is fundamental to enable compliance efforts that have clear legal paths to follow in pursuing enforcement, minimizing the room for politics to intervene in such efforts. In an executive-led system, this turn to technique could mean, again, clear rules on the responsibility of the executive in coordinating implementation, and on the roles of each branch not just in that coordination, but also in checking, pushing, and demanding action from the executive, and each other, vis-à-vis failures to implement the Court's orders.[74]

Against this background, the IACtHR could react to the ever-present role of domestic political shifts in enforcement by interacting with domestic institutions in its pursuit of a normative agenda. That is, the Court should promote and order institutional design choices embedded in clear rules regarding the structure, processes, and mechanisms for enforcement. It should require changes in domestic implementation systems to ensure that the responsibility of each branch is laid out, and with room for collaboration and implementation coalitions, enabling conventionality control by all branches. These efforts should be guided by technique, and present avenues for the legislature and judiciary to check the executive and offer express alternatives when the latter fails to comply due to lacking political will. Such measures are not only important for compliance and real effects of IACtHR judgments for victims on the

74 See section 3.3, in this chapter, on how IACtHR judgments can also be used politically in how domestic authorities deal with complex human rights issues and conflicting norms.

ground, but also reflect on the legitimacy of the implementation system and of the branch leading it, to which we turn next.

2.4 *Directness of Connection to IACtHR*

The pathways available for the IACtHR to interact with the different branches of government domestically are also important in determining and/or valuing the role of that branch in implementation efforts. The Court may seek to build or broaden pathways to communicate with different branches to consolidate partnerships with the branches and rely on them for compliance. Historically the Court has nurtured this partnership with domestic judiciaries but has more recently sought to widen that by including all branches in the doctrine of conventionality control. Moreover, technically, as an international organization, the IACtHR often liaises directly with the executive branch via the ministry of foreign affairs as well, even if a lot of those communications are more 'clerical' in nature (notification of judgments and orders against that state and any other state, advising on new requests for advisory opinions, etc.). Accordingly, where the Court finds compliance partners domestically, it may empower that partner in its orders, whom may then not only promote implementation internally, using the Court's decision to legitimize their own domestic actions and policies, but also more broadly come in the Court's defense when other branches attack it.[75] Therefore, the relationships built by the IACtHR with domestic state entities and the corresponding pathways of communication between them, can also affect the legitimacy of that branch's work in enforcement efforts, the legitimacy of the branch itself as it uses IACtHR judgments to justify its own actions, and how the Court perceives that legitimacy and uses it in shaping its ongoing work. Understanding these pathways is thus fundamental in informing not just the Court, in a descriptive agenda, but also domestic social mobilization efforts that could identify which state authorities to coalesce with in their plight.

In executive-led systems, the executive branch assumes the responsibility of coordinating implementation and ensuring that state authorities take the necessary measures to fulfil the Court's orders. Since the executive is a largely politically oriented branch, its role in implementation may depend on political interests and its perception of consequent reputational costs, which can taper the potential of its communication with the Court and affect its legiti-

75 Ximena Soley and Silvia Steininger, 'Parting Ways or Lashing Back? Withdrawals, Backlash and the Inter-American Court of Human Rights' (2018) 14(2) *International Journal of Law in Context* 237, 255. See also Hillebrecht, 'Human Rights Tribunals and the Challenge of Compliance', cit., 14.

macy as leading the implementation system. Conversely, where the executive approaches international human rights decisions and their implementation as part of its foreign affair powers, independent of action by the other branches, its communication with the Court may be strengthened because the Court may direct its attention to the executive as a potential compliance partner. In such cases, the executive becomes the first and final point of contact between the domestic and the international, and the approach it takes to implementation may be more readily covered by a cloak of legitimacy since there is no technical means for check from other branches, and since the Court itself might uphold the executive's central role in implementation, at least when the executive behaves, politically, in favor of the Court. Understanding the different models of domestic implementation systems and their pathways of communication with the IACtHR thus also relates to assessing the legitimacy of their respective structures, and of the branch of government leading that structure.

As regards the executive branch and its means of communication with the Court, the executive often works as a gatekeeper of the IACtHR's decisions entering the domestic sphere, since it is the branch that works directly with the Court and Commission receiving their judgments and recommendations, liaising with them in the efforts to resolve a rights claim or case.[76] Accordingly, the executive will exert some influence on how a new judgment is received and its implementation approached nationally.[77] In an executive-led implementation system, therefore, this branch 'exercises substantial control over the flow of cases, facilitating or hampering the delegation of compliance responsibility to other domestic actors. The more power the executive has, the more weight its preferences regarding compliance hold.'[78] Thus, the executive's approach to a new judgment may be easily perceived as legitimate depending on the amount of power the executive holds and how it chooses to use it in shaping how a judgment is received. Still, the pathways of communication between the Court and the executive can also exercise significant influence in this process, given the possibility of the Court to seek a partnership with the executive which can facilitate compliance. Ultimately, the legitimacy of the branch's engagement with IACtHR decisions and how it approaches implementation domestically will affect the actual implementation efforts, or lack thereof, since the state entity may feel undisputed and justified in whatever course of action it chooses to take if it has, or is perceived

76 Hillebrecht, 'The Domestic Mechanisms of Compliance', cit., 966.

77 Ibid.

78 Ibid, 967.

to have (by other branches, society, the Court), legitimacy. Yet, the pathways for the Court to engage with the branch may also affect enforcement, since such pathways can influence whether the Court can secure the branch's partnership in domestic implementation. Assessing these pathways and how they can affect legitimacy, and ultimately, compliance, is thus fundamental in understanding both the choices the Court has to proactively engage with domestic actors seeking positive collaborations, but also to maximize the possibilities for compliance with real effects on the ground.

For the executive, as it necessarily engages with the IACtHR by responding to the steps of a case being judged by the Court and ultimately receiving its decisions and having to liaise with it throughout monitoring, all the effects of this direct engagement can reflect the Court's influence domestically. It is only when the executive carries out efforts for implementation that its relationship with the Court stops reflecting a Velcro patch that indicates minor points of contact, and starts reflecting a stitch, as implementation takes shape. Yet, because the executive's role in communicating with the Court is so prominent in the steps prior to implementation, a lot can be understood from their relationship from a tracking of those pre-compliance moments of interaction. That is, in an executive-led system, the Velcro patch of that pre-compliance connection can show a lot of the Court's influence domestically, at least as it reflects the executive's willingness (or lack thereof) to cooperate. Although this analysis of the Velcro patch of the communications between Court and executive can be interesting and telling, and suggest the executive's legitimacy in leading domestic efforts, it says little about implementation itself or of a commitment to actual compliance.

Thus, as regards actual models of implementation, as we said above, the executive might perceive implementation of IACtHR decisions as included in its foreign affair powers, which enables action by the executive regardless of acquiescence by other branches. As follows, in the countries analyzed, one model reflects this approach, highlighting the executive's role and legitimizing its competence to lead implementation, although capable of involving other branches in it. Another model, often with less clear rules, shares competence and legitimacy to engage in implementation between the executive and other branches, which can create confusion (and potentially stagnation), but also clouding each branch's ways to communicate with the Court, although better upholding the separation of powers. Without clarity, however, this model can undermine the executive's legitimacy if its specific competence is unclear, and if its role in leading implementation can be disputed by other branches, given the unclear structure in place. That is, since it is difficult to identify for what processes each branch is competent, it also becomes difficult to legitimize their actions in operationalizing those processes.

Paraguay may exemplify the first model, where a decree directly addresses the implementation of international judgments.[79] The decree establishes the Interinstitutional Executive Commission,[80] presided by the vice-president of Paraguay and coordinated by the Ministry of Foreign Affairs, and responsible for establishing and implementing the schedule for compliance actions for any human rights commitments arising from the Inter-American System.[81] The Commission can identify the institutions, in all state branches,[82] effectively competent to implement international decisions, and such institutions must present their plans and actions toward implementation in each meeting for which they are summoned.[83] Thus, somewhat clear rules establish that the executive power is the starting point and manager of implementation, and while any state organ may be involved, at the behest of the executive, these other branches apparently still respond to the Executive Commission, which reflect a powerful executive, leading implementation and legitimized by clear rules on competence.

Nicaragua might exemplify the other model, as the Criminal Attorney Office,[84] part of the General Attorney's Office's structure in the executive branch, is responsible for processing all requests from the Inter-American System in matters within its competence.[85] Alongside the Criminal Attorney Office, the Ombudsman for the Defense of Human Rights,[86] an independent

79 Decreto N° 4367–2015 – Por cual se reestructura da Comisión Interinstitucional responsable de la ejecución de la acciones necesarias para el cumplimiento de las sentencias internacionales (CICSI).

80 'Comisión Interinstitucional Ejecutiva'.

81 Decreto N° 4367–2015 – Por cual se reestructura da Comisión Interinstitucional responsable de la ejecución de la acciones necesarias para el cumplimiento de las sentencias internacionales (CICSI), Arts. 3–5.

82 Comisión Interamericana de Derechos Humanos ['Inter-American Commission on Human Rights'], *'Mecanismos Nacionales de Implementación de Recomendaciones de Derechos Humanos'* [*'National Mechanisms for the Implementation of Human Rights Recommendations'*], Doc No OEA/Ser.L/V/II.doc.8/23, 26 February 2023, para 145.

83 Decreto N° 4367–2015 – Por cual se reestructura da Comisión Interinstitucional responsable de la ejecución de la acciones necesarias para el cumplimiento de las sentencias internacionales (CICSI), Art. 8.

84 'Procuraduría Penal'.

85 REGLAMENTO DE LA LEY ORGÁNICA DE LA PROCURADURÍA GENERAL DE LA REPÚBLICA – DECRETO EJECUTIVO N° 19–2009, Art. 27(5).

86 'Procuraduría para la Defensa de los Derechos Humanos'.

organ with administrative autonomy,[87] is entitled to protect human rights established in the constitution and 'in international human rights instruments that may be ratified in the future by Nicaragua.'[88] This Ombudsman replaces a homonymous ombudsman whose regulation connected it to the OAS bodies, but which was extinguished. At the time of writing, the new Ombudsman had not yet been regulated, leaving the relationship between it and the Criminal Attorney Office unclear, as well as the former's practical role in implementation. Nevertheless, the co-existence of an entity in the executive alongside an independent organ may reflect an effort to keep the branches in check and minimize political influence, yet it could have the effect of undermining their legitimacy in acting toward implementation, also clouding their means to engage with the Court, and hampering monitoring.

While having a check on the executive enabled by other branches' role in implementation is, a priori, a positive feature that better reflects an effort toward second generation conventionality control, and may help diminish the influence of the executive's political interests, it may also create confusion without clear rules to determine each branch's competence and hinder compliance. Conversely, a system led by the executive with less room for engagement of other branches, or with very unclear rules on how that engagement should take place, is also detrimental to implementation, not just because of its susceptibility to the executive's political will, but also because the concerted involvement of other branches is often crucial to full compliance. The model in Paraguay might reflect the best option here, though, as the executive leads implementation but there is possibility for engagement of other branches. An issue could arise, nevertheless, where political interests lead the executive to oppose the IACtHR, and reject or ignore other branches' pressure toward compliance. Without clarity and technique dictating the role of the other branches, the executive, approaching implementation as part of its foreign affairs powers, could hinder compliance entirely.

Thus, an executive-led system must benefit from clear rules laying out its pathways to communicate with the Court, so its own legitimacy is secured, but also needs clarity and technique on how other branches get involved in implementation in a coalition with the executive, also specifying their own means to engage with the IACtHR. That is because '[c]onstraints on the executive only work in facilitating compliance when domestic institutions can constrain

87 Ley N° 1174, 24 November 2023, Ley de la Procuraduría para la Defensa de los Derechos Humanos, Art. 2.

88 Ley N° 1174, 24 November 2023, Ley de la Procuraduría para la Defensa de los Derechos Humanos, Art. 4.

and partner with the executive effectively',[89] which means that their competence must also be clearly stated so their work in implementation and in checking the executive can be legitimate. Further, there must be clear pathways for communication between all branches and the Court, and, in an executive-led system, these pathways must be developed with a view to building a partnership with the IACtHR. The clarity of other branches' role in implementation is thus fundamental to keep the executive in check, and possibly minimize political interference in compliance, but also to enable full compliance and the legitimate action of other branches in a concerted effort toward implementation.

Considering these goals, the importance of joint action by all the branches in implementation can inform a descriptive agenda for the Court, as in its orders the IACtHR could consider the potential for enforcement by different state entities through the means and pathways for engagement with the Court that a certain entity offers. In turn, being aware of these pathways, the Court might explore them in its judgments, expanding means to communicate with all the branches, besides identifying avenues to more easily monitor compliance by knowing what to expect, from whom, and how to demand action from the competent entity. Further, in pursuing a normative agenda, the IACtHR should understand the role played by each branch in implementation to then order institutional design changes that facilitate communication with the Court and clarify the competence of each branch, so that the executive organizes implementation with those competences in mind, enhancing its own legitimacy, enabling full compliance and facilitating monitoring.

Although the executive has a source of legitimacy by being the first point of contact of the IACtHR in its interaction with domestic systems, the Court has historically promoted its relationship with domestic judiciaries as its natural allies. We thus turn to the judicial branch to examine its current and potential roles in implementation and further investigate its connection to the IACtHR.

3 Judicial Branch and Private International Law Technique

Domestic courts tend to be allies of international courts, but may also be gatekeepers of the latter's decisions, possibly depending on the political positioning (although usually not disclosed as such) of the judiciary or its highest judicial body vis-à-vis international law/courts or human rights, at a given

89 Hillebrecht, *Domestic Politics and International Human Rights Tribunals: The Problem of Compliance*, cit., 155.

time. Yet, centering implementation on the judicial branch can help coordinate an otherwise confusing and unstructured enforcement at the domestic level, and allow courts to advance the domestic protection of human rights, bypassing internal political debates and the political interference of other state powers. Conversely, through the judiciary, enforcement may be perceived as broader influence, limited to conversations around judicial dialogue, instead of a focus on how specific international reparation measures get effectively executed in real life. This section investigates the Latin American countries (Peru, Dominican Republic, and from one scholarly angle, Brazil)[90] which assign the responsibility for implementation of IACtHR judgements to the judicial branch.

This assignment of responsibility can be contested since unclear or overlapping legislation might fail to indicate precisely which branch leads implementation of IACtHR judgments specifically, and varying ways to interpret obscure or superficial legislation may also lead to different conclusions regarding the competent authorities to implement certain types of decision. Yet, we categorized states' implementation models considering the available information collected from each domestic system analyzed alongside international reports and scholarship on the topic, although acknowledging that the scarcity and obscurity of sources does hinder a definitive or absolute assessment oftentimes.

Approaching Peru, the Dominican Republic, and Brazil as presenting judiciary-led systems, in this section we consider the technical processes for enforcement employed, how they reflect on victims' rights on the ground and how private international law tools may contribute to exploring the judiciary's potential in implementation of international human rights judgements domestically. This analysis follows the same themes discussed above, starting with centralization of power.

3.1 *Centralized v Diffuse Authority*

Investigating whether the attribution to implement IACtHR judgments is centralized or diffuse in countries that center implementation on the judicial

90 Some scholars in Brazil argue that international human rights judgements equate to foreign judgements for the purposes of their implementation domestically, which, according to the rules on foreign judgment enforcement in the country, means that international judgments would be formally assessed by the Superior Court of Justice, and conditioned to the outcome of this assessment, could be sent to the competent federal judge for enforcement. See Rodrigo de Almeida Leite, 'As Sentenças Da Corte Interamericana de Direitos Humanos e a Execução No Brasil' (2008) 8(1) *Revista Direito e Liberdade* 1. 7.

system is relevant in considering how the state manages the current doctrine of conventionality control; that is if, although privileging the judiciary, there is a positive response to the IACtHR's contemporary rationale to spread implementation among state authorities.

It is important to investigate such an issue because, if the state chooses a centralized authority to oversee enforcement, controlling most of the implementation efforts, it may fail to follow the second generation of conventionality control. Especially as regards states highlighting the judiciary in its implementation system, a finding that they choose to keep such a structure centralized likely means they keep adhering to the first generation of conventionality control. This conclusion, in turn, suggests a continuing reliance on judicial dialogue as a primary path for international human rights influence domestically, instead of focusing on enforcement as the main method for creating points of connection between the international and the domestic. A diffuse authority would suggest otherwise: that the state may privilege the judiciary, but by following the current IACtHR doctrine, designs its implementation system ensuring that all state branches have a role to play in enforcement.

Accordingly, a centralized model conveys the state's interest in the softer tracking of influence of human rights domestically, pursued by promoting the judiciary's common behavior of relying on the IACtHR's jurisprudence through judicial dialogue, but not often willing to actually implement reparations orders. Conversely, a system based on diffuse authority for implementation may show an interest in overcoming the usual, soft, engagement with international human rights courts through judicial dialogue and citation, instead emphasizing enforcement efforts that create single, yet deeper points of connection.

In the few Latin American countries that, from the limited information available, led us to conclude that the judiciary is at the center of implementation of IACtHR judgments, we identified a general model operating. Through this model, the executive branch notifies the judiciary of the IACtHR decision, which then initiates a judicial process through which a higher court either issues a judicial order with the purpose of initiating implementation, or assigns such a responsibility to a specific judge or tribunal. In initiating implementation, however, the judiciary often needs to engage other state powers that are better placed to carry out specific reparation orders, such as the legislature where legal reform is needed. Yet, another model may center implementation efforts on the judiciary itself, at least not addressing the involvement of other state branches (although this may occur in practice). Another model still, proposed by some scholars to exist in Brazil, perceives international human rights judgements as foreign judgements that must be formally assessed by the Superior Court of Justice (including an analysis of whether the decision affects the country's *ordre public* and sovereignty), and subsequently enforced by the competent federal judge.[91] As we discuss further below, there are many similarities to the procedure for enforcement of private international law judgments from foreign domestic jurisdictions.

Breaking down the general model, on one side, there is Peru, where implementation, at the judicial branch, starts with the President of the Supreme Court, but is then distributed to a specific, competent, chamber or judge.[92] However, the rest of the enforcement procedure can change depending on whether it involves provisional measures or a full judgment, and if it includes financial compensation among the reparation orders.[93] This system further counts on a Specialized Tribunal for the enforcement of supranational judgments, which facilitates implementation of IACtHR judgments as well.[94] Depending on which type of order it is, it may be fully implemented by the judiciary (such as a provisional reparation order targeting a domestic judgment),[95] or may involve other state branches (if the order is to cease an activity performed by another state authority or to provide financial compensation).[96] An IACHR report on implementation mechanisms, in fact, highlights the executive in implementation of 'decisions' of international human rights courts, while it does acknowledge the significant role of the judiciary in the enforcement of provisional measures and 'judgments' (instead of 'decisions') from international courts, especially the IACtHR.[97]

On the other side, the Dominican Republic entitles the Constitutional Tribunal to enforce IACtHR judgements directly.[98] The specific legislation does not seem to distinguish between provisional measures and final judgments,

91 See Rodrigo de Almeida Leite, 'As Sentenças Da Corte Interamericana de Direitos Humanos e a Execução No Brasil' (2008) 8(1) *Revista Direito e Liberdade* 1. 7.

92 Peru, Código Procesal Constitucional, Artículo 115; Ley N° 27775 – Ley que regula el procedimiento de ejecución de sentencias emitidas por tribunales supranacionales, Art. 2.

93 See Peru, Ley N° 27775, artículo 2(b-e)), Art. 4.

94 Consejo Ejecutivo del Poder Judicial, Resolución Administrativa N° 089–2010-CE-PJ, Lima, 11 March 2010, Art. 1.

95 Peru, Ley N° 27775, artículo 4.

96 Peru, Ley N° 27775, artículo 2(b-e)); artículo 4.

97 Comisión Interamericana de Derechos Humanos ['Inter-American Commission on Human Rights'], '*Mecanismos Nacionales de Implementación de Recomendaciones de Derechos Humanos*' ['*National Mechanisms for the Implementation of Human Rights Recommendations*'], Doc No OEA/Ser.L/V/II.doc.8/23, 26 February 2023, paras 175, 176.

98 Ley No. 137–11, Considerando 13°.

suggesting that either way, the Constitutional Tribunal would be the organ responsible for implementation, and apparently with full discretion to structure the enforcement efforts. Finally, the legislation does not address whether such efforts could or should include other branches of government, just stating that IACtHR judgments constitute binding precedent to all public powers and organs in the state.[99] Despite these norms superficially indicating the centrality of the judiciary in the implementation system, the Constitutional Tribunal itself has decided a Direct Action of Unconstitutionality against the Dominican instrument of acceptance of the IACtHR's competence, creating grave internal controversy about the state's relationship with the IACtHR.[100]

Finally, the model proposed to exist in Brazil is contested in the scholarship. On one hand, 2023 legislation establishes that it is the attribution of an entity within the Ministry of Human Rights and Citizenship to articulate implementation of acts necessary to comply with international organizations' decisions involving human rights violations.[101] Yet, on the other, if the approach found in scholarship is considered to apply, it entitles the judiciary to control implementation through a judicial assessment of the international judgment, and avoid the interference of other branches, along with their political interests, while still enabling the use of concepts like *ordre public* that may convey some political consideration. Therefore, recent legislation assigns to an organ in the Executive the competence to articulate implementation, which may in fact suggest a diffuse system led by the executive as the articulator, but possibly involving all the branches as necessary depending on the elements of the decision that need to be implemented. Yet, here as well, the legislation does not clarify the potential involvement of other branches, just stating the authority of the executive branch entity to articulate the necessary efforts for implementation, which could also entail the exercise of this authority in a centralized way by the executive. However, an alternative view points in a completely different direction, as the scholarly approach mentioned above centralizes power on the judiciary, with no clear reference to the engagement of other branches.

---

99 Ley No. 137–11 – 'Ley Orgánica del Tribunal Constitucional y de los procedimientos constitucionales' – 11 Junio 2011, Art. 7(13).

100 Sentencia TC/0256/14, Tribunal Constitucional, Expediente núm. TC-01–2005–0013, 4 November 2014. See also Talyam Vásquez, *Reflexiones: República Dominicana y la Corte Interamericana de Derechos Humanos* (*Corte IDH*), Collección Pensamiento Internacional N° 5, Ministério de Relaciones Exteriores and Dirección de Investigación e Innovación, República Dominicana, 2022.

101 Decreto N° 11.341, 1 January 2023, Annex I, Art. 6.

Considering these three potential judiciary-led models, the one adopted in Peru seems to better reflect the second generation of conventionality control, focusing on the judiciary for the implementation efforts targeting IACtHR judgments, but clearly enabling the engagement of other state branches in implementation. This model also overcomes the use of the judiciary to pursue a connection between the international court and the domestic system through a softer discourse of human rights influence embedded in judicial dialogue and references to the IACtHR jurisprudence, and instead it actually engages the judiciary in enforcement. This approach also has the capacity to center implementation on the victim by focusing on their particular rights and by following less politicized processes compared to the possibilities centering enforcement on the executive and legislative branches. This judiciary's engagement in actual enforcement and the possibility to involve other state authorities (while avoiding their unrequested, political, interferences) amount to a system with a higher potential to create positive effects on the ground and on victims' lives.

However, the risk associated with this model is the one of uncoordinated implementation given the participation of other state branches where specific reparations that must be implemented fall within their competence. While privileging the judiciary in implementation may help minimize such a risk considering the usual position of domestic courts as allies of international ones, the risk remains as the spreading of enforcement efforts within the judiciary and to other state authorities may facilitate the influence of politics and create divergencies among all the entities involved in the enforcement of complex judgements.

Despite this risk, the well-structured, diffuse, model adopted in Peru can be useful for the IACtHR in developing a descriptive agenda as the norms establishing the forms of engagement of other state branches gives the Court plenty of guidance as to how to design the reparations orders, aware of which body would be competent to enforce it. This possibility also facilitates subsequent monitoring, as the Court would be more easily able to know and trace which organ should be carrying out a given measure and target its examination of their work. This model could also contribute to a normative agenda, if the Court finds such a system to yield positive results, as it could contribute to guiding and pushing for the development of implementation systems elsewhere adopting similar features. In any case, the model identified in Peru must rely on clear rules that do indicate the particular roles of each branch, including domestic courts, in implementation, and only with such clarity could that model inform descriptive and normative agendas for the Court.

With that context in mind, we further examine next the significance of clarity in rules for implementation in judiciary-led systems.

3.2 *Clarity of Rules for Implementation*

Clarity of rules for implementation in countries where the judiciary plays a central role in enforcement concerns assessing how well the judicial branch accommodates the duties associated with implementation of international decisions with their usual domestic attributions. We also explore here whether such rules enable an effective and integrated system in which the role played by each authority, with their particular competence, is laid out so that internal procedural debates do not hinder the efficient implementation of reparations orders.

This analysis is important to ensure that unclear, extensive, internal procedural rules on competence do not become a hindrance to the effective work of the judiciary-led implementation system, affecting its ability to present timely, practical, positive results to victims.[102] Moreover, an implementation system guided by the judiciary may easily fall back into first generation of conventionality control by stopping at the tracking of human rights influence domestically through judicial dialogue, if it cannot rely on clear rules on the available pathways for enforcement and actually operationalizing reparation orders. Meanwhile, clarity in rules of implementation can empower the judiciary to move away from a soft engagement with international human rights courts through citations and references, instead following coherent and comprehensive rules establishing steps for enforcement. In this way, the judiciary is empowered and legitimized[103] to act in response to international judgements to implement the reparation orders, creating a single, but strong and deep point of connection with the international court in such efforts.

Among the few countries centering enforcement on the judicial branch, Peru offers rather detailed information of specific aspects of implementation of IACtHR judgments, such as deadlines. The Peruvian model may facilitate technical slicing, besides covering different possibilities regarding different types of decision (provisional or final) or procedures (ordering the ceasing of an activity;[104] ensuring *restitutio in integrum*, for instance)[105] for each form of remedy. This clearer picture may promote enforcement as victims may be

102 See section 2.2, in this chapter, for more on the impact of clarity of rules in implementation.

103 See section 3.4 in this chapter on legitimacy.

104 Ley N° 27775, artículo 4.

105 Ley N° 27775, artículo 4.

more closely aware (thus capable of demanding effectiveness) of the steps being taken in the entire pathway for implementation. It is also positive because, for the processes led by the judiciary, it enables a procedure that tends to be less politicized and interfered with (unless by request of the judiciary when necessary due to another authority's competence to enforce a certain measure) by other branches of government.

Conversely, the Dominican Republic does not present very clear rules, yet, from what is available, it centers enforcement, or at least the regulation of enforcement,[106] entirely on the Constitutional Tribunal. Moreover, it does not detail the steps to be taken depending on the type of decision or reparation order to be enforced, apparently leaving for the Tribunal's discretion to structure the enforcement efforts. On top of it, as said above, a decision by the Constitutional Tribunal has declared the Dominican instrument of acceptance of the IACtHR's competence as unconstitutional,[107] generating significant obscurity in the very underlying rationale of implementation given the uncertainty created over the IACtHR's jurisdiction over the state. This severe lack of clarity is likely to create paralyzing confusion and idleness in the enforcement of reparation orders, and center political considerations in the debate on the Dominican Republic's relationship with the Court.

Finally, in Brazil, the rules to be applied in the proposed model in which the international judgment is understood as 'foreign' and assessed by the Superior Court of Justice through private international law rules prior to enforcement by the competent federal judge, are primarily clear and addressed in the Civil Procedure Act.[108] Moreover, by using private international law norms to analyze the international judgment, in this approach, judges can rely on techniques like slicing (*dépeçage*), to focus on the remedies to be made concrete to the victims and the specific technical processes to that end, instead of engaging with the merits, which helps generate a presumption that these international human rights judgments are valid. In turn, this presumption, associated with a reliance on technique from private international law tools, also minimizes room for political considerations that can muddy the enforcement efforts, which can ultimately translate into legitimacy for this implementation

106 Ley No. 137–11 – 'Ley Orgánica del Tribunal Constitucional y de los procedimientos constitucionales' – 11 Junio 2011: 'CONSIDERANDO DECIMOTERCERO: Que dentro de los procedimientos constitucionales a ser regulados se encuentra el control preventivo de los tratados internacionales y la regulación de la ejecución de las sentencias de la Corte Interamericana de Derechos Humanos'.

107 Sentencia TC/0256/14, Tribunal Constitucional, Expediente núm. TC-01–2005–0013, 4 November 2014.

108 Código de Processo Civil (2015), Art. 960.

model. However, how exactly the implementation by the federal judge will unfold considering that it may involve substantive measures possibly not common in foreign (as coming from a different country) decisions (such as adopting or changing legislation, or creating organs to support victims), is unclear. In fact, this uncertainty would be a key shortcoming of systems relying only on the judiciary for implementation, since measures that ordinarily require intervention by other branches might be left entirely unaddressed.[109]

Against this background, the Peruvian model seems to be the one with the highest potential to minimize uncoordinated execution by establishing clear rules that determine the involvement of other state branches where their competence is needed for the implementation of specific enforcement measures. It also creates particular pathways for enforcement depending on whether the decision is provisional or final, which may enable the particular fastidiousness required for provisional measures, while not overburdening the mechanisms for implementation of final judgements. The more detailed rules of this model may then promote enforcement by enabling predictability for victims and civil society to demand effectiveness from the domestic authorities, as well as monitoring from the IACtHR. This system also elevates technique as the main vector for enforcement, possibly reducing the interference of politics.

Nevertheless, a risk to consider vis-à-vis clarity of rules in judiciary-led systems, especially considering the possibility in Brazil to implement IACtHR judgments as a foreign decision, is that mixing the regional court judgments enforcement model with any other foreign judgment may downplay the authority of the IACtHR. Approaching both types of decisions as being at the same level (at least as regards implementation) puts the IACtHR on par with foreign states. This levelling, alongside the principle of *par in parem non habet iurisdictionem* (that no state's courts should exercise jurisdiction over a foreign sovereign),[110] ends up undermining the IACtHR's wanting to be the court that guides all of the Americas, and that sits atop all domestic institutions as a matter of hierarchy, to guide them. So, while sufficiently clear rules are important, there is a significant risk in adopting wholesale the rules that exist for foreign judgments arising from domestic jurisdictions, making this pathway potentially problematic for the IACtHR and its hierarchical regional influence.

Overall, considering the model identified in Peru, that judiciary-led system could be beneficial to the IACtHR in informing a descriptive agenda as the clarity in the rules can guide the Court in tailoring the reparation orders to

109 See Part IV.

110 Aaron X Fellmeth and Maurice Horwitz, *Guide to Latin in International Law* (Oxford University Press, 2009) 214.

suit the domestic implementation system and facilitate the domestic courts' work, hence enforcement, as well as subsequent monitoring. As follows, pursuing a normative agenda would lead the Court to push for institutional design changes in other countries to reflect a clearer, judiciary-led, and technique-oriented, structure for implementation. While a technique-oriented system could enable the IACtHR's resort to valuable mechanisms and tools for implementation, like slicing or *dépeçage*, in its orders, the operationalization of this system domestically would likely still be conditioned to how dependent on local political shifts the judiciary is, which leads us to an analysis of this topic in the next section.

3.3 *Dependence on Shifts in Local Politics*

Although the judiciary is also affected by local politics, and may consequently let political interests change its approach to the IACtHR and the enforcement of the Court's judgments, the judiciary still, at least in theory, needs to rely on technique and the law more directly to do its work than the other branches do. Thus, given that the judiciary has often been the most common partner of the IACtHR as they can be mutually reinforcing,[111] as discussed below, understanding how politics may affect that relationship and undermine their partnership is important in considering ways to avoid that diverging political winds sever the judiciary's alliance with the Court.

That is, the IACtHR has, historically, issued many orders that required the interference of national judiciaries to be implemented,[112] and expanded judicial power domestically by perceiving as 'judicial' actions and structures that were perhaps not seen that way by other national entities.[113] Thus, the Court has often sought support from and built connections with national courts to implement its judgments, while possibly creating some imbalance domestically by highlighting judicial action over the work of other branches. Given this usual approach, supportive of the judiciary, by the Court, a high level of political influence affecting judiciaries could create inconsistencies not only in their relationship with the IACtHR, but also with other state entities, either

111 David Kosař and Lucas Lixinski, 'Domestic Judicial Design by International Human Rights Courts' (2015) 109(4) *American Journal of International Law* 713, 714. See also Hillebrecht, 'The Domestic Mechanisms of Compliance', cit., 965; Alexandra Valeria Huneeus, 'Rejecting the Inter-American Court: Judicialization, National Courts, and Regional Human Rights' in Alexandra Valeria Huneeus, Rachel Sieder and Javier Couso (eds), *Cultures of Legality: Judicialization and Political Activism in Latin American* (2011) 112 ('Rejecting the Inter-American Court').

112 Huneeus, cit., 113.

113 Kosař and Lixinski, cit., 718–719.

way ultimately affecting enforcement. A highly political judiciary could generate imbalance, either potentially positive if over-supportive of the Court, but also possibly negative, if contrary to the Court's work. If the former, although promoting the Court's work could also positively affect enforcement, a system centered on the judiciary could cause friction with other branches, either because of political divergencies among them, or simply because the judiciary's role in implementation overshadows the possible contributions or approaches of other branches. Conversely, if the later, the Court would have to work extra hard to strengthen its relationship with the other branches, not historically perceived as such close collaborators as national judges, in order to find domestic forces to counter judicial antagonism to the IACtHR's decisions, with a view of still enabling implementation.

Further, as the soft tracking of the Court's influence often takes place in the judicial sphere through judicial dialogue, political shifts affecting domestic judiciaries could not only impact actual enforcement, but also the more diluted points of connection between the Court and the domestic legal system through an analysis of its influence. Here, a highly political judiciary opposed to the Court's work could either lead to a softer tracking of influence that results in negative reputation for the Court domestically, or could ignore the IACtHR and its domestic influence altogether, either way not helping advance implementation. A judiciary that, conversely, is very politically supportive of the Court could be positive for implementation as national judges could rely on their alliance to find legitimacy and empowerment to enforce IACtHR's orders. Yet, a highly political, even supportive, judiciary may also risk widening softer tracking of the Court's influence through judicial dialogue and perceiving that as enough engagement, while not really impacting enforcement as the latter could more directly disrupt national political dynamics with other branches possibly opposing the Court's work.

Among these possibilities and their effects, from the few Latin American countries that seem to center implementation on the judiciary, one model identified presents clearer rules on the role of the judiciary and how other branches can get involved in implementation processes, enabling the prevalence of technique and mechanisms like slicing in the coordination of enforcement. Peru is an example of this model, which relies on more detailed, clearer norms, and, by favoring technique, may help minimize the influence of political interests in enforcement. Further, Brazil could also reflect this technical approach through the scholarly understanding that 'foreign judgments' be understood to include international judgments. This approach highlights the judiciary's role in enforcement by subjecting the implementation of an IACtHR decision to a formal assessment by the Superior Court of Justice (including as regards effects to the country's *ordre public* and sovereignty), and subsequent enforcement by the competent federal judge.[114] If this understanding of Brazil's system proves right, the judiciary would rely on conflict of rules norms in enforcing IACtHR decisions, which would privilege technique over political influence.

Conversely, another model centered on the judiciary relies on somewhat less clear rules, and demonstrates a stronger involvement of other branches in the entrenchment of international human rights law domestically, which makes room for confusion and political disputes between branches regarding their role in implementation. In the Dominican Republic, the legislation leaves more discretion (than in the previous models) for the Constitutional Tribunal to decide on how to regulate or structure enforcement efforts, which could enable the reintroduction of political considerations. In that country, moreover, the entrenchment of international human rights into the national system largely relates to the connection between international human rights and domestic fundamental rights in the constitution, which reflects the work of the legislature. Ultimately, although still judiciary-led and somewhat detached from the influence of the executive or legislative branches, this model presents less focus on technique and more room for political influences and internal political disputes among branches. The Constitutional Tribunal's 2014 judgment on the unconstitutionality of the instrument accepting the IACtHR's jurisdiction[115] reflects this tension among branches as it involved the judiciary deciding about the executive's instrument of acceptance of the IACtHR's competence which, according to one of the justifications of the Tribunal, entered into force without ratification from congress.

Considering these models, the judiciary-led process that better safeguards enforcement from shifting political interests and is based on more technical processes is also likely to make implementation better by enabling tools like slicing and allowing the judiciary to coordinate enforcement efforts as the IACtHR's partner locally. Not only is this partnership beneficial for the progress of the Court's work as it will have a defender nationally, helping develop a broader acceptance of the IACtHR's decisions domestically, but it will also help legitimize the national court's judgments dealing with complicated human rights issues within the country. Still, this legitimization through technical engagement with IACtHR judgments may allow national judges to bypass political debates, at least at the stage of enforcement, or to ground

114 See Leite, cit., 7.

115 Sentencia TC/0256/14, Tribunal Constitucional, Expediente núm. TC-01-2005-0013, 4 November 2014.

judgments on the Court's work while ensuring progressive change in the internal legal system.

However, although reliance on clear rules helps the judiciary to lead enforcement efforts while trying to avoid political battles internally and with other branches, an express connection between the judiciary's role in implementation and the use of private international law mechanisms, like slicing, could further benefit this system. Making this connection more evident and as an integral part of the enforcement procedures could bring further legitimacy to the national judges' work in implementing IACtHR decisions, and better distinguish the implementation process from political undertakings.

Therefore, the IACtHR could develop a normative agenda by learning from the Peruvian and Brazilian systems and shaping its orders to reflect the judiciary-led structure those countries offer. The Court could also pursue a normative agenda, though, proposing a further connection between domestic judiciaries and private international law devices as institutional design changes in its orders, which would not only contribute to a more technical, less political enforcement procedure domestically, but would also help legitimize the national judges' work and strengthen their partnership with the Court. Considering the separate importance of legitimacy in the branches' work as part of implementation, and how legitimacy relates to the pathways of communication between the branches and the IACtHR, we turn to this topic next.

3.4 *Directness of Connection to IACtHR*

As we said above,[116] the pathways for each branch to communicate with the IACtHR can directly affect this branch's legitimacy in its role entrenching international human rights law domestically. It is also so in judiciary-led systems of implementation, especially considering the historically pronounced role domestic judiciaries have had as allies of the Court, although often promoting the Court through a softer tracking of its influence in the national legal system, rather than through enforcement itself. This alliance has been strengthened by the doctrine of conventionality control, especially in its origins, when the national judges were the ones the doctrine was directed at, and hence had to engage with the Court's case law to ensure domestic consistency with it, while also promoting the Court and its influence and legitimacy domestically.[117] At the same time, this engagement with the IACtHR judg-

116 See section 2.4, in this chapter, addressing the legitimacy of the executive in executive-led systems.

117 See Huneeus, cit., 112. See also Kosař and Lixinski, cit., 747.

ments enabled judiciaries to use those judgments to bring legitimacy to their own domestic judicial positionings and widening jurisprudence, often contrary to the positionings of other branches,[118] which makes the alliance a mutually beneficial one. Thus, it is important to consider these pathways of communication and how they may contribute to legitimizing the national courts' work in connecting the domestic and the international, and solidify the partnership between the IACtHR and national judges.

Therefore, depending on how the IACtHR and national courts communicate, legitimacy for the national judiciary itself may be undermined if its relationship with the Court is weakened, for instance by political interferences that make them antagonistic, also affecting the Court's influence domestically. That is, if national judges stop being allies of the Court, they may no longer systematically rely on IACtHR decisions to legitimize their human rights judgments and might forego their role in conventionality control. While those effects are already likely to impact the judiciary's role in enabling and coordinating enforcement, it can also affect a softer tracking of the Court's influence domestically and harm its reputation, diminishing support for it among national bodies and society. Thus, maintaining (mutually) supportive pathways of communication between the IACtHR and judiciaries is fundamental in keeping the Court's key ally domestically promoting implementation, or at least fomenting broader support for the IACtHR's work. The deterioration of this partnership can yield negative results for enforcement efforts, specifically, but also to the broader influence of the Court domestically.

Moreover, as discussed above, where the judiciary's relationship with the Court is weakened, and this weakness leads the judiciary to ignore or dismiss IACtHR decisions as tools to legitimize their own decisions, national judiciaries may also overlook their role in conventionality control, besides abandoning the broader soft tracking, through judicial dialogue, of the Court's domestic influence.

Among the Latin American countries centering their systems of implementation on the judiciary, two models exist regarding connection to the Court and the branch's legitimacy internally. One model sets a clear connection between international human rights law and fundamental/constitutional rights or issues in the country, giving direct and immediate application in the domestic sphere to IHRL treaties ratified by the state, and which further constitute binding precedent to all public powers and organs in the state. This

118 See Kosař and Lixinski, cit. 746–47. Hillebrecht, 'The Domestic Mechanisms of Compliance', cit., 969–970; Urueña, cit., 425.

judiciary-led model provides heightened legitimacy to the enforcement actions of the state's highest court which must ensure this direct and immediate application of IACtHR decisions. This model is found in the Dominican Republic,[119] where the Constitutional Court is empowered and has discretion to structure the enforcement efforts, guided by a rationale (at least in theory) of partnership with the IACtHR, embedded in the constitutional hierarchy, and direct application, of the state's international human rights obligations.[120] The 2014 unconstitutionality decision,[121] however, showcases the risk of such a model, where an empowered judiciary, with domestic legitimacy, rejects the executive's legitimacy in accepting the IACtHR jurisdiction, then casting a shadow over the whole implementation system and over the state's pathways of communication with the Court.

Another model still centers enforcement on the judiciary, but without a direct and immediate application of international human rights domestically, which ends up inviting an early intervention of the executive as the liaison between national courts and the IACtHR, and might have other branches interfering more in the implementation process. This system does not necessarily diminish the judiciary's legitimacy, but it does condition the ignition of its work to a communication by the executive. In circumstances where other branches must engage in implementation, regardless of the judiciary's prompting them, the latter loses some of its discretion and power, and becomes, again, conditioned to action by other branches, which could affect the courts' legitimacy as their control over enforcement often needs to be shared. Nevertheless, this more intertwined engagement with other branches could balance out contrary political attitudes and help avoid a scenario as happened in the Dominican Republic with the unconstitutionality decision by the Constitutional Court, as here the executive and legislative could employ also legitimate efforts to counter a similar outcome, hence possibly sustaining the broader system's legitimacy.

Peru represents this model, since it is the executive's Ministry of Foreign Affairs that owns the competence to communicate an international decision to the President of the Supreme Court, who, in turn, will send it to the compe-

119 Constitución de la República Dominicana – 2015, aart 74(3). Ley No. 137–11 – 'Ley Orgánica del Tribunal Constitucional y de los procedimientos constitucionales' – 11 Junio 2011, Art. 7(13).

120 Constitución de la República Dominicana – 2015, Art. 74(3).

121 Sentencia TC/0256/14, Tribunal Constitucional, Expediente núm. TC-01–2005–0013, 4 November 2014.

tent judge for enforcement.[122] While Peru benefits from detailed rules on procedures for enforcement, these rules require the intervention of the Ministry of Foreign Affairs in some circumstances (like in the enforcement of financial compensation that still needs to be determined, where the Ministry can contradict the amount intended by the executor),[123] which limits the national judge's (autonomy and potentially their legitimacy) in leading and advancing enforcement, although enabling some level of check from the executive of the judiciary.

Finally, the model advanced by part of the scholarship in Brazil, where IACtHR decisions are implemented as foreign judgments, may find legitimacy in the clear procedural rules for implementation, and in the technically automatic initiation of implementation once the Superior Court of Justice receives the international decision. Yet, as we discussed above, levelling IACtHR judgments with foreign judgments as regards processes for their implementation domestically can lead to an undermining of the IACtHR's role as a hierarchically superior regional court. This downplaying of the Court's role, in turn, can severely compromise the dynamics through which national judiciaries rely on IACtHR decisions to legitimize their own work, and how the IACtHR also relies on national courts to promote and implement its decisions, and to act, domestically, as its allies.

Considering these examples, an implementation system that acknowledges the direct and immediate application of the state's international human rights obligations domestically can advance implementation by providing legitimacy for the judiciary to start enforcement without having to be prompted by the executive. If the IACtHR wants to keep judges as their key allies domestically, this type of system could significantly help in strengthening the connection between national courts and the IACtHR. While other branches will likely need to be involved in implementation, conditioned to the type of orders in an IACtHR judgment, giving the judiciary that type of freedom to initiate enforcement directly once an IACtHR decision is published helps legitimize the national (often highest) courts' actions towards enforcement. This legitimacy can then also be used by the national judges to promote the Court's influence domestically, solidifying their mutually beneficial connec-

122 Código Procesal Constitucional, Artículo 115; Ley N° 27775 – Ley que regula el procedimiento de ejecución de sentencias emitidas por tribunales supranacionales, Art. 2. Ley N° 27775 – Ley que regula el procedimiento de ejecución de sentencias emitidas por tribunales supranacionales, Art. 2.

123 (Ley N° 27775, artículo 2(b-e)).

tion, while also putting national courts in a privileged position to ensure that the Court's orders are actually having their desired effect on the ground.

Still, while this type of system gives the judiciary more discretion and room for maneuver, it can backfire in contexts where the political landscape nationally also affects the judicial system, involving it in political battles that may sever or harm national courts' relationship with the IACtHR. In that case, having detailed rules specifying the procedures for enforcement, and countering that discretion could improve the system by questioning, replacing, or removing the judiciary's legitimacy if it fails to follow the rules for implementation due to political motivations.

Here the IACtHR would have an important role, mainly based on a normative agenda, to propose such a judiciary-led system in which the state's international human rights obligations are applicable directly and immediately in the state. This model would then enable the judiciary to also directly engage with enforcement once an IACtHR decision is presented against that state, yet conditioned to specific and detailed rules for implementation. In this way, the Court could promote domestic institutional design changes that help further strengthen its connection to national judiciaries, while still ensuring an alternative for enforcement if the judiciary's autonomous initiation of enforcement is hampered by political considerations.

While the pathways of communication between the IACtHR and the executive are pervasive given the latter's role in representing and defending the state before the IASPHR, and the communication between the Court and national judges is strengthened by a historical alliance between both, the IACtHR's relationship with legislatures is, instead, fairly underexplored. The next section examines this relationship through the same themes deployed in the analysis of the other branches to assess the current and potential role of the legislative branch in the implementation of IACtHR decisions domestically.

4 Legislative Branch and the Forgotten Intermediary

Assigning the implementation of IACtHR judgements domestically to the legislative branch tends to mean the legislature's compliance with such judgements as equated with general international instruments. The legislature does play this role when reparation orders require the adoption of legislation or legal reform of some type that falls into their competence. However, the legislative branch can influence implementation in other, less direct or pronounced, means – such as regulating the implementation system itself, and the very ratification of treaties that may create obligations the violations of which may originate international decisions in need of domestic efforts for implementation. While these examples reiterate the rationale in the current conventionality control doctrine to spread the competence for implementation through all the state's powers, in comparison to the two branches assessed above, the legislature still generally plays a largely weak role in this process in Latin America. The analysis below, thus, considers the Latin American countries centering or involving the legislative branch in implementation processes to examine its potential in such processes, how it is being employed by states, and whether/how its role could be optimized.

4.1 *Centralized v Diffuse Authority*

We consider the models of the countries that privilege the legislature in their implementation system to assess how they assign authority, either centralized or diffuse, within such a model, which tells us how each system responds to the current doctrine of conventionality control. The significance of examining how the power to implement international human rights decisions is distributed domestically in countries that privilege the legislature as the leading branch for implementation lies on finding how such system instrumentalizes the potential of parliaments in the entrenchment of IHRL. That is, considering the ability of congresses to influence and guide the work of other branches through legislation that, for instance, regulates the implementation system itself, or approves budgets that can be affected by the payment of compensation due to an international reparation order. Thus, it is important to assess how the power assigned to the legislature plays out in practice and in relation to other state authorities. A centralized system could mean elevating the importance of the internal political climate in how international human rights decisions are implemented, since parliaments are directly connected to, influenced by, and a thermometer of, popular will. Thus, an implementation system centered on the legislature can generate legitimacy to implementation efforts by being able to reflect the domestic political context and feeling in relation to international human rights courts.

However, as the legislature can function as gatekeepers or background operators to the work of other state branches by regulating, or in other ways interfering or checking, their operation, it may hinder the rationale behind the second generation of the doctrine of conventionality control. That is, a centralized system that focuses implementation on, and attributes much power to, this branch, may do so to the detriment of the others in ways that minimize the usefulness of the latter's contribution to implementation. A diffuse system, instead, may still enable the legislature to regulate and engage some of the work of other branches, but without undermining their role in implementation, and without letting too much of the internal political climate interfere in implementation. This limited interference can be positive where congress appears mostly contrary to international interference or even to human rights. However, a diffuse system can raise a problem of uncoordinated implementation if the primary authority is uncapable of privileging technique in articulating efforts in the system, which tends to affect victims' interests negatively.

Further, an implementation system led by the legislature and assigning to it centralized authority may become too politicized and undermine enforcement efforts and make the legislature's work in relation to international human rights judgments one closer related to the softer tracking of influence. That is, where parliaments are not mostly welcoming of such international judgements to the point of pursuing its enforcement, such decisions may be cited or referred to in parliamentary discussions and work, but not taken as precise orders to be implemented in favor of victims. Possibly, if the political climate is the opposite and fosters human rights and the work of international human rights courts, then a centralized system can work effectively to ensure enforcement. However, leaving a legislature-led system susceptible to shifting political winds can hinder consistency and commitment, and make implementation uncertain. Conversely, a diffuse system would enable other branches (most likely the judiciary) to balance out the legislature's (and the executive's) political inclinations, and offer a system more conducive of consistency with options of depoliticized (or less politicized) avenues for implementation. The diffuse system led by the legislature, however, would not necessarily do a better job in entrenching international human rights law beyond the softer tracking of the Court's influence. That is because the legislative process is often already quite procedurally complex, protracted, political, and layered, which would make the usually deep, single, connection point enabled by enforcement weaker and more diluted than what happens in enforcement by the judiciary, for instance.

Among the countries investigated, the legislative branch has enabled or somewhat centrally contributed to implementation through two general models (yet with particularities in each country) as it regards the type of authority adopted, but both models bend more toward a diffuse rather than a centralized system. One model works through legislative decrees for implementation or parliamentary human rights committees that monitor the government's compliance with its human rights obligations (which may include IACtHR decisions), but also enables the engagement of other state branches in the implementation of specific types of orders or judgements. Another model works with the participation of the legislature in some level, but mostly by creating and/or harboring self-proclaimed fully independent organs (disconnected from any state branch), and in that sense have a central, yet indirect, participation of the legislative, but not being necessarily legislative-led. These independent organs aim specifically at human rights protection and promotion, including through implementation of IACtHR decisions, but they still invite the involvement of other state authorities.

The first system is found in Guatemala, where the constitution assigns to the parliament the attribution to decree, upon request by the executive, reparations or compensation in cases originated from international complaints, apparently where there is no more room for appeal.[124] Within Congress, a Human Rights Commission has the job of communicating with international human rights organs for consultation and exchange of information,[125] recommend measures favoring human rights to state organs,[126] receive international human rights complaints targeting Guatemala, and perform conventionality control to adapt legislation to IHRL,[127] but its role in implementation is unclear. Despite the legislature's attributions, the executive branch also plays a significant role. For instance, in 2020, a 'Governmental Agreement'[128] published by the executive branch, created the temporary Presidential Commission for Peace and Human Rights (PCPHR), dependent upon the Presidency. Its aims are to assist and coordinate with several organs of the executive to promote and implement actions and mechanisms concerning human rights broadly[129] but, in practice, also working, at least in some cases, in the implementation of IACtHR judgements.[130] Here, while implementation attri-

124 Constitución Política de la República de Guatemala (1985 con reformas de 1993), Art. 171(k).

125 CONGRESO DE LA REPUBLICA DE GUATEMALA DECRETO NUMERO 54–86 – Ley de la Comisión de Derechos Humanos del Congreso de la República de Guatemala y del Procurador de los Derechos Humanos, Art. 4(g).

126 CONGRESO DE LA REPUBLICA DE GUATEMALA DECRETO NUMERO 54–86 – Ley de la Comisión de Derechos Humanos del Congreso de la República de Guatemala y del Procurador de los Derechos Humanos, Art. 4(f).

127 CONGRESO DE LA REPUBLICA DE GUATEMALA DECRETO NUMERO 54–86 – Ley de la Comisión de Derechos Humanos del Congreso de la República de Guatemala y del Procurador de los Derechos Humanos, Art. 4(b).

128 'Acuerdo Gubernativo'.

129 Acuerdo Gubernativo No 100–2020, 30 July 2020, Art. 4(a).

130 Gubierno de Guatemala, 'COPADEH avanza en cumplimiento de sentencia en caso: Masacres de Río Negro vs. Guatemala', 17 March 2023, https://prensa.gob.gt/comunicado/copadeh-avanza-en-cumplimiento-de-sentencia-en-caso-masacres-de-rio-negro-vs-guatemala. See also Comisión Interamericana de Derechos Humanos ['Inter-American

butions are scattered and somewhat unclear, the legislature does have a role to play, although other branches also intervene actively in implementing human rights decisions domestically.

Uruguay's system, in turn, is closer to the second model as it creates a National Human Rights Institute (NHRI) for the defense, promotion and protection of human rights,[131] which exists as part of the legislature, but functions autonomously.[132] In this case, the legislature or this independent organ's central role does not hinder the involvement of other branches. For instance, in 2013, a law entitled *Barbani Duarte y Otros Versus Uruguay* was enacted specifically to authorize the executive power to create a commission aimed only at complying with the eponymous IACtHR judgment.[133] Although it is the executive that is in charge of carrying out the measures necessary to enforce the decision, the first necessary step was taken by the legislative to enact the law regulating how the implementation efforts would unfold. Thus, this model relies on the legislature, an independent entity created under the remit of the legislature but detached from it, and still enables significant involvement of the executive, at least in the example mentioned, in the implementation system. Interestingly, Uruguay also has, within the executive, a National Mechanism of Information and Compliance of Recommendations[134] targeted specifically at implementation of human rights 'recommendations and observations.'[135] Yet, at present, the Mechanism includes only decisions from UN bodies, leaving the implementation of decisions and judgments from the IASPHR outside its scope, which seems to make the NHRI still the central entity for our purposes.

Commission on Human Rights'], '*Mecanismos Nacionales de Implementación de Recomendaciones de Derechos Humanos*' ['*National Mechanisms for the Implementation of Human Rights Recommendations*'], Doc No OEA/Ser.L/V/II.doc. 8/23, 26 February 2023, paras 190–91.

131 Ley N° 18446 – 2008 – Creación Institución Nacional de Derechos Humanos (INDDHH).

132 Ley N° 18446 – 2008 – Creación Institución Nacional de Derechos Humanos (INDDHH), Art. 2.

133 Ley N° 19.085 – BARBANI DUARTE Y OTROS VERSUS URUGUAY – 2013. See also I/A Court H.R., Case of Barbani Duarte et al. v. Uruguay. Merits, Reparations and Costs. Judgment of October 13, 2011. Series C No. 234; and I/A Court H.R., Case of Barbani Duarte et al. v. Uruguay. Request for Interpretation of the Judgment of Merits, Reparations and Costs. Judgment of June 26, 2012. Series C No. 243.

134 'Mecanismo Nacional de Elaboración de Informes y Seguimiento de Recomendaciones'.

135 Comisión Interamericana de Derechos Humanos ['Inter-American Commission on Human Rights'], '*Mecanismos Nacionales de Implementación de Recomendaciones de Derechos Humanos*' ['*National Mechanisms for the Implementation of Human Rights Recommendations*'], Doc No OEA/Ser.L/V/II.doc. 8/23, 26 February 2023, para 179 and 184.

Ultimately, both models reflect more of a diffuse rather than a centralized system, but with divergences within the diffuse structure. Thus, considering these divergences, and the critique to the centralized system led by the legislature addressed above, the best model may be the one adopted by Uruguay which seems to enable a more consistent, balanced and clear structure, within a diffuse system, to avoid confusion, despite the duplicity of national entities dealing with international decisions from different organs. The NHRI may be able to depoliticize the articulation of implementation efforts and engage the legislature, and the other branches, in ways to explore their potential through technique instead of politics, and focus on how the system affects victims' rights more directly.

Nonetheless, possible improvements in this system could come from awareness of the usual procedurally complex, time- and resources-consuming, aspect of legislative processes, which can weaken and dilute the point of connection with IHRL enabled by enforcement. This awareness should inform implementation efforts so that this type of processes is only employed where such features would not entail lack of redress or would reflect a further violence to the victim.

These models and their work can assist the IACtHR in its descriptive agenda by highlighting the possibilities and potential for the legislative branch in implementation, and pushing the court to consider pathways to effectively engage the legislature in operationalizing its reparation orders. The models may also contribute to the IACtHR's normative agenda by creating space for understanding of the strengths and shortcomings of the legislature's involvement in implementation, leading the Court to consider ways to propose domestic institutional design choices that optimize this involvement in ways conducive to implementation. These institutional design choices could include, for instance, clearer rules establishing the specific attributions and prerogatives of the legislature within the implementation system, since such clarity could in turn help the Court in exploring the legislative branch's potential domestically. To further examine the significance of clarity of rules in systems where the legislature has a meaningful role to play in implementation, we turn to this topic next.

4.2 *Clarity of Rules for Implementation*

Here we consider one of the issues that can contribute to optimizing the work of the legislative branch in its central involvement in a domestic implementation system: the clarity of implementation rules in that system. As mentioned above, it is important to address this topic given the often politically driven and the complex and time- and resources-consuming nature of many legislative processes, to which clear rules could contribute by advancing technique and minimizing the possible negative effects of such features.

Accordingly, clear rules addressing implementation and establishing specific processes and competence for the different types of international decisions and reparation orders, and addressing other branches' engagement, may privilege technique over politics and uncoordinated efforts in how the legislature structures implementation. Such clarity would entail consistency and predictability for victims and the international court in the domestic implementation of reparation orders, ultimately also facilitating monitoring. Yet, clarity as a means to elevate technique over politics does not necessarily means pursuing a more effective implementation system in benefit of the victim, because if the popular will leads the legislature to engage politics to seek prompt and efficient implementation, then undermining politics in favor of technique could be detrimental. However, as political winds shift, clarity is at least capable of enabling a consistent framework against which it may be easier for victims to exercise pressure and for the international court to demand implementation. Moreover, considering the complexity of many legislative processes, clear rules could contribute to minimizing negative effects of the use of such processes in implementation (such as lengthy procedures) by laying out which reparations orders should or must go through such longer processes and which require more expeditious enforcement.

Moreover, clear rules for implementation can favor an adherence to procedure over political interests, capable of overcoming a scattered assessment of international human rights judgements domestically through discrete references to it in legislative debates and processes. Thus, clarity can empower the legislature to materialize the Court's orders, creating a single, but strong and deep, point of connection between the branch and the international body, in lieu of more usual discrete references or debates around judgments, that while useful for the domestic legal system, do not reflect on redress for victims.

In the countries analyzed, there are two possible main models as regards clarity of rules. One model presents lack of clarity, although in different levels among countries, as to how the articulation of implementation from the legislature (or an independent organ in some way connected to it) involves other branches. In this model, the executive and judiciary can and often do get involved in implementation, but the source of their prerogative is obscure, and it is unclear how it relates to the legislative branch's attribution, and how their functions are coordinated so as to not to overlap or conflict. Another model offers more clarity, expressly assigning to one entity the function to coordinate implementation and affirming that other organs can be involved, as long as requested to do so by the primary entity, and based on their competence.

Guatemala exemplifies the first model, as it entitles the parliament to execute reparation orders by decree,[136] and creates a Human Rights Commission within parliament[137] but does not clarify to what extent, if at all, such a commission should assist in implementation of international human rights judgements. Further, despite these entities and their functions, a temporary commission created by the executive power has been engaged in enforcing specific IACtHR judgements.[138] Yet, we could not find clarification on how this temporary commission's attributions reconcile with the legislature's entitlement to use decrees to pursue implementation, or with the work of the Human Rights Commission. Thus, the domestic structure for enforcement of international human rights judgements in Guatemala seems scattered over different branches, with not much clarity as to how specific steps for implementation should occur, and which branch should take them, which ultimately translates into further challenges for the victim.

In turn, El Salvador's legislative branch created the Office of the Attorney General for Human Rights ('Office'),[139] a permanent and independent entity, with its own juridical personality and administrative autonomy,[140] which seems to be the primary responsible for the implementation of IACtHR judgements, despite not mentioning implementation directly in its constitutive text. The Act that regulates the work of the Office was enacted through a legislative decree at the initiative of a group of members of congress,[141] and its Attorney General is elected by Congress as well.[142] In adopting measures to fulfil its duties, the Attorney General can resort to other organs within any of the state's powers to take action in investigating and solving, within their attributions, human rights violations.[143] Thus, although created by the legisla-

136 Constitución Política de la República de Guatemala (1985 con reformas de 1993), Art. 171.

137 CONGRESO DE LA REPUBLICA DE GUATEMALA DECRETO NUMERO 54–86 – Ley de la Comisión de Derechos Humanos del Congreso de la República de Guatemala y del Procurador de los Derechos Humanos, Art. 4(g).

138 Acuerdo Gubernativo No 100–2020, 30 July 2020, Art. 1.

139 'Procuraduría para la Defensa de los Derechos Humanos'.

140 Ley De La Procuraduria Para La Defensa De Los Derechos Humanos, Art. 2.

141 Ley De La Procuraduria Para La Defensa De Los Derechos Humanos, Decreto Legislativo Nº 183 del 20 de febrero de 1992, publicado en el D.O. del 6 de marzo de 1992. Reformado por el D.L. Nº 269, del 12 de febrero de 2001, publicado el 23 de febrero de 2001.

142 Ley De La Procuraduria Para La Defensa De Los Derechos Humanos, Art. 4.

143 Ley De La Procuraduria Para La Defensa De Los Derechos Humanos, Art. 37.

tive, existing within the structure of the executive, but being entirely independent and autonomous, the Office is likely able to engage other state entities from any power in the implementation of IACtHR decisions. Differently from Guatemala, while the formal structure of the Office may involve different branches, it seems to be the only organ, independent from any specific state powers, in charge of articulating implementation, although entitled to engage other state authorities and institutions in enforcement efforts.

Against this background, considering that the role of clarity in privileging technique over politics will often, but not necessarily, be more beneficial for victims seeking effective redress, a model that promotes clarity can make implementation better. That is because clear rules can enable the provision of tools to avoid uncoordinated implementation, and possibly minimize political interference, facilitating a pursuit for consistency, predictability and accountability in enforcement and the monitoring of international reparation orders.

The risk involved in this model that cannot be addressed fully with clear rules is the up and downsides of instrumentalizing politics in implementation. While clarity of rules may help reduce the effects of contrary politics in implementation, it may not be beneficial for victims where popular political will favors an expeditious and effective implementation that cannot be pursued if contrary to procedural rules, for instance. This model would thus benefit from a mechanism or specific norms or principles to ensure flexibility where politics can be used in favor of human rights on the ground, but limit its reach where it works to undermine enforcement efforts.

Therefore, if the IACtHR seeks to widen the roles in domestic implementation efforts to include all branches of government and include the legislature as another ally, it might need to appraise these lessons in developing a normative agenda. Through this agenda, the Court could thus propose new ways to design enforcement tools capable of addressing the risks of uncoordinated and politicized implementation that may arise with the legislature leading implementation.

Considering the significant role of politics in the legislature work, as we addressed above in relation to its balance in face of clarity, the next section examines how shifting local politics can affect the legislature's potential in the implementation of IACtHR judgments.

4.3 *Dependence on Shifts in Local Politics*

As we said above, domestic legislatures reflect and are influenced by popular political will, which makes the parliament itself also a highly political state branch. In a system for the implementation of IACtHR decisions domestically that is led by or centrally involves the legislative branch, the way local politics affect the legislature's ability or potential to push that system toward effective enforcement of judgments becomes a central piece to the entrenchment of international human rights domestically. Addressing this relevance of local politics in this type of system is thus important not only in understanding how to manage and sometimes leverage politics in favor of human rights enforcement on the ground, but also to inform the Court of the potential and risks of shifting politics in legislative-centered models.

That is, the legislature's highly political character must be understood and considered by the Court, as local politics may direct the parliament's approach to human rights domestically. Further, as a reflection of the political interests of the society that elected those politicians, this approach may be legitimized locally, even if contrary to human rights. Thus, the political attitude of local parliaments is of utmost importance for the IACtHR in legislature-centered implementation models. In systems that let political inclinations fully dictate the parliaments' behavior towards international human rights entrenchment domestically, the Court must promote technique in implementation to counter solely political motivations locally when the climate opposes human rights, and when favorable, the Court still needs to ensure that the implementation of its decisions finds legitimacy on the ground. For legislature-centered models that avoid extreme political influence, technique and clear rules must be able to guide the system and legitimize the choices made by parliament.

Without technique and clarity, a highly political legislative-centered implementation system is likely to reflect only a softer tracking of the Court's influence domestically, at best. Unless there is strong political will favoring human rights entrenchment domestically, legislatures may choose to oppose or ignore the IACtHR and the implementation of its judgments, or differing political views within parliament can create a stalemate not propitious to implementation. In such cases, IACtHR orders will possibly not get implemented, and the judgments may only be referred to, debated, cited (even as basis for law reform), but not actually enforced. Therefore, outside very pro-human rights contexts, a legislature-centered system deeply influenced by local politics is likely to only enable superficial, weaker, diluted points of connection between the domestic system and international human rights decisions, if anything.

In the countries analyzed, the legislature-centered systems either count on parliamentary human rights committees to monitor the state's compliance with its international human rights obligations, or on self-proclaimed independent organs (created or hosted by the legislature but disconnected from any state branch) to protect and promote human rights, including by implementing IACtHR decisions. Both models could be influenced by shifting local politics, although the system working through an independent entity might more easily avoid political battles among branches, if willing, which the parliamentary committees would possibly not be able to avert.

More specifically, in Guatemala, despite lack of clarity as to which branch systematically leads implementation, the legislature seems to have a significant role, through a parliamentary human rights commission, to engage or at least propose implementation measures. In practice, attributions for implementation are scattered over different branches (and, according to the state, assigned on a case-by-case basis),[144] yet considering the parliamentary commission's role, it is likely to be heavily influenced by local politics. Such commissions, often composed of a variety of parliament members from different political stands, are often inherently political and, without very clear, binding, procedural rules, could easily face significant politically-motivated stalemates in implementation efforts, especially where its attributions are not well delineated vis-à-vis the executive's entities.

Uruguay can be an example of the second model, with an NHRI that exists under the aegis of the legislative power,[145] but still 'not subject to hierarchy and having an autonomous functioning not receiving orders from any authority.'[146] In practice, however, there have been cases in which the executive and judiciary took some form of leading role in implementation,[147] while the leg-

144 Comisión Interamericana de Derechos Humanos ['Inter-American Commission on Human Rights'], *'Mecanismos Nacionales de Implementación de Recomendaciones de Derechos Humanos'* [*'National Mechanisms for the Implementation of Human Rights Recommendations'*], Doc No OEA/Ser.L/V/II.doc.8/23, 26 February 2023, para 191.

145 Ley N° 18446 – 2008 – Creación Institución Nacional de Derechos Humanos (INDDHH), Art. 1.

146 Ley N° 18446 – 2008 – Creación Institución Nacional de Derechos Humanos (INDDHH), Art. 2.

147 See Resolución N° 450/011 – 2011 – CREACION DE COMISION INTERMINISTERIAL TENDIENTE A ESCLARECER EL DESTINO DE LOS DESAPARECIDOS ENTRE LOS AÑOS 1973 Y 1985, 1–2(a, c). See also Supreme Court of Justice – Judgment 506/2013: 'La Convención Americana sobre Derechos Humanos consagra como garantía de tales Derechos, primero, la irretroactividad de la ley penal y segundo, que el inculpado absuelto por sentencia firme no podrá ser sometido a nuevo juicio por los mismos hechos, tercero, consagra la prohibición de los Estados partes de desconocer el principio de la no retroactividad de la ley penal. En relación a las disposiciones internacionales los Sres. Ministros que integran la mayoría expresan, que no existe un deber de Derecho Internacional de seguir la jurisprudencia de los órganos del sistema interamericano. La intérprete última de la Convención Americana de Derechos Humanos es la Corte Interamericana de Derechos Humanos y la intérprete última de la Constitución es la Suprema Corte de Justicia. Para los ministros mencionados, la cuestión a resolver no trata de la aplicación de la Sentencia de la Corte Interamericana de Derechos Humanos, sino que dice relación

islature itself has also directly led other implementation efforts.[148] While this messy pluralism of implementation mechanisms and competences is not uncommon in Latin American countries, Uruguay's effort to create an NHRI to provide some structure to the compliance system may reflect a desire to avoid political influences in a process otherwise led inconsistently, and uncoordinatedly, by a different branch depending on the case. Ultimately, the fact that different branches have intervened to advance implementation is only a positive reflection of a confusing structure. As long as this confusion does not generate room for political interference in the NHRI's work to hinder implementation, having a (in theory) politically 'impartial' NHRI, and other branches, occasionally and in an unstructured way, leading implementation does not seem necessarily detrimental.

Thus, for these implementation systems which are led by or involve the legislature, a model that works through an independent entity would likely reflect the better option in terms of minimizing political influence in implementation. Although the title of autonomous, independent, organ, does not necessarily diminish the potential role of politics affecting its work, these organs are, at least, not functioning directly from within the inherently political sphere of parliament. This detachment from the legislature enables less political approaches and debates, and a bigger role for technique, if the members of the commission are inclined to privilege technique over political preferences, which is a lot less likely in parliamentary organs directly connected to the legislature.

Therefore, clear rules for implementation can make legislative-centered efforts, through otherwise independent entities, detached from the legislature, diminish the space often occupied by politics in the domestic implementation of IACtHR judgments. Clear rules, followed by an independent organ, may help avoid political battles among branches and within the organ itself, besides eliminating competing or confusing competences, and privileging technique in efforts to ensure compliance with IACtHR's orders, instead of just enabling a softer tracking of their influence.

As regards the IACtHR, a normative agenda would lead the Court to perceive the central role of politics in domestic implementation, especially in legislature-centered systems, and consider options to diminish this role in

---

con la comprobación o no de la adecuación de la norma legal a los derechos y garantías consagrados en la Constitución Nacional'. See Supreme Court of Justice – Judgment 4.492/2011.

148 Ley Nº 19.085 – BARBANI DUARTE Y OTROS VERSUS URUGUAY – 2013.

favor of consistent, technically oriented, compliance. Thus, by promoting the creation of an independent NHRI responsible to initiate and structure implementation efforts, and regulated by clear rules on procedures, steps and competences for compliance, the Court could push for domestic institutional design changes that, at least in theory, facilitate the focus on technique over shifting political dynamics in domestic contexts. As clear rules setting each branch's attributions can be a mechanism to legitimize the work of a branch, at least when the branch follows such rules, we turn next to an analysis of legitimacy in systems centered on the legislature, considering clarity, but also going beyond, assessing the legislature's legitimacy through its relationship with the Court.

4.4 *Directness of Connection to IACtHR*

As we mentioned above, in its connection to the IACtHR, the legislature can perform a mediator role by implementing international human rights judgments as prompted by the executive, and with the effect of guiding the national courts. Yet, in practice, the IACtHR rarely directs its orders to parliaments, which leaves the pathways of communication between them somewhat unclear, if not underexplored by the Court. Nevertheless, parliaments can utilize IACtHR decisions to legitimize changes or approaches in their work, such as for the proposition of new laws, to structure a clear, binding, model for compliance, advance legal reform and shift attitudes and practices,[149] besides being in a privileged position to oversee and pressure the government's compliance with international human rights decisions. Moreover, as a branch closely connected to the political will of society, the legislature's role in implementation can be fundamental in building legitimacy to implementation efforts when reflective of the domestic social, political, context. Thus, due to legislatures' law-making competency, their ability to shape and oversee the work of the other branches, and their political legitimacy when acting on behalf of the people in compliance efforts, it is important to consider the connections between the IACtHR and parliaments, and ways to better explore them to advance parliaments' role supporting the Court and domestic implementation.[150]

As follows, although the IACtHR has had a closer relationship with executives and judiciaries, there is much potential in its connections to legislatures. Parliaments can benefit from IACtHR decisions to bring legitimacy, or at least a political justification, to their work, including new laws and legislative

149 See Hillebrecht, 'The Domestic Mechanisms of Compliance', cit., 969–970.

150 See Ibid 971.

reform.[151] Meanwhile, the IACtHR would also possibly benefit from an alliance with parliaments given their capacity to comply with specific orders (such as legislative reform) from the Court, advance conventionality control in law-making, and oversee and pressure other branches for compliance, besides creating and changing legislation on the domestic implementation system, including the role of other branches. Conversely, lack of communication between the IACtHR and parliaments can hinder or bring compliance processes to a halt if popular political will, reflected in congress, is against compliance, or if the legislature is engaged in political battles with other branches regarding implementation and has no binding, structured, rules to follow regarding their role in those processes. The Court thus needs to connect and communicate with parliaments to make them an ally domestically,[152] liaise with them in monitoring compliance and managing political pushbacks, and in proposing a stronger role to be played by the legislature in implementation, also pushing for clear rules regulating that role and balancing out shifting political trends.

Conversely, without communication between the Court and legislature, the latter's role in compliance might be subject to being prompted to act by the executive, or might be hindered by domestic political divergences, or questioned in its legitimacy without a direct order from the Court engaging the parliament in compliance. Thus, with unclear or underexplored pathways of communication between the Court and parliaments, the role of the legislative branch in compliance can be muddied and curtailed in legislative debates, leaving only a connection to the IACtHR through a softer tracking of its influence domestically. That is, without the legislature's clear role in implementation, it may be left with room for only discrete, sparse, references to IACtHR judgments in legislative debates and processes, or in conventionality control efforts,[153] which are important but still do not quite reflect the full potential of the legislature in fulfilling the Court's orders.

In the countries we analyzed, there are systems that seek to communicate with the IACtHR more directly by expressly connecting the competence of the implementation organ to the OAS structure or the IASPHR specifically, and other systems that only identify a general competence to deal with human rights or international decisions domestically. These systems show different

151 Sabrina Ragone, 'The Importance of the Relationship Between Domestic Institutions and the Inter-American System for the Protection of Human Rights' (2016) 9(2) *Inter-American and European Human Rights Journal* 456, 466.

152 See Ibid 464.

153 Kosař and Lixinski, cit., 746.

levels of openness domestically to communicate with the IACtHR depending on whether they establish a direct connection between their responsibilities and the implementation of IACtHR decisions or not.

El Salvador is an example of the latter, as it counts on an independent organ, created by Congress, whose goal is to protect and promote human rights and their validity domestically, expressly including the rights arising from the OAS system, although not mentioning implementation explicitly.[154] Besides, this entity's role locally includes promoting the adherence to international human rights treaties,[155] and creating and developing inter-communication and inter-cooperation between national sectors and international human right organs.[156] These responsibilities show an active effort, from the domestic end, to open the pathways for communication with the Court and promote cooperation with the IASPHR.

Conversely, in Guatemala, as discussed above, the legislature's role in implementing IACtHR judgments is somewhat unclear, and the Human Rights Commission, albeit being entitled to communicate with international human rights organs for consultation and exchange of information, and propose broad human rights measures to state bodies,[157] has no clear role in actual implementation.[158] This system shows no explicit pathways of communication between the parliament and the IACtHR given the lack of clear rules determining the role of the legislature itself in implementation, which may hinder the Court's efforts to establish a connection with the local congress, if not through direct orders in its judgments.

Considering these two systems and the potential for a more active role for parliaments in implementation, a domestic model that creates, expressly, pathways for communication with the Court and enables a direct connection between the domestic and the international might also prompt a similar approach from the Court in building that bridge of communication. For this closer connection between domestic legislatures and the IACtHR to work, however, the Court itself needs to make a move in that direction, but the national system must also facilitate the liaison between the two levels. Ensur-

154 Ley De La Procuraduria Para La Defensa De Los Derechos Humanos, Art. 2.

155 Ley De La Procuraduria Para La Defensa De Los Derechos Humanos, Art. 12(5).

156 Ley De La Procuraduria Para La Defensa De Los Derechos Humanos, Art. 12(8).

157 CONGRESO DE LA REPUBLICA DE GUATEMALA DECRETO NUMERO 54–86 – Ley de la Comisión de Derechos Humanos del Congreso de la República de Guatemala y del Procurador de los Derechos Humanos, Art. 4(f).

158 CONGRESO DE LA REPUBLICA DE GUATEMALA DECRETO NUMERO 54–86 – Ley de la Comisión de Derechos Humanos del Congreso de la República de Guatemala y del Procurador de los Derechos Humanos, Art. 4(g).

ing that clear rules regulate the role of the legislature is thus fundamental to enable the parliament's work in implementation to be guided by technique rather than politics, and also to expressly state the openness of the legislature to engage with the Court as an ally in compliance.

Thus, apart from the need for the Court to change its own approach to the legislature's involvement in implementation, such as by more frequently directing orders at the legislature specifically in its judgments, the IACtHR also must follow a normative agenda to pressure states to make institutional design choices that clarify the role of legislatures in the domestic implementation system. A concerted effort embedded in clarity of rules, openness for communication, and trust in technique to lead implementation efforts is thus required from both the domestic and international spheres to widen the legislature's role, while considering and diminishing the (political) risks of its more central

5 Stitching (or Velcroing) Lessons from Branches Together

From this typology of implementation in Latin America, we have confirmation of the messy pluralism of approaches in the region to how IACtHR decisions are implemented domestically. While the executive is often the leading branch in implementation efforts, either through centralized or diffuse systems, a few countries have turned more attention to and emphasized the roles played by the judiciary and legislature in those efforts. Two main considerations arise from this finding: first, that these differences among countries regarding which branch leads or articulates implementation generate different effects and possibilities for enforcement, affecting victims and their prospects for redress differently, and inviting different types of reaction from the IACtHR in efforts to improve implementation. Thus, carefully considering the domestic framework for enforcement – understanding the possibilities, strengths and shortcomings of each model – can have significant impacts on how IHRL is entrenched domestically through IACtHR judgments. Second, there is still a lot to be done and reappraised in many of the domestic systems analyzed to promote better alignment with the IACtHR human-rights-oriented goals, like the branches' engagement with second generation conventionality control, and efforts for actual enforcement (enabling a stitch, rather than a Velcro, type of connection).

While diffuse implementation systems benefit from shared responsibilities in implementation efforts, facilitating second generation conventionality control, and might enable the materialization of a wide range of remedies awarded by the IACtHR, diverging political stands between branches can weaken the potential of a diffuse system and hinder the stitch form of implementation. Meanwhile, a centralized system can offer more structure and coordination to implementation efforts, possibly facilitating a stitch-type connection, but is also not immune to political shifts, can lead to only partial implementation if the necessary involvement of other branches is not enabled, and may jeopardize second generation conventionality control. From the analysis of specific models in place in the countries investigated, a diffuse system still seems preferable for its potential for comprehensive enforcement and better redress for victims, enabling conventionality control, and sometimes leaving room for technique to be applied in the pursuit of a stitch-type implementation. However, particularities of the current diffuse models available in the countries play a significant role in this finding, and the potential for effectiveness of a diffuse system may also depend on which branch leads, articulates, or engages the implementation efforts, as well as the correlation of this theme with the other themes studied.

Beyond the messy pluralism of implementation models, often each model lacks clarity in its own domestic rules regulating the structure, authorities and processes of the implementation system. This lack of clarity is largely unproductive, except where an overly formalistic approach hinders or lingers enforcement due to the need to follow those rules while the political climate favors implementation and pushes for more effective and speedier enforcement efforts. Generally, however, unclear rules are significantly detrimental to implementation, especially in efforts seeking enforcement in a stitch type of connection. Therefore, clear and comprehensive rules coordinating implementation are preferable and more likely to minimize the role played by politics in domestic efforts and facilitate a stitch type of entrenchment of IHRL domestically.

The role of politics remains pervasive and significant in how the implementation systems are structured and operated, and more often than not, works to the detriment of a stitch kind of connection. In a nutshell, judiciary-led models seem to be the most able to reduce the role of politics in favor of technique, yet no model or branch is safe from detrimental political influences affecting the possibilities for enforcement. While entirely eliminating the role of politics in the domestic implementation systems is impossible and perhaps not always desirable (mainly when politics favor human rights), clear rules aligned with a focus on technique enabled by resort to private international law rules, can offer a potentially productive counter-point to politics. Through technique, not only the implementation system gains legitimacy and structure, but also victims and the IACtHR gain better avenues to monitor compliance and better prospects for a stitch form of connection between IHRL and its concrete effects on the domestic system.

Finally, while the findings and considerations in this section focus on the domestic systems, this analysis necessarily takes us to how such domestic systems speak to the IACtHR. First, this connection is necessary because the pathways for communication between the two spheres, domestic and international, help explain the IACtHR's past trends of relationship with domestic branches and shed light on the potential for the future, but also relate to internal dynamics that can generate mutual benefits and legitimacy between these two spheres. In this regard, while the Court has been closer to the executive and judiciary, it has been progressively turning attention to the legislature as a potential domestic ally, and as a necessary agent in conventionality control. The models found in the countries analyzed confirm the historic closeness between the Court and the executive, and to an extent, the judiciary; while showing a shy and incipient involvement of the legislature as well. Second, identifying these pathways can inform an assessment of what the IACtHR can do to improve implementation, including a stitch-type connection, and conventionality control. Accordingly, from our analysis, while there is much potential in the legislature as a possible partner in domestic implementation for the Court, clarity and technique are essential in countering the prevalence of politics in the work of this branch to also enable a stitch where, otherwise, a Velcro model is more likely. To strengthen the pathway of communication between IACtHR and legislatures, however, a more active and consistent move from the Court itself is needed.

The analysis of these Latin American countries' solutions, read through the perspective of the different branches of government and the two main bodies of scholarship on which we rely (foreign relations law and conflict of laws style), yields numerous useful insights for the Inter-American Court, states under its jurisdiction, and victims of human rights violations and their advocates. In the next chapter, we seek to turn those insights into normative lessons. In teasing out those lessons we also consider the possible significant implications beyond the geographical confines of the Inter-American system, for both the problem (enhancing the effectiveness of international courts' judgments to enhance international law's ability to engender transformation), and the scholarly fields (of studies on international courts and tribunals, alongside foreign relations law and conflict of laws style).

CHAPTER 4

Impacts on the Problem and the Field

In the previous chapter, we indicated many of our preferences in terms of domestic enforcement. We declared those preferences in relation to the options different states have designed within each branch of government, and in relation to four specific factors. These are: the degree of centralization of authority for enforcement; the clarity of domestic rules on implementation; the volatility of those mechanisms in relation to domestic politics; and the implementer's legitimacy based on its connection to the IACtHR.

What we are still to do, however, is to compare these solutions across different branches, with a view to forming a more holistic understanding of the possibilities and pitfalls of enforcing IACtHR judgments domestically. This chapter is devoted to drawing those lessons together.

In doing so, we first foreground the question of the IACtHR's legitimacy. Our intention in focusing on legitimacy first is because it is at the core of the enforcement question: the IACtHR needs its judgments to be enforced if it is to be able to muster the gravitas to demand that the next state in the next case also implements a judgment. Here, the issue of stitches and Velcro starts to blend a little. The overall influence of the IACtHR depends on its legitimacy, and the legitimacy depends on enforcement. In some ways, and at the risk of belaboring the metaphor, a discussion of the IACtHR's legitimacy amounts to thinking about how we stitch a Velcro patch in place. Further, legitimacy is in some respects the price of admission for enforcement: if states believe the IACtHR's actions are legitimate, they are more likely to enforce them in the next case.

Next, we refocus on the problem: what deeper thinking about, and more clarity on, pathways for enforcement mean for (alleged) victims and their advocates. With an eye to tactic- and strategy-building, that section discusses the levers that participants in the IASPHR have available to them in pursuit of tangible outcomes to redress human rights violations and improve human rights in the region.

The third section tries to distill the lessons from the previous two sections into a workable model for enforcement. We do so very mindful (and even wary) of the idiosyncrasies of domestic law and politics that render such a model only an archetype. States, we believe, are unlikely to use this model in its integrity. However, much like model laws as a key instrument of comparative law and international organizations seeking to influence states parties,

© AYLA DO VALE ALVES AND LUCAS LIXINSKI, 2025 | DOI:10.1163/9789004741829_005

here we believe that a model is useful fodder for conversations about the possibilities and limits of domestic solutions. And, for the most part, our key addressee in this section is not states – it is the IACtHR. By distilling a baseline model, we hope we can offer the Court subsidies for its own thinking when designing, ordering, and monitoring compliance with reparations. We also then partly address other human rights bodies and their remedial practices.

Lastly, the fourth section takes a step back and asks how the insights of this book might be useful beyond human rights adjudication. Here we recenter the field, and ask what the lessons we have learned in this book mean for the two key bodies of scholarship we have used (foreign affairs law and conflict of laws style). We then discuss what this book's insights mean for how we think about international law as a whole.

1 Legitimacy Impacts

The IACtHR's legitimacy, as one of us has argued elsewhere, does not derive from states parties.[1] Rather, the IACtHR seeks as its main source of legitimacy an idealized (and to a large extent undefined) archetype of international legal ordering oriented towards ever greater protection of human rights. This specific take on the source of the Court's legitimacy, which contrasts with other similar courts, has specific consequences when it comes to remedial practice and its enforcement.

First and foremost, recall the quote from *Velásquez Rodríguez v Honduras*'s reparations judgment in Chapter 2. Already in its very first case, the IACtHR made it clear that the American Convention's remedies mandate 'does not refer to or limit the ability to ensure the effectiveness of the means of reparation available under the internal law of the State Party responsible for the violation, so it is not limited by the defects, imperfections or deficiencies of national law, but functions independently of it.'[2] This quote reinforces the idea that the IACtHR does not rely on states parties for its understanding of self, and of its own legitimacy. Rather, it is mistrusting of states.

That attitude is hard-won. Remember that most countries in Latin America at the time were military dictatorships, known for widespread human rights abuses. Manfredo Velásquez Rodríguez himself was a victim of enforced dis-

1 Lucas Lixinski, 'The Consensus Method of Interpretation by the Inter-American Court of Human Rights', 3(1) *Canadian Journal of Comparative and Contemporary Law*, (2017) 65–96.
2 Velásquez Rodríguez, cit., para. 30.

appearance at the (presumed) hands of the state. That these states ratified the American Convention, and accepted the jurisdiction of the Court, speaks to their self-belief that their dictatorial regimes protected human rights by keeping the hemisphere safe from the threat of communism.[3] The Court did not share said belief, from its very beginning.

Regardless of how merited the IACtHR's suspicion is, the fact remains that the Court is adamant about not engaging with domestic law, and ordering reparations apart from it. In doing so, the IACtHR preserves its independence vis-à-vis states, but does so at the cost of its own legitimacy with them, and its ability to promote the human rights transformation it set out to promote. States have in fact pushed against the Court's use of its broad mandate on reparations, precisely on legitimacy grounds.[4]

Beyond this legitimacy gambit having been met with resistance at a broader, more political level, it also has a harmful impact on the Court's own wishes. Specifically, by not being more precise on directions for implementation of reparations (because it sees itself as fully independent from domestic law), the IACtHR makes it harder for states to know how to implement those orders in full compliance with human rights, and to the Court's satisfaction. Doctrines like conventionality control, if applied well domestically, enhance awareness of the Court's doctrines, and increase its influence, but still fall short of giving detailed operational insight that the Court itself refuses to produce.

The IACtHR's lack of direction at the reparations phase inevitably makes its own supervision of compliance with judgments more difficult. Whereas the Court, as we indicated above, normally adds a section on 'modalities of compliance' to its judgments nowadays, these directions still fall short of distributing responsibility to specific authorities, and risk creating a version of the bystander effect we also discussed in Chapter 2.

The legitimacy of the Court is also impacted by the timing of the reparations orders, particularly in relation to domestic politics in the affected state. In the pushback against the IACtHR's reparations orders we indicated above, a group of states issued a joint statement admonishing the Court against being too aggressive in its orders. Those states were all experiencing democratic backslides at the time. In the Court's defense, thus, it may be that not being too specific in its engagement with domestic institutions is a means to preserve the reparations orders against changes in political winds domestically.

3 On this point, see generally Pasqualucci, cit.
4 Lixinski, 'Mechanisms', cit.

Remember for instance that the state's lead representative before the IACtHR is usually a diplomat, who is a member of the executive branch and one whose job requires them to be particularly attuned to the politics of the day. Even though diplomats are not the ones that prepare the entire defense, nor are necessarily even the actual advocates before the Court, the filtering of the case through foreign ministries and embassies creates a political wind within or even against which the IACtHR must navigate its aspirations.

Nonetheless, we suggest that this caution, if it is a factor, partly misses the point. The point we have been making about domestic implementation is that it is, in fact, politically charged, but ultimately it is a series of bureaucratic moves. Those moves can be more impervious to politics, and the conflict of law's style analysis in particular shows those possibilities, suggesting even that there is a sense of inherent legitimacy in the (temporary) suspension of politics in favor of technique to promote change.

This suspension of politics is arguably a dangerous game. The Court (as most human rights organizations, at least to some extent) declares itself to be apolitical, or above politics. Doing so is a legitimacy-grabbing tool, of course. But it can also mean an excessive focus on substantive human rights law standards, and ensuing remedies, that are doable without really rocking the proverbial boat. In doing so, the IACtHR in fact preserves the state of which it is suspicious, by avoiding the more transformational possibilities of human rights law (and particularly remedies) to remake society. It is thus necessary to be very mindful of politics in the implementation of technique. The suspension can be nothing but temporary, and focused on the implementation, rather than the design, of remedies.

Our suggestion to suspend the politics of the implementation of remedies is one that relies on the possibilities of bureaucratic allyship, but is still mindful of the political winds that affect implementation (it just tries to shield enforcement from those forces temporarily). This modality opens the door for victims and strategy-building to think more proactively about reparation enforcement in all stages of their litigation, too.

2 Impacts on Victims and Strategy-Building

The possibilities of technique suspending politics do not solve all issues, but can sometimes create specific levers. For one, remember that a powerful tool for an international human rights court is reputational damage. Much like all of human rights law, "naming and shaming" is an important element for rule-following (as is arguably the case for all of international law).[5] The question then is whether reputation is tied to a government, or to a state. If the former, then the political winds of the day are much more influential in assessing the cost of compliance.

A lesson, in other words, is for activists to shame the state, and not the government, connecting governments to the long lineage they are meant to represent and defend. In countries experiencing the rise of populism, it is worth remembering that the populist appeal is a nostalgic recalling of the past, which evokes a supposedly harmonious time (and worth adding that in said past people did enjoy human rights, even if by another name).

The IACtHR already does it, of course. It does not refer to the government of the day, but rather to the state in broader terms. In other words, it pulls its reputational lever. As the relatively low compliance record with IACtHR judgments shows, however, it is not the most effective lever.

An important yet unexplored lever, in our view, is for the Court to give more detailed instructions on enforcement. We will return to that topic in the next section. Part of that lever, as we discuss below, is to benefit from the goodwill and natural allyships between the IACtHR as a judicial body and domestic judges. The IACtHR leverages some of these relationships when it speaks about judicial design, for instance, and in doing so it empowers itself.[6]

Turning specifically to the roles of victims and their advocates, there is one important caveat to make. We are not suggesting in any way that the bulk of the burden for compliance lays with victims. To expect them to do so is to shift a significant burden onto a party that, by definition within human rights law, is not a peer to the wrongdoer in terms of its resources. The primary responsibility for compliance lies with the state at all times.

At the same time, victims and their advocates could explore being savvier in their implementation strategies. Victims can lead enforcement by making direct representations to domestic authorities, for instance, instead of waiting for the state to voluntarily initiate enforcement. In doing so, victims' representatives have significant power in triggering specific state authorities towards compliance. They can arguably select the branches of government, and agencies within it, that are more likely to offer the most satisfactory remedy (whether in terms of the action itself, or speed, or strength of the action – whether systemic change or individual redress, for instance).

5 See generally Andrew T Guzmán, *How International Law Works: A Rational Choice Theory* (Oxford University Press, 2008).

6 David Kosař and Lucas Lixinski, cit.

Victims already appear, too, in the IACtHR's own internal mechanism of monitoring of compliance with judgments. There, they tend to make representations about the extent to which the state is still to comply with reparations, in a position of checking for compliance, instead of guiding it. Arguably, victims could do more to bring to the Court's attention not just that states have failed to comply, but also how the Court can maneuver states towards compliance. Here and more broadly, victims would do well to remember that the IACtHR is more likely to offer a sympathetic ear than the state being accused of violating human rights (whether in general, or even more so the specific authorities allegedly responsible for the violation).

Further, victims can be more mindful of compliance possibilities in their advocacy from the very beginning of a case. Victims already do it to a significant extent, of course: by pointing out which authority within the state is the perpetrator of the human rights violation, and framing (or not) the specific violation against a broader background of systemic violations, victims already give important elements to shape the Court's reparations orders. Further, victims always make representations on reparations in their petitions to the IACtHR, as part of its regular procedure. It is arguable, however, that victims can do even more in this respect, by offering richer descriptions not just of a violation, but of the structural factors that contributed to that specific violation. To be clear, here we do not mean the broader context of violations; rather, we mean the institutions, actors, and actions that connect the broader context of violations to the specific moment of violation. A clear sequence paints a more vivid story not just of which authorities are to blame, but indirectly also which authorities can promote change. Further, in the claims for remedies, victims could revisit those accounts to identify the specific pressure points within a state that can lead to change therein; instead of asking the Court that the police force change its culture of discrimination, for instance, representatives can indicate which body oversees the police force, and has carriage over training and retraining.

These are just some possibilities, of course. As we already said, the burden still lies with the state. But savvier victims and their representatives can contribute to more expedient enforcement, as is in their interest. To do so optimally, however, they would also benefit from the IACtHR clearly signaling its expectations on enforcement better, and offering at least elements of a model for judgment enforcement. To imagining such a model we turn next.

3 An Optimal Model of International (Human Rights) Judgment Enforcement in Domestic Law?

The Court, we have been arguing throughout, ought to give states clearer guidance on the implementation of the remedies it orders. For the most part, the IACtHR does not spend much energy on directing states on how to implement remedies, even if it does give guidance on judicial and other institutional design. The reasons why the Court will only do so selectively are varied, as we indicated above.

One of those factors worth stressing again is that, from a doctrinal legal perspective, the IACtHR is already doing all it can. To the extent it treats the state as a monolith, which is what international law (and its own previous case law) requires it to do, there is not much more the Court can do in directing states, whether across branches of government or in federal contexts. However, the Court can do much more on implementation, both in offering a direct roadmap in its judgments, and via indirect action.

We will return to indirect action below. For now, suffice to say that the Court ought to rely more on the friendly interlocutors it already has, and that it could expand capacity-building activities it already undertakes, making them more purposive. Indirect activities, by our account, mean activities that facilitate the Court's activity by educating its addressees.

For the most part, however, the IACtHR relies on its own judgments. Reparations are, by their very nature, allocations of resources. What they are not always, however, are allocations of authority. The Court, by this account, will determine financial compensation, or order the state to reopen a police investigation (allocation of resources), but will not spell out who exactly is to do those things (allocation of authority).

Over the past few years, the IACtHR has started offering more direction.[7] In the *Case of the Employees of the Fireworks Factory of Santo Antônio de Jesus v. Brazil*, for instance,[8] the Court still falls short of allocating specific authority, but gives specific direction on the make-up of a development fund for the victims, including capacity-building courses so they can retrain towards other industries, awareness-raising campaigns on workers' rights, and meas-

7 We are thankful to Lucas Mendes Felippe for this insight and for sending us very useful materials.

8 I/A Court H.R., Case of the Employees of the Fireworks Factory of Santo Antônio de Jesus and their families v. Brazil. Preliminary Objections, Merits, Reparations and Costs. Judgment of July 15, 2020. Series C No. 407.

ures against school attrition.[9] While worthwhile, and a gradual evolution, these instructions do not go much further than what the Court usually spells out in its judgments under 'Modality of Compliance', right after the reparations sections of its judgments.

It is easier for the Court to give direction for some reparations orders than for others. When it comes to the reopening of domestic cases (even the ones with a final judgment), for instance, the Court is quicker to point out to implementation as a relatively simple (from a policy perspective, anyway) mechanism, and to map practice in the Americas and even in Europe that enables this type of compliance.[10] In order to comply with this type of measures, the Court has praised (but not directed) the bypassing of police authorities, and the ability in some countries (like Brazil) for the public attorney[11] to reopen and lead the investigation, without police participation. In this specific case, it is worth noting, it was the representatives of the victims who made the push for the development of this institutional pathway, by the Court's own admission.[12] However, representatives of victims did so based on the Court's prompt in an earlier case, where the Court framed this pathway as an 'example' of how to guarantee independence from the police when the police had been the institution responsible for the rights violation.[13]

The Court notes in this regard that the development of parallel institutional pathways is important to preserve independence, and goes further. The Court specifies that this separation must be supported 'by police, technical-criminal and administrative staff', acknowledging the importance of bureaucratic structures and calling them to task.[14]

Creating these alternative pathways makes sense in some respects. It allows for enforcement that is not dependent on the authorities responsible for the original violation, for one. It also creates mechanisms to oversee the violating

---

9 Id., para. 289.

10 I/A Court H.R., Case of Sales Pimenta v. Brazil. Preliminary Objections, Merits, Reparations and Costs. Judgment of June 30, 2022. Series C No. 454, paras. 179–180 (particularly footnote 262 to para. 180).

11 In Portuguese, the *Ministério Público*.

12 I/A Court H.R., Case of Honorato et al. v. Brazil. Preliminary Objections, Merits, Reparations and Costs. Judgment of November 27, 2023. Series C No. 508, para. 189 (building on I/A Court H.R., Case of Favela Nova Brasília v. Brazil. Preliminary Objections, Merits, Reparations and Costs. Judgment of February 16, 2017. Series C No. 333, and mirrored in I/A Court H.R., Case of Tavares Pereira et al. v. Brazil. Preliminary Objections, Merits, Reparations and Costs. Judgment of November 16, 2023. Series C No. 507).

13 Case of Favela Nova Brasilia, cit., para. 319.

14 Case of Tavares Pereira, cit., para. 209.

authorities, which can then translate into changes to those authorities themselves. It is thus a mix of individualized (independence for the specific case) and systemic (changes to the authorities) effects, even if there seems to be more focus on the former over the latter. Further, to create a separate route is easier for the Court to dictate as a measure, since it requires less in-depth knowledge of the operation of each of the state's institutions.

Conversely, however, this type of separation has some possible downsides. First of all, to create an alternative pathway will only secondarily impact the violating authority, as we suggested in the previous paragraph. If the point is, for instance, to change the culture in the military, then to say an external authority will have limited oversight only with respect to one set of proceedings might not be enough. That said, states who have created these parallel pathways seem to have them as permanent oversight mechanisms that can, in fact, change culture. Most crucially, though, the authorities who oversee these parallel pathways need to have the powers to compel the original authorities to make the necessary changes to comply with the ambitious asks of IACtHR judgments, too. There is a risk here that the IACtHR will only multiply bureaucratic pathways, making the system unwieldy from the perspective of states, and, particularly, victims. However, the Court can address these issues by clear mandates for local authorities to be able to coordinate and override other bodies of the state machinery.

Another factor to consider is whether implementation of an IACtHR judgment should be performed by a dedicated permanent organ with the power to compel state authorities, or by ad hoc commissions designed for each separate judgment and their idiosyncratic reparations. An ad hoc body would be able to adapt more easily to what each judgment requires, avoiding the risk of formulaic or 'box-ticking' types of enforcement. But a fresh body might also find it harder to compel state authorities with whom it has limited experience. On balance, we would suggest that a permanent body with some flexibility in its composition, like the Colombian Working Groups we discussed above, would be optimal institutional design for reparations that are executive- or legislative-centric.

But the independence of enforcement pathways and their form (permanent or ad hoc) are not the only considerations at stake for the IACtHR. Drawing together the four themes through which we analyzed the different solutions across the continent, and comparing considerations therein across the three branches of government, also yields important insights as to how the IACtHR might go about being more proactive in nudging states towards specific institutional and legal enforcement pathways.

Revisiting our discussion above about centralized or diffuse authority, it seems that centralized authority works best from the Court's perspective, at least in the short term. The IACtHR only needs to address one authority. Likewise, victims only need to access one body. This shape thus seems to favor the stitch-type enforcement in the short term. However, diffuse domestic authority, while more difficult at first, is more in line with the doctrinal mandates of conventionality control, which gives the IACtHR a clearer normative entry point to pursue enforcement. Further, in the long run, diffuse enforcement authority also further entrenches the IACtHR, thus combining stitch-type enforcement with long-term Velcro-type influence.

Turning to the clarity of rules for implementation, it would seem obvious from the discussion in this section that we prefer clarity in the enforcement rules. Clarity facilitates implementation, particularly to the extent we expect bureaucratic or technical personnel to lead enforcement. Doing so also avoids the bystander effect we discussed above, because the IACtHR points to specific authorities that ought to comply, prompting them to do so as direct addressees of the Court's order. However, excessive clarity can also backfire in some instances, by becoming too rigid. Some flexibility is helpful particularly considering the complexity of some of the reparations measures (particularly guarantees of non-repetition). And flexibility can give more power to the Court in the medium to long term because it gives the Court more opportunities, in its supervision of compliance with judgments, to nudge state institutions in multiple ways. Further, clarity seems to favor enforcement led by the legislative or judicial branches far more than the executive branch, where flexibility seems more attractive given the nature of that branch.

Third, the influence of shifts in local politics hits executive-led enforcement harder, compared to the other branches. The latest wave of rise in populist politics in Latin America, as well as the corresponding democratic backsliding, make it apparent how susceptible the executive branch is to the personalities of officials elected to form government, despite best efforts by bureaucrats committed to the state. At the same time, however, human rights are inherently political, otherwise this body of law loses much of its transformative potential, particularly relevant in a vision of reparations as world-making. Therefore, it is also unwise to shun politics altogether from enforcement, as we discussed above. Rather, what we need is clearer inter-relationships among branches (checks and balances) that help keep political interference at a healthy level. Further, politics is an optimal pathway for civil society to exert pressure over government, and a fully technical government would present much more limited participation opportunities outside of comparably technical civil society organizations, which again would take away some of the transformative power of human rights and resolve it as a series of individualized technical issues rather than wholesale changes to society. But politics under this version finds more traction, we would suggest, in thinking about the role of legislatures than executive branches, given the power of legislatures to dispel the personality-centric nature of presidential politics in the Americas.

Lastly, in terms of lines of communication with the IACtHR, it is clear that the judiciary tends to be in an optimal position vis-à-vis the Court. Judges like to speak to, and understand better, other judges, to put it bluntly. But the IACtHR also has a good pathway of communication with the Executive because of the formalities of diplomatic representation. It is the legislature that has little opportunity to speak directly to the Court. These pathways are important for the overall legitimacy of the Court, and, of course, for conventionality control. They can exclude victims, however, if they function too well, so one must be wary of their efficiency as a bilateral enforcement pathway, which compromises their usefulness by excluding important voices that are central to the stitch-type enforcement on which we focus in this book.

Considering these four factors, a question that comes to mind is whether, in the abstract, there is one branch of government whom the IACtHR should favor in its design of reparations orders. Judiciaries are more natural allies, and the Court has more experience in institutional design with them. Legislatures have more democratic legitimacy, though, and therefore a better ability to entrench the Court's legitimacy. And executives have greater powers (including financial) to enforce judgments. All in all, though, our separation of these three branches for our analysis shows that there is no clear winner here. The most important factor that emerges is the ability of whichever branch takes the lead to compel the others.

The IACtHR would thus do well to make this power to compel clear in its reparation orders. It may be that the Court sees this power as implied or a given, but it would be useful to make it part of reparations orders that the state assign specific authority to one branch, or an institution therein, with clear legislated powers to compel the other branches, on the basis of domestic constitutional provisions on fundamental rights (to sidestep domestic litigation on the basis of separation of powers). Based on this type of order, the Court can then create a clear specific domestic authority who has primary carriage of enforcement, also facilitating the IACtHR's monitoring of compliance with judgments. This measure is, in our view, the single most important thing the Court can do to facilitate the enforcement of its own judgments, from the standpoint of its direct judicial action.

One way for the Court to go further in reparation orders would be for it to make greater use of the section in judgments on 'Modality of Compliance'.

At present, as we indicated in Chapter 2, the IACtHR generally only uses this section to discuss payment modalities and deadlines. It could go further there, and develop more detailed instructions on institutional design with a view to enforcement. Doing so would not be unlike what the Court does in other contexts, namely, of using the reparations part of a judgment (since the section on modes of compliance is within the reparations part) to backdoor development of the law more broadly. Here, the IACtHR would be using the equivalent of a small window on the backdoor to make the backdoor more efficient (which may or may not lead to development of its legal standards more broadly, particularly on institutional design).

A similar but more tentative and gradual approach would be for the IACtHR to give more direction in its resolutions on monitoring of compliance with judgments.[15] Because these are resolutions, they are lower-stakes documents, and the Court could start developing guidance to states there in the first instance, eventually moving on to judgments themselves. This tactic would also benefit cases for which there is already a judgment on the merits, but compliance is still pending, thus allowing the Court to experiment with currently existing cases that might be closer to full compliance, and on the basis of more compliance information after several rounds of compliance monitoring.

Elsewhere, though, the Court can also engage in a range of other activities. The IACtHR could tap further into its soft power, as we indicated earlier in this section. By soft power we mean the activity of the Court not as a judicial institution, but as a more complex international organization. Soft power activities include the Court's sessions outside of Costa Rica to raise further awareness of its work, for instance, with ensuing capacity-building activities with local government authorities and civil society. Soft activities also include the work of the IACtHR's press office. These powers are an important part of the enforcement puzzle, and one that makes sense if we understand enforcement as not just a legal-technical activity, but fundamentally a bureaucratic activity aimed at social and political transformation. Reading the IACtHR enforcement through a foreign relations law prism helps understand these powers better.

One example is capacity-building, and what the Court already does in this area.[16] The IACtHR, when doing itinerant sessions in countries in the Americas, always engages in capacity-building with civil society and government

15 We are thankful to Suellen Moura for prompting this insight.

16 We are thankful to Pedro Sousa Salgueiro Pawlowski for prompting these insights on capacity-building.

officials. It would do well to turn that capacity-building away from general awareness about the Court and its case law (useful for conventionality control and Velcro-type influence) towards specific discussions about enforcement. At the very least, it ought to make enforcement pathways part of those presentations. The Court has a talented and diverse Secretariat, with highly qualified lawyers from most of the countries under its jurisdiction. These lawyers, because of their training, would be in a good place to speak to changes to domestic law as suggestions to their audiences, and to receive feedback on how to finesse those measures. These members of the Secretariat can then take this knowledge back to the Court and the drafting of reparations measures, and attendees to these sessions will also be in a better position to pursue enforcement in the course of their regular work with the IACtHR.

Further, the Court could order capacity-building by organs of the IASPHR as a measure of reparations, to further entrench the system, conventionality control, and to help develop enforcement pathways by teaching a range of state authorities about the importance of compliance with the Court's judgments.[17] Of course, it would not be appropriate for the Court's Secretariat to undertake these activities as a measure of reparations, given conflict of interests. However, it would be very appropriate for the Commission to do so, especially considering the Commission already has a clear mandate on human rights education and capacity-building in the Americas.

The insights in this section are useful not just for the IACtHR itself, but also for other human rights bodies. United Nations Treaty Bodies and other human rights bodies lacking the power to issue binding judgments in particular would benefit from more intentional deployment of their soft powers. But even the African and European courts would in theory enhance the enforcement of their judgments by thinking more deeply about their relationships to domestic branches of government, taking the elements in this section into account.

Assuming these insights are both feasible in actuality, and have some impact in improving the state of human rights in the Americas and beyond, we would be more than happy. However, there are further lessons we can draw from our analysis, of significance beyond the realm of human rights adjudication. In the next section, we focus on what we believe are the poten-

17 For an example of Commission involvement, see I/A Court H.R., Case of Julien Grisonas Family v. Argentina. Preliminary Objections, Merits, Reparations and Costs. Judgment of September 23, 2021. Series C No. 437; and I/A Court H.R., Case of Julien Grisonas family v. Argentina. Interpretation of the Judgment on Preliminary Objections, Merits, Reparations and Costs. Judgment of November 21, 2022. Series C No. 479.

tials of this book to thinking about the fields of foreign relations law and conflict of laws style. We also query whether these insights can be useful to thinking about international adjudication more broadly, beyond human rights law.

4 Lessons beyond International Human Rights Adjudication

To understand the influence of international human rights courts beyond a series of Velcro patches, and to think again of stitches, does significant work for our thinking about international law more broadly. These contributions affect not only the two main bodies of scholarship we have deployed in this book, but also the goalposts we set for international law, its relationship to domestic law, and its capacity to constitute effective global ordering.

With respect to foreign relations law, its main contribution to this book is unpacking the state. And this book's main contribution to foreign affairs law is in thinking seriously about institutional design, an admitted gap in foreign affairs law. Further, in terms of how unpacking the state through a human rights adjudication prism helps our understanding of foreign relations law, it is worth assessing each of the four factors through which we studied the practice of states in enforcing IACtHR judgments.

First, with respect to the centralization or diffusion of authority, foreign relations law's impulse to unpack the monolith of the state (and therefore fragment it) benefits from this analysis because we stressed the importance, at least in the first instance, of centralization as the best way to gain some immediate traction in having international law influence domestic institutions and practices. Put it a different way, even if we opt for a Velcro patch, we still need an initial stitch to have it adhere to the pieces of fabric we are trying to connect. In fact, we need multiple stitches. So, even if the objective is ultimately Velcro-type influence and a richer and more accurate description of a complex state apparatus, at least initially centralized power is helpful.

Second, with respect to the clarity of rules for implementation, our analysis showcases the possibilities of flexibility to deal with complexity, which reinforces foreign affairs law's insights. At the same time, our analysis contributes to foreign affairs law by highlighting the importance of a politically charged bureaucracy committed to the same principles, and able to vary their practices at the service of that principle.

Shifts in local politics as a significant factor in enforcement of IACtHR judgments help foreign affairs law by highlighting the importance of checks and balances among domestic branches of government to counter unhelpful politicization. At the same time, our insights reinforce foreign affairs law's insights of how different branches of government leverage international law and institutions to bypass each other. They also reinforce the idea that politics are inextricably tied to international legal practice when it intersects with the state, and any suspension can only be temporary (and therefore ought to be intentionally so).

Fourth, our analysis of communication lines to the IACtHR contributes to foreign affairs law simply by creating another avenue through which branches of government can use international law to bypass each other. These insights also highlight, however, the risks of defaulting in foreign affairs law scholarship to a binary between a (diverse and complicated) state and an international institution, reminding us of the importance of considering other actors (particularly civil society).

The other body of scholarship from which we benefitted in this book could also use some of its insights. The conflict of laws style scholarship can benefit from our analysis of international courts to contrast with the bulk of existing work, which is on the activities of domestic courts. Beyond this obvious descriptive contribution, however, we also believe our book helps advance some of the normative insights of conflict of laws style scholarship.

In relation to the centralization or diffusion of enforcement authority, our analysis is useful to the conflict of laws style by reminding us that, if the ultimate goal is to have multiple authorities enforcing judgments, then we ought to create appropriate legal and institutional pathways to facilitate the checks of recognition and enforcement of an international judgment. We cannot depend simply on the abstract knowledge of private international law – institutional safeguards pushing it must be in place.

Second, the debate on clarity of rules for implementation tells the conflict of laws style that clarity, while important, still needs to make room for complexity. The conflict of laws scholarship makes room for this complexity by mandating analyses of *ordre public*, for instance, which contains the complexity within a specific window. But conflict of laws scholarship would also do well to understand that, as per our analysis, this embrace of complexity ultimately benefits courts above other institutions, which can generate checks and balances problems.

Relatedly, our insights on dependence on shifts in local politics benefit conflict of laws style by showing how the different branches operate to try to reach equilibrium on political matters. It is therefore not just the slicing of issues that allows for a suspension of politics; there is also an equilibrium that state institutions themselves ought to reach, to allow for politics to productively enter the scene. The technique on which the conflict of laws style relies cannot on its own resolve the politics it simultaneously seeks to suspend or exchange for technical steps. We need instead to think of other branches as part of the conversation about politics and its suspension and deployment.

Finally, in relation to the directness of connection to the IACtHR, the conflict of laws style scholarship can benefit from understanding that pathways for communication can be exclusionary, and that technique itself can backfire if it does not leave room for victims to exercise their procedural rights. Otherwise, the style's contribution to legitimacy can miss out on the reason why legitimacy is important in the first place: so international institutions can deploy their acquired legitimacy credits to transform human lives and the world.

Beyond these two bodies of scholarship, though, there are also useful insights from this book to how we think about international law and its institutional operation through and beyond international adjudication. We do not subscribe to a court-centric understanding of (international) law and its operation,[18] which probably helps us think about the potential implications of our insights. International courts, in some respects, are just another form of international institution, all vying for influence in domestic law and for the ability to transform lives. Courts use specific language, procedures, and even rituals, but the objective is similar. Our book thus yields insights that are useful to all of international law, potentially.

First, this book contributes to thinking about better pathways for the enforcement of international law in domestic law. Pathways for enforcement are also pathways for implementation, and ultimately influence. And international courts and other international institutions, we suggest, ought to invest more in giving direction to states on institutional development. There is admittedly a risk of imperialism here. The World Bank's Structural Adjustment Programs come to mind, in which international institutions used the threat of withholding needed money to transform domestic institutions at the service of a neoliberal enterprise that benefitted primarily if not exclusively Global North countries.[19] We certainly do not want to suggest we go down that path again. However, it is well known that the World Bank's direction was, however well-intentioned, fundamentally misguided. It focused, functionally, on improving the state as a monolith, and assumed that thereby it would improve people's lives. Instead, our book cracks open the state as a monolith in its relationships to international law and institutions. Further,

---

18 Probably a byproduct of our Civil Law training, but something we ought to scrutinize elsewhere.

19 See, for instance, Marc Darrow, *Between Light and Shadow: The World Bank, The International Monetary Fund and International Human Rights Law* (Hart / Bloomsbury, 2003)

what we suggest here is to focus on the improvement of people's lives in the first instance, as the guide to what ought to improve the state. The IACtHR's focus on human beings and human rights (enshrined in its pro persona interpretive principle)[20] allows it to do that. More broadly, though, all of international law can, and much of it seems to be moving towards, a version of itself that puts people first.[21]

To make greater allowance for enforcement also improves the influence of international organizations. Our distinction between Velcro and stitches seeks to dispel the temptation to focus on influence as a feasible 'good news story' that in fact hides the deficiencies of international institutions in achieving more deeply entrenched influence (and, in the long term, harms this ability).

Finally, our book offers an account of the potentials of better understanding by international legal organs (particularly courts) of their pathways to influence domestic law, and how international law cannot be separated from domestic law. This assertion rings even more true if we consider that international law's claims to universality, which might have explained an international organ's resistance to engaging with domestic law, are not actually true, and international law draws from and reflects domestic legal traditions all the time.[22]

---

20 For an analysis, see Jorge Contesse, 'Conventionality Control and the Limits of Pro Persona Jurisprudence', 3(1) *The Italian Review of International and Comparative Law*, (2023) 121–132.

21 See, generally, Antonio Cassese, *The human dimension of international law: selected papers of Antonio Cassese* (Oxford University Press, 2008); and Edith Brown-Weiss, *Establishing norms in a kaleidoscopic world* (Brill, 2022).

22 For one of the more compelling analyses of this phenomenon, see Anthea Roberts, *Is International Law International?* (Oxford University Press, 2017).

CHAPTER 5

Conclusions

In this book, we focused on the enforcement of judgments of the international judicial body with the widest and most ambitiously deployed competence for reparations: the Inter-American Court of Human Rights. This Court has a reputation for ambitious standard-setting, and for determinedly seeking to transform people's lives.

Despite this reputation, the enforcement record of the IACtHR's judgments lags. Part of the reason is the ambition of the reparations measures, which require fundamental transformations of societies, legislation, and institutional cultures that are difficult to measure, let alone accomplish in a timely manner. Nevertheless, the Court perseveres.

Seeking a 'good news story,' many observers of the Court, as well as of other international human rights bodies, have increasingly opted for a narrative of influence over compliance. Despite the many merits of thinking about influence, we showed in this book that compliance is a fundamental piece of the puzzle, and that to ignore this dimension is to betray the aspiration of influence itself.

If we are serious about influence, we need to think of it as necessitating compliance as well. Otherwise, influence vanes. Further, influence may serve a feel-good story, and even accomplish something in the long run, but it leaves behind current and past victims of human rights violations. A body of law that is serious about transformation, and about centering human beings, cannot afford to dispose of human beings as just stepping stones towards an idealized (not to mention unattainable) idea of influence that, without changing victims' lives, is hollow.

In order to scrutinize the possibilities of enforcement of IACtHR judgments, and to unpack some of the challenges, we resorted to scholarship in foreign affairs law, and on the conflict of laws style of international law. Both bodies of scholarship helped us understand the importance of unpacking the state as an international legal monolith, and particularly of imagining the state as a series of politically charged bureaucratic institutions and pathways.

Politics does not go away from the conversation about enforcement, nor should it. Transformation without politics is, too, hollow. But we are able to temporarily suspend the politics that guides the creation of reparations measures in their implementation.

© AYLA DO VALE ALVES AND LUCAS LIXINSKI, 2025 | DOI:10.1163/9789004741829_006

Victims, their representatives, and the Court itself can afford to be more proactive in designing pathways for the implementation of international judgments. Doing so enables well-meaning states, while further shaming states that do not mean so well by exposing their reluctance for what it is, rather than giving them the benefit of hiding behind confusion and lack of clarity.

The practice of states in the Americas shows us a wide diversity of implementation pathways, with varying degrees of success. But key elements are the creation of dedicated institutions with a clear mandate to coordinate across multiple branches of government. Which branch of government leads the enforcement of judgments is almost immaterial, in this respect. However, because the IACtHR has often relied on natural affinities with other (domestic) judges and courts, then courts offer a possibility that the IACtHR ought to exploit. The Court can leverage these allyships to create better pathways for victims to access reparations, as well as for institutional reform.

In thinking through these issues, we hope to contribute not just to the work of the IACtHR, but also to other courts, within and beyond international human rights law. Further, other international institutions who seek to influence domestic law and practice could also benefit from our insights on the importance of direction on institutional design, and of attempting to demystify the state instead of expecting the state to demystify itself.

It would be useful for future research to take some of these insights and deploy them in other contexts. Other regional human rights courts, as well as the United Nations Human Rights Treaty Bodies, would be obvious next loci for research. But it would also be useful to extrapolate the lessons learned from and for foreign affairs law and the conflict of laws style to other international institutions.

Finally, because we relied on domestic law-in-the-books for our analysis to enable the breadth of our analysis, naturally more socio-legal studies of implementation and enforcement in individual jurisdictions, hopefully in comparative perspective and deploying the insights and overarching framework of this book, would be useful. To do so would go a long way in advancing our key message in this book: that human rights law, and its influence and enforcement, should first and foremost serve people on the ground, and transform their lives. We believe human rights law, institutions, and advocates are up to the task. We hope to be able to help them do so.

APPENDIX

Latin American State Practice and Primary Sources in Enforcing Inter-American Court Judgments

Latin American state practice and primary sources in enforcing Inter-American Court judgments

Country	Branch of government that does implementation	Basic constitutional provisions on international law and IHRL	Specific legislation/decrees/ regulations on IACtHR and domestic law	Judicial cases on implementation of IACtHR judgments	Differences between provisional measures and full judgment on the merits
			EXECUTIVE-LED		
Argentina	Executive – the Ministry of Foreign Affairs (and to some extent, the Ministry of Justice and Human Rights (with its Secretary of Human Rights)) is responsible for implementing the	Constitución de la Nación Argentina, Art. 75. 'Artículo 75. Corresponde al Congreso: […] 22. Aprobar o desechar tratados concluidos con las demás naciones y con las organizaciones	Ley de Ministerios, Ley 22.520, Texto Ordenado Por Decreto 438/92. 'Artículo 18. Compete al MINISTERIO DE RELACIONES EXTERIORES, COMERCIO INTERNACIONAL Y CULTO asistir al Presidente de la Nación, y al Jefe de Gabinete de Ministros en orden a sus competencias, en todo lo inherente a las relaciones exteriores de la Nación y su	Corte Suprema de Justicia de la Nación Argentina 386/1998 (34-M)/CS1, 14 febrero 2017 – Sentencia dictada en el caso 'Fontevecchia y D' Amico vs. Argentina' por la Corte Interamericana de Derechos Humanos. https://sjconsulta.csjn .gov.ar/sjconsulta/docu	No information found in legislation. The case law found suggests that both full judgments and provisional measures may be submitted to the judiciary for implementation. The case of *Fontevecchia and D'Amico* (full

Latin American state practice and primary sources in enforcing Inter-American Court judgments (*cont.*)

Country	Branch of government that does implementation	Basic constitutional provisions on international law and IHRL	Specific legislation/decrees/ regulations on IACtHR and domestic law	Judicial cases on implementation of IACtHR judgments	Differences between provisional measures and full judgment on the merits
	decisions of the IACtHR.[a] There has also been a case where the President issued a decree ordering implementation.[b]	internacionales y los concordatos con la Santa Sede. Los tratados y concordatos tienen jerarquía superior a las leyes. La Declaración Americana de los Derechos y Deberes del Hombre; la Declaración Universal de Derechos Humanos; la Convención Americana sobre Derechos Humanos; [...] en las	representación ante los gobiernos extranjeros, la SANTA SEDE y las entidades internacionales en todos los campos del accionar de la República, y en particular: [...] 8. Intervenir, en su área, en las decisiones sobre el uso de la fuerza armada, en las materias relacionadas con el estado de guerra y su declaración, en la solución de las controversias internacionales, los ajustes de paz, la aplicación de sanciones decididas por organismos internacionales competentes y otros actos contemplados por el derecho internacional. [...]	mentos/verUnicoDocumentoLink.html?idAnalisis=735716&cache=1630819081447 Corte Suprema de Justicia de la Nación Argentina 120/2017/CS1, 5 diciembre 2017 Sala, *Milagro Arnalia Ángela y otros* s/ p. s. a. asociación ilícita, fraude a la administración pública y extorsión – refers to the IACtHR's order for provisional measures on the '*Matter of Milagro Sala regarding Argentina.*'	judgment) is particularly controversial because the Supreme Court decided against implementing the IACtHR judgment.

a Ley 22.520, Art. 18(8).
b Argentina, Nacional Decree 99/2006, 25 January 2006.

Latin American state practice and primary sources in enforcing Inter-American Court judgments (*cont.*)

Country	Branch of government that does implementation	Basic constitutional provisions on international law and IHRL	Specific legislation/decrees/ regulations on IACtHR and domestic law	Judicial cases on implementation of IACtHR judgments	Differences between provisional measures and full judgment on the merits
		condiciones de su vigencia, tienen jerarquía constitucional, no derogan artículo alguno de la primera parte de esta Constitución y deben entenderse complementarios de los derechos y garantías por ella reconocidos. Sólo podrán ser denunciados, en su caso, por el Poder Ejecutivo Nacional, previa aprobación de las dos terceras partes de la totalidad de los miembros de cada	35. Participar en la formulación de políticas, elaboración de planes y programas, y en la representación del Estado Nacional ante los organismos internacionales en materia de Derechos Humanos y en aquellos relativos a la condición y situación de la mujer, e intervenir en la reforma de la legislación nacional en dichas materias.' https://www.argentina.gob.ar/normativa/nacional/ley-22520-48853/actualizacion Decreto 50/2019 – DCTO-2019-50-APN-PTE – Estructura organizativa, Anexo II. Secretaría de Derechos Humanos, Art. 4. 'MINISTERIO DE JUSTICIA Y DERECHOS HUMANOS SECRETARÍA DE DERECHOS	https://sjconsulta.csjn.gov.ar/sjconsulta/documentos/verDocumentoById.html?idDocumento=7422712&cache=1630820234046	

Latin American state practice and primary sources in enforcing Inter-American Court judgments (*cont.*)

Country	Branch of government that does implementation	Basic constitutional provisions on international law and IHRL	Specific legislation/decrees/regulations on IACtHR and domestic law	Judicial cases on implementation of IACtHR judgments	Differences between provisional measures and full judgment on the merits
		Cámara. Los demás tratados y convenciones sobre derechos humanos, luego de ser aprobados por el Congreso, requerirán el voto de las dos terceras partes de la totalidad de los miembros de cada Cámara para gozar de la jerarquía constitucional.' https://www.oas.org/dil/esp/constitucion_de_la_nacion_argentina.pdf	HUMANOS OBJETIVOS: [...] 4. Ejercer la representación del ESTADO NACIONAL ante los Organismos Internacionales de Derechos Humanos, sustentando a nivel mundial la política de la REPÚBLICA ARGENTINA en materia de derechos humanos mediante la participación en foros internacionales de la ORGANIZACIÓN DE LAS NACIONES UNIDAS (ONU), la ORGANIZACIÓN DE ESTADOS AMERICANOS (OEA) y el MERCOSUR.' Subsecretaría de Protección y Enlace Internacional en Derechos Humanos, Arts. 2, 6–7. '2. Asistir a la Secretaría en el ejercicio de la representación del ESTADO NACIONAL ante los		

Latin American state practice and primary sources in enforcing Inter-American Court judgments (*cont.*)

Country	Branch of government that does implementation	Basic constitutional provisions on international law and IHRL	Specific legislation/decrees/regulations on IACtHR and domestic law	Judicial cases on implementation of IACtHR judgments	Differences between provisional measures and full judgment on the merits
			organismos internacionales de derechos humanos, incluido el seguimiento de los programas de mediano y largo plazo de la ORGANIZACIÓN DE LAS NACIONES UNIDAS (ONU), la ORGANIZACIÓN DE LOS ESTADOS AMERICANOS (OEA) y el MERCOSUR y la participación en reuniones especializadas. [...] 5. Asistir a la Secretaría en la propuesta de medidas preventivas, administrativas y/o reparatorias o en la realización de denuncias penales ante hechos violatorios de derechos humanos que, por su gravedad institucional, revistan especial interés público. 6. Coordinar las acciones con el MINISTERIO DE RELACIONES EXTERIORES, COMERCIO INTERNACIONAL Y CULTO y con		

Latin American state practice and primary sources in enforcing Inter-American Court judgments (*cont.*)

Country	Branch of government that does implementation	Basic constitutional provisions on international law and IHRL	Specific legislation/decrees/regulations on IACtHR and domestic law	Judicial cases on implementation of IACtHR judgments	Differences between provisional measures and full judgment on the merits
			el MINISTERIO DE DEFENSA, en temas de su competencia. 7. Asesorar y patrocinar en los asuntos de carácter jurídico nacional, regional e internacional de competencia de la Secretaría.' https://www.boletinoficial.gob.ar/detalleAviso/primera/224026/20191220 Decreto Nacional 99/2006, 25 enero 2006, Cumplimiento de Sentencia de la Corte Interamericana de Derechos Humanos – refers to case of '*Cantos Vs. Argentina.*' 'Artículo 1º – Dése cumplimiento a la sentencia de la CORTE INTERAMERICANA DE DERECHOS HUMANOS recaída en el Caso CANTOS – CDH 11.636, mediante los siguientes cursos de acción: [...]' https://tinyurl.com/2s78rsb3		

Latin American state practice and primary sources in enforcing Inter-American Court judgments (*cont.*)

Country	Branch of government that does implementation	Basic constitutional provisions on international law and IHRL	Specific legislation/decrees/ regulations on IACtHR and domestic law	Judicial cases on implementation of IACtHR judgments	Differences between provisional measures and full judgment on the merits
Bolivia	Executive – the Presidential Decrees suggest that the President is responsible for implementation by passing a decree establishing the specific measures to be taken by different internal organs for the execution of IACtHR judgments.	Constitución Política del Estado Plurinacinal de Bolivia, Arts. 13–14, 218, 222(3), 256, 410. 'Artículo 13. [...] Los tratados y convenios internacionales ratificados por la Asamblea Legislativa Plurinacional, que reconocen los derechos humanos y que prohíben su limitación en los Estados de Excepción prevalecen en el orden interno. Los derechos y deberes consagrados en esta	Decreto Supremo No 0840, 06 de Abril de 2011, Arts. 1, 3, 5. 'Artículo 1. (OBJETO).- El presente Decreto Supremo tiene por objeto establecer el mecanismo financiero de pago de las medidas indemnizatorias a los beneficiarios señalados en la Sentencia de 1 de septiembre de 2010, Fondo, Reparaciones y Costas, emitida por la Corte Interamericana de Derechos Humanos en el caso "Ibsen Cárdenas e Ibsen Peña Vs. Bolivia".' 'Artículo 3. (AUTORIZACIÓN).-I. Se autoriza e instruye al Ministerio de Relaciones Exteriores, en coordinación con el Ministerio de Justicia, a efectuar los pagos establecidos en los numerales 1 al 9 del Parágrafo II del Artículo 2	Tribunal Constitucional de Bolivia, Sentencia Constitucional Nº 1190/ 01-R de 12 de noviembre de 2001. – Expediente: 2001-03164-07-RAC – refers to the case of *Trujillo Oroza v. Bolivia*, but mainly relies on domestic criminal prescription norms. https://funsolon.files.wordpress.com/2015/01/sc-1190-01-r.pdf Tribunal Constitucional de Bolivia, Sentencia Constitucional Nº 0110/ 2010-R de 10 de mayo de 2010 – Expediente: 2006-13381-27- RAC – also refers to the case of *Trujillo Oroza v Bolivia*,	No information found on implementation of provisional measures.

Latin American state practice and primary sources in enforcing Inter-American Court judgments (*cont.*)

Country	Branch of government that does implementation	Basic constitutional provisions on international law and IHRL	Specific legislation/decrees/ regulations on IACtHR and domestic law	Judicial cases on implementation of IACtHR judgments	Differences between provisional measures and full judgment on the merits
		Constitución se interpretarán de conformidad con los Tratados internacionales de derechos humanos ratificados por Bolivia.' 'Artículo 14. [...] III. El Estado garantiza a todas las personas y colectividades, sin discriminación alguna, el libre y eficaz ejercicio de los derechos establecidos en esta Constitución, las leyes y los tratados internacionales de derechos humanos.'	del presente Decreto Supremo, considerando los términos y condiciones establecidos en la Sentencia del 1 de septiembre de 2010, pronunciada en la Corte Interamericana de Derechos Humanos.' 'Artículo 5. (CELERIDAD DE TRÁMITES).-Se instruye al Ministerio de Justicia coordinar con las instancias competentes, la atención a los trámites necesarios para el cumplimiento de la sentencia de la Corte Interamericana de Derechos Humanos. Los Señores Ministros de Estado en los Despachos de relaciones Exteriores, de Economía y Finanzas Públicas y de Justicia, quedan encargados de la ejecución y cumplimiento del presente Decreto Supremo.'	but addresses specifically the effects of the IACtHR's decisions in Bolivia (from p. 8). https://funsolon.files.wordpress.com/2015/01/sentencia0110-2010-r.pdf	

Latin American state practice and primary sources in enforcing Inter-American Court judgments (*cont.*)

Country	Branch of government that does implementation	Basic constitutional provisions on international law and IHRL	Specific legislation/decrees/ regulations on IACtHR and domestic law	Judicial cases on implementation of IACtHR judgments	Differences between provisional measures and full judgment on the merits
		'Sección I: Defensoría del Pueblo Artículo 218. I. La Defensoría del Pueblo velará por la vigencia, promoción, difusión y cumplimiento de los derechos humanos, individuales y colectivos, que se establecen en la Constitución, las leyes y los instrumentos internacionales. [...]' 'Artículo 222. Son atribuciones de la Defensoría del Pueblo, además de	https://www.derechoteca.com/gacetabolivia/decreto-supremo-0840-del-06-abril-2011/ Decreto Supremo Nº 27001, 17 de abril de 2003, Arts. 1–2, 4. 'Artículo 1º.- (Objeto) El presente Decreto Supremo tiene por objeto establecer los mecanismos para el cumplimiento de la Sentencia de Reparaciones dictada por la Corte Interamericana de Derechos Humanos, en fecha 27 de febrero de 2002.' 'Artículo 2º.- (Pago de daños) En cumplimiento a la Sentencia de Reparaciones de 27 de febrero de 2002, dictada por la Corte Interamericana de Derechos Humanos en el caso Trujillo Oroza vs. Estado Boliviano, se instruye el pago por concepto de daños		

Latin American state practice and primary sources in enforcing Inter-American Court judgments (*cont.*)

Country	Branch of government that does implementation	Basic constitutional provisions on international law and IHRL	Specific legislation/decrees/ regulations on IACtHR and domestic law	Judicial cases on implementation of IACtHR judgments	Differences between provisional measures and full judgment on the merits
		las que establecen la Constitución y la ley: […] 3. Investigar, de oficio o a solicitud de parte, los actos u omisiones que impliquen violación de los derechos, individuales y colectivos, que se establecen en la Constitución, las leyes y los instrumentos internacionales, e instar al Ministerio Público al inicio de las acciones legales que correspondan.' 'Artículo 256. I. Los tratados e	ocasionados a las siguientes personas: […]' 'Artículo 4°.- (Previsiones presupuestarias) Para llevar adelante lo establecido en el Artículo precedente, el Poder Ejecutivo, a través del Ministro de Hacienda, deberá efectuar las previsiones presupuestarias correspondientes. El Ministerio de la Presidencia deberá realizar las respectivas cancelaciones. Los Señores Ministros de Estado en los Despachos de la Presidencia y Hacienda, quedan encargados de la ejecución y cumplimiento del presente Decreto Supremo.' https://www.lexivox.org/norms/BO-DS-27001.html Ley N° 971, 16 de Agosto de 2017. Evo Morales		

Latin American state practice and primary sources in enforcing Inter-American Court judgments (*cont.*)

Country	Branch of government that does implementation	Basic constitutional provisions on international law and IHRL	Specific legislation/decrees/ regulations on IACtHR and domestic law	Judicial cases on implementation of IACtHR judgments	Differences between provisional measures and full judgment on the merits
		instrumentos internacionales en materia de derechos humanos que hayan sido firmados, ratificados o a los que se hubiera adherido el Estado, que declaren derechos más favorables a los contenidos en la Constitución, se aplicarán de manera preferente sobre ésta. II. Los derechos reconocidos en la Constitución serán interpretados de acuerdo a los tratados	'DECRETA: Artículo Único. I. Se autoriza al Ministerio de Economía y Finanzas Públicas, a través del Tesoro General de la Nación – TGN, realizar el traspaso presupuestario interinstitucional de forma anual al Ministerio de Salud, para cubrir el costo de la prestación de servicios de salud de la Señora Irma Lily Vélez de Villa Rojas y sus familiares, según lo determinado en la Sentencia de 30 de noviembre de 2016 sobre Excepciones Preliminares, Fondo, Reparaciones y Costas, emitida por la Corte Interamericana de Derechos Humanos, en el Caso I.V. Vs. Bolivia. II. Si la evaluación psicológica y/o psiquiátrica a los familiares de la Señora Irma Lily Vélez de Villa Rojas, concluyese que deben recibir terapia, la		

Latin American state practice and primary sources in enforcing Inter-American Court judgments (*cont.*)

Country	Branch of government that does implementation	Basic constitutional provisions on international law and IHRL	Specific legislation/decrees/ regulations on IACtHR and domestic law	Judicial cases on implementation of IACtHR judgments	Differences between provisional measures and full judgment on the merits
		internacionales de derechos humanos cuando éstos prevean normas más favorables.' 'Artículo 410. […] II. La Constitución es la norma suprema del ordenamiento jurídico boliviano y goza de primacía frente a cualquier otra disposición normativa. El bloque de constitucionalidad está integrado por los Tratados y Convenios internacionales en materia de Derechos Humanos y las	prestación de servicios de salud establecida en el Parágrafo anterior, deberá ampliarse a éstos, tal como establece el Párrafo 332 de la citada Sentencia. III. El Ministerio de Salud, tiene la responsabilidad de gestionar las evaluaciones psicológicas y/o psiquiátricas que se requieran, así como regular, coordinar, supervisar y controlar la aplicación de la presente Ley.' http://www.gacetaoficialdebolivia.gob.bo/normas/busquedag1?data%5BGobierno%5D%5Bid_gobierno%5D=&data%5BTipoNorma%5D%5Bid_tipo_norma%5D=&q=corte+interamericana&s=0 Ley Nº 091, 2 de Marzo de 2011. Refers to cases *Ticona Estrada y Otros v Bolivia* and *Ibsen Cárdenas*		

Latin American state practice and primary sources in enforcing Inter-American Court judgments (*cont.*)

Country	Branch of government that does implementation	Basic constitutional provisions on international law and IHRL	Specific legislation/decrees/ regulations on IACtHR and domestic law	Judicial cases on implementation of IACtHR judgments	Differences between provisional measures and full judgment on the merits
		normas de Derecho Comunitario, ratificados por el país. La aplicación de las normas jurídicas se regirá por la siguiente jerarquía, de acuerdo a las competencias de las entidades territoriales: 1. Constitución Política del Estado. 2. Los tratados internacionales.' https://www.mindef.gob.bo/mindef/sites/default/files/Consitucion_2009_Orig.pdf	*e Ibsen Peña v Bolivia.* – 'DECRETA: Artículo Único. 1. Se autoriza al Ministerio de Economía y Finanzas Públicas, a través del Tesoro General de la Nación, realizar el traspaso presupuestario interinstitucional de forma anual al Ministerio de Salud y Deportes para cubrir el costo de las prestaciones de servicios de salud de las personas determinadas en las sentencias sobre fondo, reparaciones y costas de la Corte Interamericana de Derechos Humanos del 27 de noviembre de 2008 y del 1 de septiembre de 2010, en el caso Ticona Estrada y Otros Vs. Bolivia; y el caso Ibsen Cárdenas e Ibsen Peña Vs. Bolivia.' *Other Presidential Decrees		

Latin American state practice and primary sources in enforcing Inter-American Court judgments (*cont.*)

Country	Branch of government that does implementation	Basic constitutional provisions on international law and IHRL	Specific legislation/decrees/ regulations on IACtHR and domestic law	Judicial cases on implementation of IACtHR judgments	Differences between provisional measures and full judgment on the merits
			implementing IACtHR's decisions: Decreto Supremo N° 3260, 26 de Julio de 2017 – refers to the case of *I.V. v Bolivia.* 'ARTÍCULO 1.- (OBJETO). El presente Decreto Supremo tiene por objeto establecer el mecanismo de pago de la medida indemnizatoria, costas y gastos, y reintegro, previstos en la Sentencia de 30 de noviembre de 2016, Excepciones Preliminares, Fondo, Reparaciones y Costas, emitida por la Corte Interamericana de Derechos Humanos en el caso "I.V. vs. Bolivia".' Decreto Supremo N° 3264, 26 de Julio de 2017 – refers to the case of *Andrade Salmón v Bolivia.* 'ARTÍCULO 1.- (OBJETO). El presente Decreto Supremo tiene		

Latin American state practice and primary sources in enforcing Inter-American Court judgments (*cont.*)

Country	Branch of government that does implementation	Basic constitutional provisions on international law and IHRL	Specific legislation/decrees/ regulations on IACtHR and domestic law	Judicial cases on implementation of IACtHR judgments	Differences between provisional measures and full judgment on the merits
			por objeto establecer el mecanismo de pago de la medida indemnizatoria y el pago de costas y gastos previstos en la Sentencia de 1 de diciembre de 2016, Fondo, Reparaciones y Costas, emitida por la Corte Interamericana de Derechos Humanos en el caso "Andrade Salmón vs. Bolivia".' Decreto Supremo N° 1935, 19 Marzo 2014 – refers to the case of *Familia Pacheco Tineo v Estado Plurinacional De Bolivia.* 'ARTÍCULO 1.- (OBJETO). El presente Decreto Supremo tiene por objeto establecer el mecanismo de pago determinado en la Sentencia de 25 de noviembre de 2013, Excepciones Preliminares, Fondo, Reparaciones y Costas, emitida por la Corte Interamericana de Derechos		

Latin American state practice and primary sources in enforcing Inter-American Court judgments (*cont.*)

Country	Branch of government that does implementation	Basic constitutional provisions on international law and IHRL	Specific legislation/decrees/ regulations on IACtHR and domestic law	Judicial cases on implementation of IACtHR judgments	Differences between provisional measures and full judgment on the merits
			Humanos en el "CASO FAMILIA PACHECO TINEO VS. ESTADO PLURINACIONAL DE BOLIVIA".' Decreto Supremo N° 0262 – refers to the case of *Ticona Estrada y otros v Bolivia*. 'ARTÍCULO 1.- (OBJETO). El presente Decreto Supremo tiene por objeto establecer el mecanismo financiero de pago de las medidas indemnizatorias a los beneficiarios señalados en la Sentencia de 27 de noviembre de 2008, Fondo, Reparaciones y Costas, emitida por la Corte Interamericana de Derechos Humanos en el caso "Ticona Estrada y otros vs Bolivia".' All found here: http://www.gacetaoficialdebolivia.gob.bo/normas/busquedag1?data%5BGobierno%5D%5Bid_gobierno%5D=&data%		

Latin American state practice and primary sources in enforcing Inter-American Court judgments (*cont.*)

Country	Branch of government that does implementation	Basic constitutional provisions on international law and IHRL	Specific legislation/decrees/ regulations on IACtHR and domestic law	Judicial cases on implementation of IACtHR judgments	Differences between provisional measures and full judgment on the merits
			5BTipoNorma%5D%5Bid_tipo _norma%5D=&q=corte+interamer icana&s=0		
Chile	Executive-led – The Subsecretary of Human Rights, as part of the Ministry of Justice and Human Rights, and in collaboration with the Ministry of Foreign Affairs, to implement decisions by the IASPHR.[c]	Constitución Política de la Republica de Chile, 2005, Art. 5. 'Artículo 5° [...] El ejercicio de la soberanía reconoce como limitación el respeto a los derechos esenciales que emanan de la naturaleza humana. Es deber de los	Decreto con Fuerza de Ley N° 3, 2 de diciembre de 2016, Arts. 2(d), (p), 8(f), 15(e). FIJA EL TEXTO REFUNDIDO, COORDINADO Y SISTEMATIZADO DE LA LEY ORGÁNICA DEL MINISTERIO DE JUSTICIA Y DERECHOS HUMANOS MINISTERIO DE JUSTICIA Y DERECHOS HUMANOS. 'Artículo 2°.- Al Ministerio de Justicia y Derechos Humanos corresponden las siguientes	No relevant case law found either in the civil or the constitutional courts when searching for results with each of the cases in which Chile has been sentenced by the IACtHR. Rol Interno: C-7564-2019 / 30° Juzgado Civil de Santiago. —Briefly mentions the IACtHR and the states parties'	Decree with Force of Law N° 3 mentions both without making a distinction.

c Decreto con Fuerza de Ley N° 3, 2 de Deciembre de 2016, Fija el Texto Refundido, Coordinado y Sistematizado de la Ley Orgánica del Ministerio de Justicia y Derechos Humanos; Ley Organica del Ministerio de Justicia y Derechos Humanos, DL 3346, as amended by Act 20.885/2016.

Latin American state practice and primary sources in enforcing Inter-American Court judgments (*cont.*)

Country	Branch of government that does implementation	Basic constitutional provisions on international law and IHRL	Specific legislation/decrees/ regulations on IACtHR and domestic law	Judicial cases on implementation of IACtHR judgments	Differences between provisional measures and full judgment on the merits
		órganos del Estado respetar y promover tales derechos, garantizados por esta Constitución, así como por los tratados internacionales ratificados por Chile y que se encuentren vigentes.' – https://www.oas.org/dil/esp/constitucion_chile.pdf	funciones: [...] d) Colaborar con el Ministerio de Relaciones Exteriores, dentro del ámbito de su competencia, en la elaboración y seguimiento de los informes periódicos ante los órganos y mecanismos de derechos humanos, en la ejecución de medidas cautelares y provisionales, soluciones amistosas y sentencias internacionales en que Chile sea parte, y en la implementación, según corresponda, de las resoluciones y recomendaciones originadas en el Sistema Interamericano y en el Sistema Universal de Derechos Humanos, sin perjuicio de las atribuciones de otros órganos del Estado; [...] p) Dictar las resoluciones necesarias para el cumplimiento	general duty to implement the remedies established by the Court.	

Latin American state practice and primary sources in enforcing Inter-American Court judgments (*cont.*)

Country	Branch of government that does implementation	Basic constitutional provisions on international law and IHRL	Specific legislation/decrees/ regulations on IACtHR and domestic law	Judicial cases on implementation of IACtHR judgments	Differences between provisional measures and full judgment on the merits
			de las sentencias ejecutoriadas que condenen al Fisco;' 'Artículo 8°.- Son funciones de la Subsecretaría de Derechos Humanos prestar asesoría y colaboración directa al Ministro de Justicia y Derechos Humanos en el diseño y elaboración de las políticas, planes y programas relativos a la promoción y protección de los derechos humanos. [...] Corresponde a la Subsecretaría de Derechos Humanos: [...] f) Colaborar con el Ministerio de Relaciones Exteriores según lo dispuesto en la letra d) del artículo 2°, en la elaboración y seguimiento de los informes periódicos ante los órganos y mecanismos de derechos humanos, en la ejecución de		

Latin American state practice and primary sources in enforcing Inter-American Court judgments (*cont.*)

Country	Branch of government that does implementation	Basic constitutional provisions on international law and IHRL	Specific legislation/decrees/ regulations on IACtHR and domestic law	Judicial cases on implementation of IACtHR judgments	Differences between provisional measures and full judgment on the merits
			medidas cautelares y provisionales, soluciones amistosas y sentencias internacionales en que Chile sea parte, y en la implementación, según corresponda, de las resoluciones y recomendaciones originadas en el Sistema Interamericano y en el Sistema Universal de Derechos Humanos, sin perjuicio de las atribuciones de otros órganos del Estado.' 'Artículo 15.- El Plan Nacional de Derechos Humanos tendrá una duración de cuatro años y contendrá el diseño e implementación de las políticas encaminadas al respeto, promoción y protección de los derechos humanos [...] El Plan Nacional se materializará en la elaboración de políticas que		

Latin American state practice and primary sources in enforcing Inter-American Court judgments (*cont.*)

Country	Branch of government that does implementation	Basic constitutional provisions on international law and IHRL	Specific legislation/decrees/ regulations on IACtHR and domestic law	Judicial cases on implementation of IACtHR judgments	Differences between provisional measures and full judgment on the merits
			abordarán al menos especialmente las siguientes materias: [...] e) La promoción del cumplimiento de las medidas cautelares y provisionales, soluciones amistosas y sentencias internacionales en que Chile sea parte, dictadas en virtud del Sistema Interamericano y del Sistema Universal de Derechos Humanos, de conformidad con la letra f) del artículo 8°.' – https://www.bcn.cl/leychile/navegar?idNorma=1099611 Ley Organica del Ministerio de Justicia y Derechos Humanos, Decreto Ley 3346, 1980. Fija el Texto de la Leu Orgánica del Ministerio de Justicia y Derechos Humanos. —https://www.bcn.cl/leychile/navegar?		

Latin American state practice and primary sources in enforcing Inter-American Court judgments (*cont.*)

Country	Branch of government that does implementation	Basic constitutional provisions on international law and IHRL	Specific legislation/decrees/ regulations on IACtHR and domestic law	Judicial cases on implementation of IACtHR judgments	Differences between provisional measures and full judgment on the merits
			idNorma=7098 Ley 20.885/2016 – Crea la Subsecretaría de Derechos Humanos y Adecúa la Ley Orgánica del Ministerio de Justicia. —https://www.bcn.cl/ley chile/navegar?idNorma=1086063		
Colombia	Executive – A committee composed by the Ministries of the Interior, Foreign Affairs, Justice and Law, and Ministry of National Defence must adopt a 'decision'[d]	Constitución Política de Colombia, Arts. 93, 164. 'Artículo 93. Los tratados y convenios internacionales ratificados por el Congreso, que reconocen los	LEY N° 288, 5 Junio 1996, Arts. 2–3, 8. 'Por medio de la cual se establecen instrumentos para la indemnización de perjuicio a las víctimas de violaciones de derechos humanos en virtud de lo dispuesto por determinados órganos internacionales de Derechos Humanos: [...]	Sentencia de Tutela 558 de 2003 – On the incorporation of Commission's and Court's Precautionary measures into domestic law. https://www.corte constitucional.gov.co/ relatoria/2003/T-558-03 .htm#_ftn20	Sentencia de Tutela 558 de 2003 distinguishes between precautionary measures and provisional measures. For the procedures for incorporation of Precautionary measures:

d 'Concepto' in the original.

Latin American state practice and primary sources in enforcing Inter-American Court judgments (*cont.*)

Country	Branch of government that does implementation	Basic constitutional provisions on international law and IHRL	Specific legislation/decrees/ regulations on IACtHR and domestic law	Judicial cases on implementation of IACtHR judgments	Differences between provisional measures and full judgment on the merits
	favourable to the compliance with the international decision.[e] With a favourable decision from the Committee, the 'National Government' will require a conciliation hearing with the Public Prosecutor's Office (who will then summon the interested parties to present evidence) before the	derechos humanos y que prohíben su limitación en los estados de excepción, prevalecen en el orden interno. Los derechos y deberes consagrados en esta Carta, se interpretarán de conformidad con los tratados internacionales sobre derechos humanos ratificados por Colombia. […]	ARTÍCULO 20. Para los efectos de la presente Ley solamente se podrán celebrar conciliaciones o incidentes de liquidación de perjuicios respecto de aquellos casos de violaciones de derechos humanos en relación con los cuales se cumplan los siguientes requisitos: 1. Que exista una decisión previa, escrita y expresa del Comité de Derechos Humanos del Pacto Internacional de Derechos Civiles y Políticos o de la Comisión Interamericana de Derechos Humanos, en la que se concluya respecto de un caso concreto que el Estado colombiano ha incurrido en una	Expediente T-2499665, Sentencia T-367/10, 11 de Mayo 2010 – refers to the *Case of Ituango Massacres v. Colombia*. 'Como se puede apreciar a partir del examen del cumplimiento de los estándares y obligaciones internacionales de derechos humanos se determina la responsabilidad internacional del Estado por violación de los derechos humanos	'Agrega que las medidas cautelares decretadas por la CIDH difieren de las medidas provisionales que decreta la Corte Interamericana de Derechos Humanos, a solicitud de la Comisión, las cuales no han sido adoptadas en el presente asunto. […] En síntesis, el Ministerio de Relaciones Exteriores alega que con fundamento en el

e Ley N° 288, 5 Junio 1996, Art. 2–3.

Latin American state practice and primary sources in enforcing Inter-American Court judgments (*cont.*)

Country	Branch of government that does implementation	Basic constitutional provisions on international law and IHRL	Specific legislation/decrees/ regulations on IACtHR and domestic law	Judicial cases on implementation of IACtHR judgments	Differences between provisional measures and full judgment on the merits
	Contentious Administrative Tribunal to settle the dispute that is the object of the conciliation within 30 days.[f]	Artículo 164. El Congreso dará prioridad al trámite de los proyectos de ley aprobatorios de los tratados sobre derechos humanos que sean sometidos a su consideración por el Gobierno.’	violación de derechos humanos y se establezca que deben indemnizarse los correspondientes perjuicios. 2. Que exista concepto previo favorable al cumplimiento de la decisión del órgano internacional de derechos humanos proferido por un Comité constituido por: a) El Ministro del Interior; b) El Ministro de Relaciones Exteriores; c) El Ministro de Justicia y del Derecho; d) El Ministro de Defensa Nacional. […] PARÁGRAFO 20. Cuando el Comité considere que se no (sic) reúnen los presupuestos a que hace	de las personas sujetas a su jurisdicción, y una vez establecida se busca la reparación integral de las víctimas que, además de la indemnización, supone la restitución, la reparación, la rehabilitación y la garantía de no repetición. En nuestro sistema jurídico una reparación similar sólo se lograría con la conjunción de la acción de reparación directa por daño	artículo 59 de la Ley 489 de 1998, sus funciones se limitan a transmitir a las autoridades nacionales competentes las decisiones adoptadas por la CIDH y a informar a esta última los avances que se han presentado en cuanto a la ejecución de las mismas en el orden interno.’ https://www.cortecon stitucional.gov .co/relatoria/2003/T

f Ley N° 288, 5 Junio 1996, Art. 3.

Latin American state practice and primary sources in enforcing Inter-American Court judgments (*cont.*)

Country	Branch of government that does implementation	Basic constitutional provisions on international law and IHRL	Specific legislation/decrees/ regulations on IACtHR and domestic law	Judicial cases on implementation of IACtHR judgments	Differences between provisional measures and full judgment on the merits
			referencia el parágrafo anterior, deberá comunicarlo así al Gobierno Nacional para que presente la demanda o interponga los recursos del caso contra la aludida decisión ante órgano internacional competente, si lo hubiere. En todo caso, si no existiere segunda instancia prevista en el tratado internacional aplicable o se hubiere agotado el término para impugnar la decisión, el Comité deberá rendir concepto favorable al cumplimiento de la decisión del órgano internacional. […] ARTÍCULO 30. Si el Comité emite concepto favorable al cumplimiento de la decisión del órgano internacional, el Gobierno Nacional solicitará la audiencia de conciliación ante el agente del	antijurídico que se ejerce ante la jurisdicción contenciosa administrativa (centrada en la indemnización monetaria o reparación material) y la acción penal (investiga y sanciona a los responsables, cumpliendo con la garantía de no repetición).' https://www.corteconstitucional.gov.co/Relatoria/2010/T-367-10.htm https://www.corteidh.or.cr/corteidh/docs/casos/articulos/seriec_148_ing.pdf	-558-03.htm#_ftn20 For full judgments on the merits: as it appears, after a favourable decision by the Committee with the Ministries, the Judgment is sent to the Contentious Administrative Tribunal to settle the dispute, although a criminal dispute may also arise where the IACtHR's judgment includes accountability for those responsible and guarantees of non-repetition. For provisional measures: it seems

Latin American state practice and primary sources in enforcing Inter-American Court judgments (*cont.*)

Country	Branch of government that does implementation	Basic constitutional provisions on international law and IHRL	Specific legislation/decrees/ regulations on IACtHR and domestic law	Judicial cases on implementation of IACtHR judgments	Differences between provisional measures and full judgment on the merits
			Ministerio Público adscrito al Tribunal Contencioso Administrativo que sería competente, de acuerdo con el derecho interno, para dirimir la controversia objeto de la conciliación, en un término que no exceda los treinta (30) días. [...] ARTÍCULO 80. El auto aprobatorio de la conciliación tendrá los alcances de un crédito judicialmente reconocido y efectos de cosa juzgada y, por ende, pondrá fin a todo proceso que se haya iniciado contra el Estado por los beneficiarios de la indemnización en relación con los hechos materia de la conciliación.' DECRETO 321, 25 Febrero 2000, Diario Oficial No. 43.918 de 2 de marzo de 2000, Art. 20. 'Por el cual se crea la Comité	Provisional Measures: Sentencia T-327/04. 'Envíese al señor Ministro de Defensa Nacional copia de esta providencia, así como la copia de la Resolución de la Corte Interamericana de Derechos Humanos, del 18 de junio de 2002, sobre "Medidas Provisionales solicitadas por la Comisión Interamericana de Derechos Humanos respecto de Colombia – Caso de la Comunidad de Paz de San José de Apartadó", para los fines relacionados con el cumplimiento de esta	that the Ministries (at least the Ministry of National Defense, Ministry of Foreign Affairs, and Ministry of the Interior and Justice) are the central actors in receiving the resolution with the provisional measures and then reaching out to the state organs capable of implementing the measures (such as the 'public force', or the army more specifically); there is no specific mention of a role played by the Contentious Administrative

Latin American state practice and primary sources in enforcing Inter-American Court judgments (*cont.*)

Country	Branch of government that does implementation	Basic constitutional provisions on international law and IHRL	Specific legislation/decrees/ regulations on IACtHR and domestic law	Judicial cases on implementation of IACtHR judgments	Differences between provisional measures and full judgment on the merits
			Intersectorial Permanente para la Coordinación y Seguimiento de la Política Nacional en Materia de Derechos Humanos y Derecho Internacional Humanitario. [...] ARTÍCULO 20. La Comisión tendrá las siguientes funciones: [...] 7. Promover la adecuación de la legislación nacional a los instrumentos internacionales de derechos humanos de los cuales Colombia sea Parte y coadyuvar al cumplimiento de los compromisos internacionales en estas materias. 8. Analizar las recomendaciones que formulen los organismos internacionales en materia de Derechos Humanos y Derecho Internacional Humanitario y evaluar la posibilidad de su implementación en el orden interno.'	tutela.' – https://www.corteconstitucional.gov.co/relatoria/2004/T-327-04.htm On the same case: Sentencia T-1025/07. 'En los informes presentados por el Ministerio de Relaciones Exteriores se mencionan algunas obras realizadas por las entidades estatales, en el marco del cumplimiento de las medidas provisionales solicitadas por la Corte Interamericana de Derechos Humanos en relación con la Comunidad de Paz de San José de Apartadó.	Tribunal in the implementation of provisional measures.

Latin American state practice and primary sources in enforcing Inter-American Court judgments (*cont.*)

Country	Branch of government that does implementation	Basic constitutional provisions on international law and IHRL	Specific legislation/decrees/ regulations on IACtHR and domestic law	Judicial cases on implementation of IACtHR judgments	Differences between provisional measures and full judgment on the merits
			http://wp.presidencia.gov.co/sitios/normativa/leyes/Documents/Juridica/Decreto%20321%20de%202000.pdf	[...] De la misma manera, se anexan a la respuesta: – un documento en el que se relacionan tanto una serie de jornadas humanitarias adelantadas por la Fuerza Pública para brindar servicios de salud, cultura y recreación a los habitantes del corregimiento, como un conjunto de directrices y órdenes de carácter permanente dictadas en la Brigada XVII con el fin de implementar las medidas provisionales de la Corte Interamericana de	

Latin American state practice and primary sources in enforcing Inter-American Court judgments (*cont.*)

Country	**Branch of government that does implementation**	**Basic constitutional provisions on international law and IHRL**	**Specific legislation/decrees/ regulations on IACtHR and domestic law**	**Judicial cases on implementation of IACtHR judgments**	**Differences between provisional measures and full judgment on the merits**
				Derechos Humanos y las órdenes impartidas en la sentencia T-327 de 2004. [...] Anotó que existe una instancia interinstitucional que coordina la acción estatal para dar cumplimiento a la sentencia y las medidas provisionales y que 'en dicho escenario se tiene definido que la protección de la mencionada comunidad se encuentra a cargo del Ministerio del Interior y Justicia, sin desmedro de la eventual intervención del	

Latin American state practice and primary sources in enforcing Inter-American Court judgments (*cont.*)

Country	Branch of government that does implementation	Basic constitutional provisions on international law and IHRL	Specific legislation/decrees/ regulations on IACtHR and domestic law	Judicial cases on implementation of IACtHR judgments	Differences between provisional measures and full judgment on the merits
				programa de protección y asistencia de la Fiscalía para situaciones relacionadas con las investigaciones penales a su cargo. https://www.corteconstitucional.gov.co/Relatoria/2007/T-1025-07.htm	
Costa Rica	Executive – it is the 'Interinstitutional Commission for the Monitoring and Implementation of International Human Rights Obligations', as part of the Ministry of Foreign Affairs and Worship that is responsible for	Constitución Política de la República de Costa Rica, 1949, Arts. 7, 18. 'artículo 7.- Los tratados públicos, los convenios internacionales y los concordatos, debidamente aprobados por la Asamblea	Decreto Presidencial 36776-RE, 9 de agosto de 2011, Arts. 4, 6, 8. '4°-Que de conformidad con el artículo 7 de la Constitución Política los tratados públicos, los convenios internacionales y los concordatos, debidamente aprobados por la Asamblea Legislativa, tienen autoridad superior a las leyes y que, de acuerdo con jurisprudencia reiterada de la Sala Constitucional,	Sala Constitucional de la Suprema Corte de Justicia – Resolución Nº 14953 – 2011 – Expediente: 11-008049-0007-CO – refers to the case of *Herrera Ulloa v Costa Rica*, and whether the state failed to implement (omitted itself from	The Presidential Decree N° 36776 does not make a distinction. The domestic judgement found on the implementation of IACtHR's provisional measures in *Manfred Amhrein and others v Costa Rica* does not

Latin American state practice and primary sources in enforcing Inter-American Court judgments (*cont.*)

Country	Branch of government that does implementation	Basic constitutional provisions on international law and IHRL	Specific legislation/decrees/ regulations on IACtHR and domestic law	Judicial cases on implementation of IACtHR judgments	Differences between provisional measures and full judgment on the merits
	coordinating the implementation of the country's international human rights obligations at the domestic level.[g]	Legislativa, tendrán desde su promulgación o desde el día que ellos designen, autoridad superior a las leyes.' 'ARTÍCULO 48.- Toda persona tiene derecho al recurso de hábeas corpus para garantizar su libertad e integridad personales, y al recurso de amparo para mantener o restablecer el goce de los otros derechos consagrados en esta	en aquellos casos donde dichos tratados amplíen la protección de los Derechos Humanos, estos se consideran incluso por encima de la Constitución Política de la República.' '6º-Que resulta pertinente desarrollar mecanismos de coordinación nacional con el fin de preparar informes, elaborar posiciones de Estado, implementar sentencias y recomendaciones de órganos del Sistema Interamericano de Derechos Humanos y del Sistema de Naciones Unidas de Derechos Humanos y concertar acciones a nivel nacional en materia de	implementing) the IACtHR's decision on that case. https://nexuspj.poder-judicial.go.cr/document/sen-1-0007-525680 Tribunal Contencioso Administrativo, II Circuito, EXPEDIENTE Nº 13-003114-1027-CA, Nº19-2020-V – refers to the case of *Artavia Murillo and others v Costa Rica*, and the reach of the IACtHR's decision domestically. https://nexuspj.poder-judicial.go.cr/docu	point to any difference.

g Presidential Decree 36776-RE, 2011, Art. 2 Annex.

Latin American state practice and primary sources in enforcing Inter-American Court judgments (*cont.*)

Country	Branch of government that does implementation	Basic constitutional provisions on international law and IHRL	Specific legislation/decrees/ regulations on IACtHR and domestic law	Judicial cases on implementation of IACtHR judgments	Differences between provisional measures and full judgment on the merits
		Constitución, así como de los de carácter fundamental establecidos en los instrumentos internacionales sobre derechos humanos, aplicables en la República. Ambos recursos serán de competencia de la Sala indicada en el artículo 10.' http://www.asamblea.go.cr/sd/Publicaciones%20a%20Texto%20Completo%20%20Revistas/Constituci%C3%B3n%20Pol%C3%	derechos humanos, que respondan a las obligaciones internacionales en la materia.' 8º-Que estas tareas de cumplimiento de instrumentos internacionales sobre derechos humanos requiere de procesos responsables y consensuados, con la participación de funcionarios gubernamentales y estatales, de organizaciones de la sociedad civil, de expertos y de la academia. Por tanto, DECRETAN: 'Creación de la Comisión Interinstitucional para el seguimiento e implementación de las obligaciones internacionales de Derechos Humanos, el Comité Asesor y el Ente Permanente de Consulta.' 'Artículo 1º-Es misión y función del Estado implementar las	ment/sen-1-0034-966374 Sala Tercera de la Corte, Resolución Nº 00723, 2014, Expediente: 13-000572-0006-PE – also refers to the case of *Artavia Murillo and others v Costa Rica*, and its binding effect domestically. https://nexuspj.poder-judicial.go.cr/document/sen-1-0034-616628 Sala Constitucional, Resolución Nº 12166 – 2016 – Expediente: 16-010715-0007-CO – refers to the case of *Manfred Amhrein and others v Costa Rica*, especially the provisional	

Latin American state practice and primary sources in enforcing Inter-American Court judgments (*cont.*)

Country	Branch of government that does implementation	Basic constitutional provisions on international law and IHRL	Specific legislation/decrees/ regulations on IACtHR and domestic law	Judicial cases on implementation of IACtHR judgments	Differences between provisional measures and full judgment on the merits
		ADtica%20de%20la%20Rep%C3%BAblica%20de%20Costa%20Rica,Reglamento%20de%20la%20Asamblea%20Legislaiva.pdf	obligaciones internacionales en derechos humanos que emanan del Sistema Universal y del Sistema Regional de Derechos Humanos. Artículo 2º-Se crea, como órgano asesor permanente del Poder Ejecutivo, adscrito al Ministerio de Relaciones Exteriores y Culto, la Comisión Interinstitucional para el seguimiento e implementación de las obligaciones internacionales de Derechos Humanos (en adelante Comisión Interinstitucional sobre Derechos Humanos o Comisión Interinstitucional) con el objeto de coordinar la implementación en el ámbito nacional de las obligaciones internacionales en derechos humanos, así como coordinar las acciones que se	measures in the case. https://nexuspj.poder-judicial.go.cr/document/sen-1-0007-673818	

Latin American state practice and primary sources in enforcing Inter-American Court judgments (*cont.*)

Country	Branch of government that does implementation	Basic constitutional provisions on international law and IHRL	Specific legislation/decrees/regulations on IACtHR and domestic law	Judicial cases on implementation of IACtHR judgments	Differences between provisional measures and full judgment on the merits
			lleven a cabo a nivel internacional en materia de derechos humanos, con el fin de fortalecer la promoción y defensa de estos derechos.' 'Artículo 4º-La coordinación y dirección de la Comisión Interinstitucional estará a cargo del Ministerio de Relaciones Exteriores y Culto. La Comisión estará presidida por el/la Ministro (a) o el/la Viceministro(a) de Relaciones Exteriores o por su representante, quien necesariamente deberá tener un rango no inferior al de Director y deberá tener experiencia en órganos y mecanismos internacionales de derechos humanos y en el funcionamiento del Estado. La Secretaría Ejecutiva la ostentará un(a) funcionario(a)		

Latin American state practice and primary sources in enforcing Inter-American Court judgments (*cont.*)

Country	Branch of government that does implementation	Basic constitutional provisions on international law and IHRL	Specific legislation/decrees/regulations on IACtHR and domestic law	Judicial cases on implementation of IACtHR judgments	Differences between provisional measures and full judgment on the merits
			de la Dirección General de Política Exterior de ese Ministerio, preferiblemente con experiencia en derechos humanos. La Presidencia y la Secretaría Ejecutiva de la Comisión Interinstitucional se denominarán Coordinación Nacional.' Artículo 6º […] La Comisión Interinstitucional podrá invitar, como instituciones de apoyo o como observadores permanentes, a instituciones de los otros poderes públicos como la Corte Suprema de Justicia, la Fiscalía General de la República, la Asamblea Legislativa, el Tribunal Supremo de Elecciones y la Defensoría de los Habitantes de la República. Cuando así sea requerido, se solicitará a estas instituciones aportar información		

Latin American state practice and primary sources in enforcing Inter-American Court judgments (*cont.*)

Country	Branch of government that does implementation	Basic constitutional provisions on international law and IHRL	Specific legislation/decrees/ regulations on IACtHR and domestic law	Judicial cases on implementation of IACtHR judgments	Differences between provisional measures and full judgment on the merits
			de importancia y coadyuvar en la implementación de las obligaciones de derechos humanos, de conformidad con sus mandatos y sus respectivos ámbitos de acción. http://www.pgrweb.go.cr/scij/Busqueda/Normativa/Normas/nrm_texto_completo.aspx?param1=NRTC&nValor1=1&nValor2=71193&nValor3=86331&strTipM=TC Ley Nº 6889, Convenio entre el gobierno de la República de Costa Rica y la Corte Interamericana de Derechos Humanos, 9 de septiembre de 1983. Art. 27. 'Artículo 27.- Las resoluciones de la Corte y, en su caso, de su Presidente, una vez comunicadas a las autoridades administrativas o judiciales correspondientes de la		

Latin American state practice and primary sources in enforcing Inter-American Court judgments (*cont.*)

Country	Branch of government that does implementation	Basic constitutional provisions on international law and IHRL	Specific legislation/decrees/ regulations on IACtHR and domestic law	Judicial cases on implementation of IACtHR judgments	Differences between provisional measures and full judgment on the merits
			república, tendrán la misma fuerza ejecutiva y ejecutoria que las dictadas por los tribunales costarricenses.' https://www.corteidh.or.cr/docs/otros/convenio.pdf		
Ecuador	Executive – the Ministry of Justice and Human Rights is responsible for 'coordinating the execution' of any decisions from the Inter-American System.[h] In this 'coordination', the	Constitución de la República del Ecuador, Arts. 11(3), 93, 417, 424, 426, 436. Art. 11(3). 'El ejercicio de los derechos se regirá por los siguientes principios: [...] 3. Los derechos y garantías	Decreto Ejecutivo 560, 2018 changed arts. 1 and 2 of the Decreto Ejecutivo No 1317. Decreto Ejecutivo 1317, 2008, Arts. 1–2. 'Art. 1.- Confiérase al Ministerio de Justicia y Derechos Humanos la responsabilidad de coordinar la ejecución de sentencias, medidas cautelares, medidas provisionales, acuerdos amistosos,	Corte Constitucional, 008-13- SAN-CC – relates to case of *Mejía Idrovo v. Ecuador*. http://doco.corteconstitucional.gob.ec:8080/alfresco/d/d/workspace/SpacesStore/b5b37285-55ea-4f6f-bdd0-b7143837358c	No information about different procedures; according to the Executive Decree n. 1317, the Ministry of Justice and Human Rights is responsible for both.

h Executive Decree N° 1317, Art. 2(1)–(2).

Latin American state practice and primary sources in enforcing Inter-American Court judgments (*cont.*)

Country	Branch of government that does implementation	Basic constitutional provisions on international law and IHRL	Specific legislation/decrees/ regulations on IACtHR and domestic law	Judicial cases on implementation of IACtHR judgments	Differences between provisional measures and full judgment on the merits
	Ministry refers the decision/resolution to the competent authority or the state entity that is competent to undertake the necessary measures to fulfil the obligations arising from the IASPHR's decisions. An option in the Judiciary: An action for non-compliance may also be brought before the Constitutional Court for IACtHR decisions that provide an obligation of action	establecidos en la Constitución y en los instrumentos internacionales de derechos humanos serán de directa e inmediata aplicación por y ante cualquier servidora o servidor público, administrativo o judicial, de oficio o a petición de parte.' Acción por incumplimiento – 'Art. 93.- La acción por incumplimiento tendrá por objeto garantizar la aplicación de las normas que integran	recomendaciones y resoluciones originados en el Sistema Interamericano de Derechos Humanos y en el Sistema Universal de Derechos Humanos, y demás obligaciones surgidas por compromisos internacionales en esta materia.' 'Art. 2.- El Ministerio de Justicia y Derechos Humanos cumplirá las siguientes funciones: 1. Remitir a la autoridad competente las resoluciones para que ordene el inicio de investigaciones y la determinación de responsabilidades individuales relacionadas con la violación de derechos humanos; y, dar seguimiento al curso de tales investigaciones y determinación de responsabilidades. [...] 3. Coordinar con la entidad del	/0010-10-AN-sen.pdf?guest=true Corte Constitucional, 11-18-CN/19 – relates to IACtHR *Advisory Opinion OC24/17*. https://portal.corteconstitucional.gob.ec/FichaRelatoria.aspx?numdocumento=11-18-CN/19	

Latin American state practice and primary sources in enforcing Inter-American Court judgments (*cont.*)

Country	Branch of government that does implementation	Basic constitutional provisions on international law and IHRL	Specific legislation/decrees/ regulations on IACtHR and domestic law	Judicial cases on implementation of IACtHR judgments	Differences between provisional measures and full judgment on the merits
	or of lack of action (positive or negative) that is clear, express, and demandable/ enforceable.[i] Also, any person can bring an international decision containing an obligation of material reparation to the Attorney General.[j]	el sistema jurídico, así como el cumplimiento de sentencias o informes de organismos internacionales de derechos humanos, cuando la norma o decisión cuyo cumplimiento se persigue contenga una obligación de hacer o no hacer clara, expresa y exigible. La acción se interpondrá ante	Estado competente la realización de medidas necesarias para dar cumplimiento integral a las obligaciones. 4. Preparar proyectos de reforma legal para adecuar el sistema normativo a los estándares internacionales de derechos humanos. [...] 11. Con el apoyo del Ministerio de Relaciones Exteriores, Comercio e integración, poner en conocimiento de las entidades públicas y la sociedad civil, las recomendaciones que emanen de comités u órganos internacionales de derechos humanos, así como		

i Constitución de la República del Ecuador, Arts. 93 and 436(5). See also Ley Organica de Garantias Jurisdiccionales y Control Constitucional, Art. 68.

j Ecuador, Ley Organica de Garantias Jurisdiccionales y Control Constitucional, Art. 68.

Latin American state practice and primary sources in enforcing Inter-American Court judgments (*cont.*)

Country	Branch of government that does implementation	Basic constitutional provisions on international law and IHRL	Specific legislation/decrees/ regulations on IACtHR and domestic law	Judicial cases on implementation of IACtHR judgments	Differences between provisional measures and full judgment on the merits
		la Corte Constitucional.' 'Art. 417.- Los tratados internacionales ratificados por el Ecuador se sujetarán a lo establecido en la Constitución. En el caso de los tratados y otros instrumentos internacionales de derechos humanos se aplicarán los principios pro ser humano, de no restricción de derechos, de aplicabilidad directa y de cláusula abierta establecidos en la Constitución. […]'	realizar la evaluación de su cumplimiento.' https://www.atencionintegral.gob.ec/wp-content/uploads/2020/01/21.-Decreto-1317.pdf Reglamento Organico Funcional de la Procuraduria General Del Estado, 2017, Art. 31. Art. 31.- 'Corresponde al Director Nacional de Derechos Humanos cumplir las funciones señaladas en la Ley Orgánica de la Procuraduría General del Estado y las siguientes: […] 6. Coordinar con los organismos y entidades del sector público competentes, a nivel, interno, la implementación de las acciones necesarias para cumplir sentencias, resoluciones, recomendaciones u otras medidas que hayan dictado organismos		

Latin American state practice and primary sources in enforcing Inter-American Court judgments (*cont.*)

Country	Branch of government that does implementation	Basic constitutional provisions on international law and IHRL	Specific legislation/decrees/regulations on IACtHR and domestic law	Judicial cases on implementation of IACtHR judgments	Differences between provisional measures and full judgment on the merits
		'Art. 424. […] La Constitución y los tratados internacionales de derechos humanos ratificados por el Estado que reconozcan derechos más favorables a los contenidos en la Constitución, prevalecerán sobre cualquier otra norma jurídica o acto del poder público.' 'Art. 426.- […] Los derechos consagrados en la Constitución y los	internacionales para la prevención y protección de los derechos fundamentales;' —http://www.pge.gob.ec/images/documentos/LeyTransparencia/2018/mayo/a3/REGLAMENTO_ORGANICO_FUNCIONAL_DE_LA_PGE.pdf Ley Organica de Garantias Jurisdiccionales y Control Constitucional, 2009 (última modificación 2020), Arts. 1, 4, 26, 39, 52–53, 68. 'Art. 1.- Objeto y finalidad de la ley.- Esta ley tiene por objeto regular la jurisdicción constitucional, con el fin de garantizar jurisdiccionalmente los derechos reconocidos en la Constitución y en los instrumentos internacionales de derechos humanos y de la naturaleza; y garantizar la eficacia		

Latin American state practice and primary sources in enforcing Inter-American Court judgments (*cont.*)

Country	Branch of government that does implementation	Basic constitutional provisions on international law and IHRL	Specific legislation/decrees/regulations on IACtHR and domestic law	Judicial cases on implementation of IACtHR judgments	Differences between provisional measures and full judgment on the merits
		instrumentos internacionales de derechos humanos serán de inmediato cumplimiento y aplicación. […]' 'Art. 436.- La Corte Constitucional ejercerá, además de las que le confiera la ley, las siguientes atribuciones: […] 5. Conocer y resolver, a petición de parte, las acciones por incumplimiento que se presenten con la finalidad de garantizar la aplicación de normas o actos	y la supremacía constitucional.' 'Art. 4.- Principios procesales.- La justicia constitucional se sustenta en los siguientes principios procesales: […] 2. Aplicación directa de la Constitución.- Los derechos y garantías establecidas en la Constitución y en los instrumentos internacionales de derechos humanos, serán de directa e inmediata aplicación por y ante cualquier servidora o servidor público, administrativo o judicial, de oficio o a petición de parte.' 'Art. 26.- Finalidad.- Las medidas cautelares tendrán por objeto evitar o cesar la amenaza o violación de los derechos reconocidos en la Constitución y en instrumentos internacionales		

Latin American state practice and primary sources in enforcing Inter-American Court judgments (*cont.*)

Country	Branch of government that does implementation	Basic constitutional provisions on international law and IHRL	Specific legislation/decrees/ regulations on IACtHR and domestic law	Judicial cases on implementation of IACtHR judgments	Differences between provisional measures and full judgment on the merits
		administrativos de carácter general, cualquiera que sea su naturaleza o jerarquía, así como para el cumplimiento de sentencias o informes de organismos internacionales de protección de derechos humanos que no sean ejecutables por las vías judiciales ordinarias.' https://educacion.gob.ec/wp-content/uploads/downloads/2012/08/Constitucion.pdf	sobre derechos humanos. [...]' 'Acción de protección Art. 39.- Objeto.- La acción de protección tendrá por objeto el amparo directo y eficaz de los derechos reconocidos en la Constitución y tratados internacionales sobre derechos humanos, que no estén amparados por las acciones de hábeas corpus, acceso a la información pública, hábeas data, por incumplimiento, extraordinaria de protección y extraordinaria de protección contra decisiones de la justicia indígena' 'Art. 52.- Objeto y ámbito.- La acción por incumplimiento tiene por objeto garantizar la aplicación de las normas que integran el sistema jurídico, así como el cumplimiento de sentencias,		

Latin American state practice and primary sources in enforcing Inter-American Court judgments (*cont.*)

Country	Branch of government that does implementation	Basic constitutional provisions on international law and IHRL	Specific legislation/decrees/ regulations on IACtHR and domestic law	Judicial cases on implementation of IACtHR judgments	Differences between provisional measures and full judgment on the merits
			decisiones o informes de organismos internacionales de protección de derechos humanos. Esta acción procederá cuando la norma, sentencia, decisión o informe cuyo cumplimiento se persigue contengan una obligación de hacer o no hacer, clara, expresa y exigible' 'Art. 53.- Legitimación pasiva.- La acción por incumplimiento procederá en contra de toda autoridad pública y contra de personas naturales o jurídicas particulares cuando actúen o deban actuar en ejercicio de funciones públicas, o presten servicios públicos. Procederá contra particulares también en el caso de que las sentencias, decisiones o informes de organismos internacionales de		

Latin American state practice and primary sources in enforcing Inter-American Court judgments (*cont.*)

Country	Branch of government that does implementation	Basic constitutional provisions on international law and IHRL	Specific legislation/decrees/ regulations on IACtHR and domestic law	Judicial cases on implementation of IACtHR judgments	Differences between provisional measures and full judgment on the merits
			protección de derechos humanos impongan una obligación a una persona particular determinada o determinable.' 'Repetición contra servidoras y servidores públicos por violación de derechos […] Art. 68.- Legitimación activa.- La máxima autoridad de la entidad responsable asumirá el patrocinio de esta causa a nombre del Estado y deberá interponer la demanda ante la Sala de lo Contencioso Administrativo de la Corte Provincial competente para que se reintegren al Estado los recursos erogados por concepto de reparación. […] Cualquier persona puede poner en conocimiento de la Procuradora o Procurador General la existencia de una sentencia, auto definitivo o		

Latin American state practice and primary sources in enforcing Inter-American Court judgments (*cont.*)

Country	Branch of government that does implementation	Basic constitutional provisions on international law and IHRL	Specific legislation/decrees/ regulations on IACtHR and domestic law	Judicial cases on implementation of IACtHR judgments	Differences between provisional measures and full judgment on the merits
			resolución de un organismo internacional competente en la cual se ordena la reparación material.'		
Honduras	Executive-led (through Independent Organ) – The National Commission for Human Rights is an independent organ created by Executive decree and whose members are voted by the Congress, and it is the organ in charge of ensuring state compliance with	Constitución de Honduras – 1982 (actualizada hasta 2005), Arts. 15, 18, 59, 313(4). 'ARTÍCULO 15.- Honduras hace suyos los principios y practicas del derecho internacional que propenden a la solidaridad humana, al respecto de la autodeterminacion de los pueblos, a la no intervencion y al	Ley Orgánica del Comisionado Nacional de los Derechos Humanos, 21 Noviembre 1995, Arts. 1, 9, 16. 'ARTÍCULO 1. El Comisionado Nacional de los Derechos Humanos es una institución nacional, establecida para garantizar la vigencia de los derechos y libertades reconocidas en la Constitución de la República y los Tratados y Convenios Internacionales ratificados por Honduras.' ATRIBUCIONES Y PRERROGATIVAS 'ARTICULO 9. El Comisionado	Statement of the Judiciary about the implementation of the IACtHR's judgment on the case of *López and Others v. Honduras*: http://www.poderjudicial.gob.hn/Documents/ComunicadoSentenciaCumplimientoSentenciaCIDHLopezLone.pdf Search engine for case law presented difficulties – no decision found concerning implementation of a	Provisional measures are to be implemented by the General Direction of the System of Protection, whereas IASPHR's decisions more generally (including judgments) are the responsibility of the state branches and their institutions assisting the National System of Protection.[1]

Latin American state practice and primary sources in enforcing Inter-American Court judgments (*cont.*)

Country	Branch of government that does implementation	Basic constitutional provisions on international law and IHRL	Specific legislation/decrees/ regulations on IACtHR and domestic law	Judicial cases on implementation of IACtHR judgments	Differences between provisional measures and full judgment on the merits
	international human rights.[k] The Law for the Protection of Human Rights Defenders says that the organ responsible for implementing the IACtHR's provisional measures is the 'General Direction of the National System for the Protection of Human Rights	afianzamiento de la paz y la democracia universales. Honduras proclama como ineludible la validez y obligatoria ejecucion de las sentencias arbitrales y judiciales de caracter internacional' 'ARTÍCULO 18.- En caso de conflicto entre el tratado o convencion y la Ley prevalecerá el primero.' 'ARTÍCULO 59.- La	Nacional de los Derechos Humanos, tiene las atribuciones siguientes: 1. Velar por el cumplimiento de los Derechos y Garantías establecidas en la Constitución de la República y la presente Ley, la Declaración Universal de los Derechos Humanos y demás Tratados y Convenios ratificados por Honduras; [...] 4.- Velar porque los actos y resoluciones de la administración pública sean acordes con el contenido de los tratados, convenios y acuerdos internacionales en materia de derechos humanos ratificados por	IACtHR's judgment, only briefly commenting on decisions against other countries.	

k Ley Orgánica del Comisionado Nacional de los Derechos Humanos, 1995, Art. 9(1).

Latin American state practice and primary sources in enforcing Inter-American Court judgments (*cont.*)

Country	Branch of government that does implementation	Basic constitutional provisions on international law and IHRL	Specific legislation/decrees/regulations on IACtHR and domestic law	Judicial cases on implementation of IACtHR judgments	Differences between provisional measures and full judgment on the merits
	Defenders',[m] in coordination with the Attorney General, while all state branches and their institutions are responsible for assisting the National System for the Protection of Human Rights Defenders in implementing the decisions of the IACtHR.[n] The Executive also has led	persona humana es el fin supremo de la sociedad y del Estado. Todos tienen la obligacion de respetarla y protegerla. La dignidad del ser humano es inviolable. Para garantizar los derechos y libertades reconocidos en esta Constitucion, crease la Institucion del Comisionado	Honduras; [...] 8. Coordinar cuando sea necesario, con las instancias y organismos nacionales e internacionales, y con la colaboración de organismos no gubernamentales, las medidas relacionadas con la protección de los Derechos Humanos, en su más amplio concepto, incluyendo la seguridad alimentaria de las clases desposeidas y de los niños desprotegidos, así como el respeto a la dignidad e imagen de la persona humana;' 'ARTÍCULO 16. El Comisionado Nacional de los Derechos Humanos podrá iniciar de oficio o		

m 'Dirección General del Sistema de Protección para Personas Defensoras de Derechos Humanos.'

n Ley de Protección para las y los Defensores de Derechos Humanos, Periodistas, Comunicadores Sociales y Operadores de Justicia, Arts. 29, 52, 53.

Latin American state practice and primary sources in enforcing Inter-American Court judgments (*cont.*)

Country	Branch of government that does implementation	Basic constitutional provisions on international law and IHRL	Specific legislation/decrees/ regulations on IACtHR and domestic law	Judicial cases on implementation of IACtHR judgments	Differences between provisional measures and full judgment on the merits
	implementation by creating an Interinstitutional Committee to enforce an IACtHR decision.	Nacional de los Derechos Humanos. La organizacion, prerrogativa y atribuciones del Comisionado Nacional de los Derechos Humanos sera objeto de una ley especial' 'ARTÍCULO 313.- La Corte Suprema de Justicia, tendrá las atribuciones siguientes: [...] 4. Conocer de las causas de extradición y de las demás que deban juzgarse conforme al Derecho Internacional.'	a petición de parte, cualquier investigación conducente al esclarecimiento de hechos que impliquen ejercicio ilegítimo, arbitrario, abusivo, defectuoso, negligente o discriminatorio de parte de la administración pública y entidades privadas que presten servicios públicos, del mismo modo en lo referente a violaciones de los Derechos Humanos, en su más amplio concepto.' —https://www.acnur.org/fileadmin/Documentos/BDL/2001/0152.pdf Ley de Protección para las y los Defensores de Derechos Humanos, Periodistas, Comunicadores Sociales y Operadores de Justicia, 15 mayo 2015, Decreto No. 34-2015, Arts. 19, 29(6), 52–53. 'ARTÍCULO 19.- 'DEL SISTEMA		

Latin American state practice and primary sources in enforcing Inter-American Court judgments (*cont.*)

Country	Branch of government that does implementation	Basic constitutional provisions on international law and IHRL	Specific legislation/decrees/regulations on IACtHR and domestic law	Judicial cases on implementation of IACtHR judgments	Differences between provisional measures and full judgment on the merits
		https://www.oas.org/dil/esp/constitucion_de_honduras.pdf	NACIONAL DE PROTECCIÓN PARA PERSONAS DEFENSORAS DE DERECHOS HUMANOS. [...] El Sistema Nacional de Protección para Personas Defensoras de Derechos Humanos está integrado por: 1. La Secretaría de Estado en los Despachos de Derechos Humanos, Justicia, Gobernación y Descentralización, como órgano rector; 2. El Consejo Nacional de Protección para las y los Defensores de Derechos Humanos, Periodistas, Comunicadores Sociales y Operadores de Justicia; 3. La Dirección General del Sistema de Protección; 4. El Comité Técnico del		

Latin American state practice and primary sources in enforcing Inter-American Court judgments (*cont.*)

Country	Branch of government that does implementation	Basic constitutional provisions on international law and IHRL	Specific legislation/decrees/ regulations on IACtHR and domestic law	Judicial cases on implementation of IACtHR judgments	Differences between provisional measures and full judgment on the merits
			Mecanismo de Protección; y, 5. El Departamento de Derechos Humanos de la Secretaría de Estado en el Despacho de Seguridad. […]' 'ARTÍCULO 29.- […] Son atribuciones de la Dirección General del Sistema de Protección las siguientes: […] 6. Solicitar y dar seguimiento permanente a las medidas provisionales de la Corte Interamericana de Derechos Humanos, medidas cautelares de la Comisión Interamericana de Derechos Humanos y las correspondientes medidas decretas de seguridad por los órganos jurisdiccionales del Estado, respectivamente;' 'ARTÍCULO 52.- SOBRE LA IMPLEMENTACIÓN DE LAS MEDIDAS CAUTELARES Y		

Latin American state practice and primary sources in enforcing Inter-American Court judgments (*cont.*)

Country	Branch of government that does implementation	Basic constitutional provisions on international law and IHRL	Specific legislation/decrees/ regulations on IACtHR and domestic law	Judicial cases on implementation of IACtHR judgments	Differences between provisional measures and full judgment on the merits
			PROVISIONALES DEL SISTEMA INTERAMERICANO DE DERECHOS HUMANOS.- El cumplimiento de las medidas cautelares y provisionales de la Comisión y la Corte Interamericana de Derechos Humanos respectivamente es competencia del Sistema Nacional de Protección para Personas Defensoras de Derechos Humanos, que debe coordinar con la Procuraduría General de la República como representante del Estado ante el Sistema Interamericano de Protección de Derechos Humanos la recepción y tramitación de las mismas. Cuando se reciba la notificación respectiva, la Procuraduría General de la República debe trasladar inmediatamente a la		

Latin American state practice and primary sources in enforcing Inter-American Court judgments (*cont.*)

Country	Branch of government that does implementation	Basic constitutional provisions on international law and IHRL	Specific legislation/decrees/ regulations on IACtHR and domestic law	Judicial cases on implementation of IACtHR judgments	Differences between provisional measures and full judgment on the merits
			Dirección General del Sistema de Protección el mandato emanado por la Comisión o Corte Interamericana de Derechos Humanos, con el objeto de implementarlo en los plazos, modo y forma determinada por éstas. El Comité Técnico del Mecanismo de Protección debe realizar un análisis de riesgo adicional con el objeto de determinar si las medidas de protección ordenadas por dichos órganos son suficientes para impedir que se produzcan daños irreparables a sus derechos, asegurando en todo momento el consentimiento informado de las personas beneficiarias, sus familiares o la organización que las representan.		

Latin American state practice and primary sources in enforcing Inter-American Court judgments (*cont.*)

Country	Branch of government that does implementation	Basic constitutional provisions on international law and IHRL	Specific legislation/decrees/ regulations on IACtHR and domestic law	Judicial cases on implementation of IACtHR judgments	Differences between provisional measures and full judgment on the merits
			Ni la Dirección General del Sistema de Protección, ni el Comité Técnico del Mecanismo de Protección pueden suspender, revocar o de cualquier manera disminuir la protección otorgada por las Medidas Cautelares o Provisionales de la Comisión y Corte Interamericana de Derechos Humanos, respectivamente.' 'ARTÍCULO 53.- DE LA OBLIGACIÓN DE COOPERACIÓN DE LOS ORGANISMOS, INSTITUCIONES Y ENTES DEL ESTADO.- Los tres (3) Poderes del Estado y demás instituciones, están obligados a auxiliar con carácter preferente y urgente al Sistema Nacional de Protección para Personas Defensoras de Derechos Humanos a fin de dar cumplimiento a la presente Ley,		

Latin American state practice and primary sources in enforcing Inter-American Court judgments (*cont.*)

Country	Branch of government that does implementation	Basic constitutional provisions on international law and IHRL	Specific legislation/decrees/ regulations on IACtHR and domestic law	Judicial cases on implementation of IACtHR judgments	Differences between provisional measures and full judgment on the merits
			así como a las decisiones de los órganos del Sistema Interamericano de Protección de Derechos Humanos.' —https://www.sedh.gob.hn/documentos-recientes/263-ley-de-proteccion-para-las-y-los-defensores-de-derechos-humanos-periodistas-comunicadores-sociales-y-operadores-de-justicia/file Reglamento General de la Ley Orgánica del Comisionado Nacional de los Derechos Humanos, Acuerdo No 142–96, 26 Noviembre 1996, Art. 8. 'ARTÍCULO 8. OTRAS ATRIBUCIONES DEL COMISIONADO NACIONAL DE LOS DERECHOS HUMANOS: Además de las establecidas en la Ley Orgánica del Comisionado Nacional de los Derechos		

Latin American state practice and primary sources in enforcing Inter-American Court judgments (*cont.*)

Country	Branch of government that does implementation	Basic constitutional provisions on international law and IHRL	Specific legislation/decrees/regulations on IACtHR and domestic law	Judicial cases on implementation of IACtHR judgments	Differences between provisional measures and full judgment on the merits
			Humanos, corresponde al Comisionado: [...] e. Investigar de oficio o a solicitud del interesado, las acciones materiales, actos y omisiones de la actividad administrativa del sector público, para lo cual podrá inspeccionar oficinas, citar funcionarios y requerir cualquier tipo de información.' —https://www.tsc.gob.hn/web/leyes/Reglamento_Ley_del_CONADEH.pdf Reglamento General de la Ley De Protección para las y los Defensores de Derechos Humanos, Periodistas, Comunicadores Sociales y Operadores de Justicia – Acuerdo Ejecutivo No.059–2016, Arts. 4(7), 8(2), 23(4), 53. 'ARTÍCULO 4.- [...] 7. Crear grupos de trabajo para el estudio e implementación en cumplimiento		

Latin American state practice and primary sources in enforcing Inter-American Court judgments (*cont.*)

Country	Branch of government that does implementation	Basic constitutional provisions on international law and IHRL	Specific legislation/decrees/ regulations on IACtHR and domestic law	Judicial cases on implementation of IACtHR judgments	Differences between provisional measures and full judgment on the merits
			de lo señalado en el Artículo 14 de la Ley, sobre las Resoluciones del Sistema de Derechos Humanos de las Naciones Unidas y del Sistema Interamericano de Protección de los Derechos Humanos a efecto de observar las recomendaciones y establecer acciones, programas y estrategias de prevención sobre violaciones a los derechos humanos, combate a la impunidad y agresiones a los sujetos protegidos por la Ley;' 'ARTÍCULO 8.- DEL ROL DEL CONSEJO EN EL TRATAMIENTO DE LOS CASOS. […] 2. El Consejo debe recomendar y asesorar a la Dirección General para que en el proceso de remisión de los casos relacionados con la implementación de Medidas Cautelares y Provisionales		

Latin American state practice and primary sources in enforcing Inter-American Court judgments (*cont.*)

Country	Branch of government that does implementation	Basic constitutional provisions on international law and IHRL	Specific legislation/decrees/regulations on IACtHR and domestic law	Judicial cases on implementation of IACtHR judgments	Differences between provisional measures and full judgment on the merits
			emitidas por los órganos del Sistema Interamericano de Protección establecidos en el Artículo 29 de la Ley, este proceso se realice de manera ordenada, con una metodología adecuada de trabajo y garantizando que se mantengan las medidas de protección implementadas por el 66 Departamento de Derechos Humanos de la Secretaría de Estado en el Despacho de Seguridad;' 'ARTÍCULO 23.- UNIDAD DE IMPLEMENTACIÓN Y SEGUIMIENTO. La Unidad de Implementación y Seguimiento es un órgano técnico auxiliar de la Dirección General, tendrá las siguientes funciones, en apoyo a las facultades que la Ley y el Reglamento asignan a la Dirección		

Latin American state practice and primary sources in enforcing Inter-American Court judgments (*cont.*)

Country	Branch of government that does implementation	Basic constitutional provisions on international law and IHRL	Specific legislation/decrees/ regulations on IACtHR and domestic law	Judicial cases on implementation of IACtHR judgments	Differences between provisional measures and full judgment on the merits
			General: [...] 4. Dará seguimiento al cumplimiento de las medidas de prevención y protección ordenadas por el Sistema Interamericano y coordinará las acciones con las instancias competentes;' 'ARTÍCULO 59.- Para la implementación de las Medidas Cautelares y Provisionales del Sistema Interamericano de Derechos Humanos se actuará conforme a lo establecido en el Artículo 52 de la Ley, entendiéndose exclusivamente a aquellas medidas otorgadas en beneficio de las personas referidas en el Artículo 2 de la Ley' – https://www.sedh.gob.hn/documentos-recientes/263-ley-de-proteccion-para-las-y-los-defensores-de-derechos-humanos-periodistas		

Latin American state practice and primary sources in enforcing Inter-American Court judgments (*cont.*)

Country	Branch of government that does implementation	Basic constitutional provisions on international law and IHRL	Specific legislation/decrees/ regulations on IACtHR and domestic law	Judicial cases on implementation of IACtHR judgments	Differences between provisional measures and full judgment on the merits
			-comunicadores-sociales-y-operadores-de-justicia/file Decreto Ejecutivo 01-2016, Arts. 1–2. 'ARTÍCULO 1.- Crear la Comisión Interinstitucional para el Cumplimiento de las Sentencias Internacionales emitidas por la Corte Interamericana de Derechos Humanos, en los casos Comunidad Garífuna Triunfo de la Cruz y sus miembros vs. Honduras y Comunidad Garífuna de Punta Piedra y sus miembros vs. Honduras, de fecha 08 de octubre de 2015.' ARTÍCULO 2.- 'La comisión será la responsable de la ejecución de las acciones necesarias para el cumplimiento de las sentencias internacionales dictadas por la Corte Interamericana de Derechos		

Latin American state practice and primary sources in enforcing Inter-American Court judgments (*cont.*)

Country	Branch of government that does implementation	Basic constitutional provisions on international law and IHRL	Specific legislation/decrees/ regulations on IACtHR and domestic law	Judicial cases on implementation of IACtHR judgments	Differences between provisional measures and full judgment on the merits
			Humanos, en los casos Comunidad Garífuna Triunfo de la Cruz y sus miembros vs. Honduras y Comunidad Garífuna de Punta Piedra y sus miembros vs. Honduras.' —https://tzibalnaah.unah.edu.hn/bitstream/handle/123456789/4705/20161210.pdf?sequence=2&isAllowed=y (pp. 9–11).		
Mexico	Executive-led – the Secretary of Government, through its internal organs (possibly in conjunction with the Secretary of Foreign Affairs – unclear) promotes actions to comply with the	Constitución Política de los Estados Unidos Mexicanos, Arts. 1, 103. 'Artículo 1o. En los Estados Unidos Mexicanos todas las personas gozarán de los derechos humanos	Ley Orgánica de la Administración Pública Federal, Art. 27. 'Artículo 27.- A la Secretaría de Gobernación corresponde el despacho de los siguientes asuntos: [...] VII. Vigilar el cumplimiento de los preceptos constitucionales por parte de las autoridades del país; coordinar, en vinculación con las organizaciones de la sociedad	Supreme Court's Public Session 489/2010. 'Trámite y medidas que deben seguirse por el Poder Judicial de la Federación para atender una sentencia de la Corte Interamericana de Derechos Humanos' – not a judgment, but	The Internal Rules of the Secretary of Government only differentiates between both in Art. 45, where it identifies the 'General Adjunct Directory for Attention to Cases of International Human

Latin American state practice and primary sources in enforcing Inter-American Court judgments (*cont.*)

Country	Branch of government that does implementation	Basic constitutional provisions on international law and IHRL	Specific legislation/decrees/ regulations on IACtHR and domestic law	Judicial cases on implementation of IACtHR judgments	Differences between provisional measures and full judgment on the merits
	'recommendations of international organizations.'[o] The document from the Supreme Court's Public Session 489/ 2010 suggests that the Secretary of Foreign Affairs informs the 'Secretary of Government' about the judgment, and the latter, through its internal organs,	reconocidos en esta Constitución y en los tratados internacionales de los que el Estado Mexicano sea parte, así como de las garantías para su protección, cuyo ejercicio no podrá restringirse ni suspenderse, salvo en los casos y bajo las condiciones que esta Constitución	civil, la promoción y defensa de los derechos humanos y dar seguimiento a la atención de las recomendaciones que emitan los organismos competentes en dicha materia, así como dictar las medidas administrativas necesarias para tal efecto;' – http://www.diputados.gob.mx/ LeyesBiblio/pdf/153_110121.pdf Reglamento Interior de la Secretaría de Gobernación, Arts. 5 (XI), 43(VI), (XII), 45(I), (III), (VIII), 51(X), 52(VI), 53(VII). 'Artículo 5.- Son facultades	relevant concerning implementation of IACtHR's decisions by the Judiciary – refers to the case of *Radilla Pacheco v México*. https://www.scjn.gob .mx/PLENO/ver_taqui graficas/ag014.pdf Supreme Court, Expediente 1396/2011, Decision 11 May 2015 – refers to cases *Rosendo Cantú and others v Mexico*, and *Fernández*	Rights Organs'[q] as in charge of managing the actions in response to provisional measures.[r] https://www.dof.gob .mx/nota_detalle.php? codigo= 5561631&fecha=31/05/ 2019#gsc.tab=0

o Secretaría de Gobernación. Reglamento Interior de la Secretaría de Gobernación, 31 May 2019, Art. 43, VI, and XII, Art. 45, I, III, VIII, Art. 51, X, Art. 52, VI, Art. 53, VII.

q 'Dirección General Adjunta para la Atención de Casos en Organismos Internacionales de Derechos Humanos.'

r Reglamento Interior de la Secretaría de Gobernación, 31 May 2019, Art. 45.

Latin American state practice and primary sources in enforcing Inter-American Court judgments (*cont.*)

Country	Branch of government that does implementation	Basic constitutional provisions on international law and IHRL	Specific legislation/decrees/ regulations on IACtHR and domestic law	Judicial cases on implementation of IACtHR judgments	Differences between provisional measures and full judgment on the merits
	coordinates the publishing and enforcement of the IACtHR's judgment by referring it to the national organs capable of enforcing it.[p]	establece. […] En consecuencia, el Estado deberá prevenir, investigar, sancionar y reparar las violaciones a los derechos humanos, en los términos que establezca la ley.' 'Artículo 103. Los Tribunales de la Federación resolverán toda controversia que se suscite I. Por normas generales, actos u omisiones de la	indelegables de la persona Titular de la Secretaría: […] XI. Fijar la política que deberá aplicar la Secretaría a efecto de vigilar el cumplimiento de los preceptos constitucionales por parte de las autoridades del país, especialmente en lo que se refiere a los derechos humanos;' 'De las unidades administrativas adscritas a la Subsecretaría de Derechos Humanos, Población y Migración. 'Artículo 43.- La Unidad para la Defensa de los Derechos Humanos tiene las atribuciones siguientes: […] VI. Proponer a la persona Titular	*Ortegaand others v Mexico*. https://www2.scjn.gob.mx/ConsultaTematica/PaginasPub/DetallePub.aspx?AsuntoID=134051 Supreme Court, Expediente 1107/2019 – refers to the case of *García Cruz and Sánchez Silvestre v Mexico*, and limits the participation of the Judiciary in the enforcement of the IACtHRs decisions. https://www2.scjn.gob.mx/Juridica/Votos/	

p Mexico, Supreme Court's Public Session 489/2010, pp. 12–18, 23–24, https://www.scjn.gob.mx/PLENO/ver_taquigraficas/ag014.pdf

Latin American state practice and primary sources in enforcing Inter-American Court judgments (*cont.*)

Country	Branch of government that does implementation	Basic constitutional provisions on international law and IHRL	Specific legislation/decrees/ regulations on IACtHR and domestic law	Judicial cases on implementation of IACtHR judgments	Differences between provisional measures and full judgment on the merits
		autoridad que violen los derechos humanos reconocidos y las garantías otorgadas para su protección por esta Constitución, así como por los tratados internacionales de los que el Estado Mexicano sea parte; […]'. Ley sobre la Celebración de Tratados, 2 de enero de 1992, Art. 11. 'ARTÍCULO 11.- Las sentencias, laudos arbitrales y demás resoluciones	de la Subsecretaría de Derechos Humanos, Población y Migración los mecanismos para el cumplimiento y seguimiento de los compromisos asumidos por el Estado mexicano en materia de derechos humanos, así como las recomendaciones emitidas por organismos internacionales; […] XII. Promover ante dependencias y entidades de la Administración Pública Federal acciones de cumplimiento de los compromisos internacionales en materia de derechos humanos, así como definir y consensar la colaboración para la ejecución de dichas acciones a través de los instrumentos jurídicos que al efecto se formalicen;' 'Artículo 45. La Dirección General Adjunta para la Atención de Casos	HojasVotacion/2021/26de6df4-125c-eb11-800a-0050569eace9.pdf Relevant link: https://www.scjn.gob.mx/derechos-humanos/buscadores-juridicos/sentencias-relevantes-en-materia-de-derechos-humanos	

Latin American state practice and primary sources in enforcing Inter-American Court judgments (*cont.*)

Country	Branch of government that does implementation	Basic constitutional provisions on international law and IHRL	Specific legislation/decrees/ regulations on IACtHR and domestic law	Judicial cases on implementation of IACtHR judgments	Differences between provisional measures and full judgment on the merits
		jurisdiccionales derivados de la aplicación de los mecanismos internacionales para la solución de controversias legales a que se refiere el artículo 8o,. tendrán eficacia y serán reconocidos en la República, y podrán utilizarse como prueba en los casos de nacionales que se encuentren en la misma situación jurídica, de conformidad con el Código Federal de Procedimientos	en Organismos Internacionales de Derechos Humanos tiene las atribuciones siguientes: I. Instrumentar, en coordinación con las instituciones y las autoridades competentes del Estado mexicano, las acciones para el cumplimiento y seguimiento de los compromisos asumidos por el Estado frente a organismos internacionales de derechos humanos; [...] III. Instrumentar, en coordinación con las instituciones y las autoridades competentes del Estado mexicano, las acciones para la atención de las solicitudes de medidas precautorias o cautelares emitidas por organismos internacionales de derechos humanos; [...] VIII. Proponer, previo acuerdo con		

Latin American state practice and primary sources in enforcing Inter-American Court judgments (*cont.*)

Country	Branch of government that does implementation	Basic constitutional provisions on international law and IHRL	Specific legislation/decrees/regulations on IACtHR and domestic law	Judicial cases on implementation of IACtHR judgments	Differences between provisional measures and full judgment on the merits
		Civiles y los tratados aplicables.'	la persona Titular de la Unidad para la Defensa de los Derechos Humanos, los mecanismos de vinculación y de seguimiento con la unidad administrativa competente en materia de derechos humanos adscrita a la Secretaría de Relaciones Exteriores para el eficiente cumplimiento de las recomendaciones que emitan los organismos competentes en materia de derechos humanos.' 'Artículo 51. La Dirección General de Política Pública de Derechos Humanos tiene las atribuciones siguientes: [...] x. Implementar los mecanismos para el cumplimiento y seguimiento de los compromisos asumidos por el Estado mexicano en materia de derechos humanos, así como las recomendaciones		

Latin American state practice and primary sources in enforcing Inter-American Court judgments (*cont.*)

Country	Branch of government that does implementation	Basic constitutional provisions on international law and IHRL	Specific legislation/decrees/ regulations on IACtHR and domestic law	Judicial cases on implementation of IACtHR judgments	Differences between provisional measures and full judgment on the merits
			emitidas por organismos internacionales;' 'Artículo 52. La Dirección General Adjunta de Diseño e Implementación de Política Pública de Derechos Humanos tiene las atribuciones siguientes: […] VI. Dirigir las acciones para verificar el cumplimiento y seguimiento de los compromisos asumidos por el Estado mexicano en materia de derechos humanos, así como las recomendaciones emitidas por organismos internacionales;' 'Artículo 53. La Dirección General Adjunta de Seguimiento y Evaluación de Política Pública de Derechos Humanos tiene las atribuciones siguientes: […]		

Latin American state practice and primary sources in enforcing Inter-American Court judgments (*cont.*)

Country	Branch of government that does implementation	Basic constitutional provisions on international law and IHRL	Specific legislation/decrees/ regulations on IACtHR and domestic law	Judicial cases on implementation of IACtHR judgments	Differences between provisional measures and full judgment on the merits
			VII. Coordinar mecanismos interinstitucionales para el seguimiento y evaluación del cumplimiento de los compromisos asumidos por el Estado mexicano en materia de derechos humanos, así como las recomendaciones emitidas por organismos internacionales.' —https://www.dof.gob.mx/nota_detalle.php?codigo=5561631&fecha=31/05/2019		
Nicaragua	Executive-led—The Criminal Attorney Office of the Attorney General's Office is responsible for processing the requests from the Court and Commission in matters under its	Constitución Política de Nicaragua, 1987, con enmiendas hasta 2014, Arts. 5, 10, 46, 182. 'Artículo 5 [...] Nicaragua fundamenta sus relaciones	Reglamento de la Ley Orgánica de la Procuraduría General de la República, Decreto Ejecutivo N° 19-2009. 'Artículo 27. Funciones. Son funciones de la Procuraduría Penal, las siguientes: [...] 5. Tramitar todas las solicitudes procedentes de la Comisión y la Corte Interamericana de Derechos	We were unable to find access to the search engine for case law. https://www.poderjudicial.gob.ni/bijun2/sentencias2013.asp No cases found dealing with an IACtHR judgment.	No information found.

Latin American state practice and primary sources in enforcing Inter-American Court judgments (*cont.*)

Country	Branch of government that does implementation	Basic constitutional provisions on international law and IHRL	Specific legislation/decrees/ regulations on IACtHR and domestic law	Judicial cases on implementation of IACtHR judgments	Differences between provisional measures and full judgment on the merits
	competence. The 'Office of the Attorney for Human Rights Protection',[s] an independent entity, also seems to play an important role dealing with human rights protection, although its constitutive Law makes no reference to implementation of IACtHR's decisions.	internacionales en la amistad, complementariedad y solidaridad entre los pueblos y la reciprocidad entre los Estados. Por tanto, se inhibe y proscribe todo tipo de agresión política, militar, económica, cultural y religiosa, y la intervención en los asuntos internos de otros Estados. [...]';	Humanos en materia de su competencia, así como de cualquier organismo o Corte Internacional en donde el Estado de Nicaragua sea parte. [...] 7. Dar seguimiento en lo que corresponda y sea pertinente a las resoluciones de la Procuraduría para la Defensa de los Derechos Humanos.' http://legislacion.asamblea.gob.ni/Normaweb.nsf/3133c0d121ea3897062568a1005e0f89/f5a0a05d8cf0cba6062575ae005eb079?OpenDocument Ley N° 212, 1995, Ley de la Procuraduría para la Defensa de los Derechos Humanos, Arts. 1,	Cases briefly mentioning provisions from the ACHR: https://www.poderjudicial.gob.ni/pjupload/scons1/pdf/bot03.pdf and https://www.poderjudicial.gob.ni/pjupload/scons1/pdf/bdic02.pdf	

s 'Procuraduría para la Defensa de los Derechos Humanos.'

Latin American state practice and primary sources in enforcing Inter-American Court judgments (*cont.*)

Country	**Branch of government that does implementation**	**Basic constitutional provisions on international law and IHRL**	**Specific legislation/decrees/ regulations on IACtHR and domestic law**	**Judicial cases on implementation of IACtHR judgments**	**Differences between provisional measures and full judgment on the merits**
		'Artículo 10 [...] La República de Nicaragua únicamente reconoce obligaciones internacionales sobre su territorio que hayan sido libremente consentidas y de conformidad con la Constitución Política de la República y con las normas de Derecho Internacional. Asimismo, no acepta los tratados suscritos por otros países en los cuales Nicaragua no sea Parte	3–4, 18(9–10, 12, 14). 'Artículo 1.- Créase la Procuraduría para la Defensa de los Derechos Humanos como organismo independiente, con personalidad jurídica propia y autonomía funcional y administrativa.La Procuraduría para la Defensa de los Derechos Humanos estará a cargo de un Procurador y Subprocurador electo por la Asamblea Nacional en la forma establecida en la Constitución Política y en la presente Ley.' 'Artículo 3.- El Procurador es un Comisionado de la Asamblea Nacional electo por ésta para la promoción, defensa y tutela de las garantías constitucionales de los ciudadanos y sus derechos humanos, a cuyos efecto podrá vigilar y controlar la actividad de		

Latin American state practice and primary sources in enforcing Inter-American Court judgments (*cont.*)

Country	Branch of government that does implementation	Basic constitutional provisions on international law and IHRL	Specific legislation/decrees/ regulations on IACtHR and domestic law	Judicial cases on implementation of IACtHR judgments	Differences between provisional measures and full judgment on the merits
		Contratante.' 'Artículo 46 En el territorio nacional toda persona goza de la protección estatal y del reconocimiento de los derechos inherentes a la persona humana, del irrestricto respeto, promoción y protección de los derechos humanos, y de la plena vigencia de los derechos consignados en la Declaración Universal de los Derechos Humanos; en la Declaración	la administración pública, dando cuenta a la Asamblea Nacional. Ejercerá las funciones que les encomienda la Constitución Política y la presente Ley.' 'Artículo 4.- La Procuraduría debe contribuir, con las instituciones estatales y la sociedad civil, a garantizar dentro de un Estado de Derecho, la seguridad de las personas y los derechos humanos incorporados en el Artículo 46 de la Constitución Política.' 'Artículo 18.- Son Atribuciones del Procurador: [...] 9) Conocer los informes que el Estado envía al Comité de Derechos Humanos de la Organización de Naciones Unidas y a la Organización de Estados Americanos. 10) Procurar la conciliación entre las personas cuyos derechos han sido violados		

Latin American state practice and primary sources in enforcing Inter-American Court judgments (*cont.*)

Country	Branch of government that does implementation	Basic constitutional provisions on international law and IHRL	Specific legislation/decrees/ regulations on IACtHR and domestic law	Judicial cases on implementation of IACtHR judgments	Differences between provisional measures and full judgment on the merits
		Americana de Derechos y Deberes del Hombre; en el Pacto Internacional de Derechos Económicos, Sociales y Culturales y en el Pacto Internacional de Derechos Civiles y Políticos de la Organización de las Naciones Unidas y en la Convención Americana de Derechos Humanos de la Organización de Estados Americanos.' 'Artículo 182 La Constitución Politica es la carta	o puestos en peligro con los presuntos responsables de la administración pública. [...] 12) Proponer reformas ante los órganos administrativos, tendientes a promover la tutela de los derechos humanos y recomendar la rectificación de acciones ilegales o arbitrarias. [...] 14) Proponer la suscripción y ratificación de tratados y convenios sobre derechos humanos.' —http://legislacion.asamblea.gob.ni/normaweb.nsf/d0c69e2c91d9955906256a400077164a/29360a59fbb47a5406257116005385eb?OpenDocument We were unable to access the website of the Ministry of Exterior Relations as the website found requires login.		

Latin American state practice and primary sources in enforcing Inter-American Court judgments (*cont.*)

Country	Branch of government that does implementation	Basic constitutional provisions on international law and IHRL	Specific legislation/decrees/ regulations on IACtHR and domestic law	Judicial cases on implementation of IACtHR judgments	Differences between provisional measures and full judgment on the merits
		fundamental de la República; las demas leyes están subordinadas a ella. No tendrán valor alguno las leyes, tratados, decretos, reglamentos, órdenes o disposiciones que se le opongan o alteren sus disposiciones.' https://www.constituteproject.org/constitution/Nicaragua_2014.pdf?lang=es			
Panama	Executive – The Department of International Legal Counselling of the Ministry of Foreign	Constitución Política de Panamá, Art. 4. 'ARTICULO 4. La República de	Decreto Ejecutivo No 367, 17 de Agosto de 2018, Arts. 6, 79–80, 86, 116. Que reorganiza la Estructura Orgánica y Funcional del	Corte Suprema de Justicia, Panamá, 18 Octubre 2004 – Supreme Court Judgment regarding the	No information found in legislation. Case law points to no difference.

Latin American state practice and primary sources in enforcing Inter-American Court judgments (*cont.*)

Country	Branch of government that does implementation	Basic constitutional provisions on international law and IHRL	Specific legislation/decrees/ regulations on IACtHR and domestic law	Judicial cases on implementation of IACtHR judgments	Differences between provisional measures and full judgment on the merits
	Affairs seems to be the one responsible for the implementation of IACtHR decisions.[t]	Panamá acata las normas del Derecho Internacional.' Resolución N° 01, 15 Enero 2018. 'Que establece los principios rectores de la Política Institucional de Derechos Humanos, Acceso a la Justicia y Género del Ministerio Público.' https://ministeriopublico.gob.pa/wp-content/uploads/2018/02/Res.-1-15-01-2018-Establece-los-princi	Ministerio de Relaciones Exteriores: 'Artículo 6. Son funciones del Consejo Nacional de Relaciones Exteriores las seguintes: […] d) Estudiar las medidas que sean necessarias adoptar para la plena efectividad de los Tratados y Acuerdos que haya celebrado el Estado.' 'Artículo 79. Departamento de Asesoría legal Internacional. Le corresponde al Departamento de Asesoría legal Internacional brindar asesoría en materias de Derecho Internacional Comparado, Público y Privado que le sean formuladas en el ejercicio	enforcement of the IACtHR decision on *Baena Ricardo et al. v. Panama* (2001). 'Esta circunstancia parece indicar, que el Estado Panameño se encuentra en proceso de cumplimiento de la sentencia internacional, bajo la supervisión de la Corte Interamericana de Derechos Humanos, y que aún se mantiene activo en el referido tribunal internacional, el caso R.B. y Otros (270 trabajadores -vs-	

t Decreto Ejecutivo No. 367, Article 80(f).

Latin American state practice and primary sources in enforcing Inter-American Court judgments (*cont.*)

Country	Branch of government that does implementation	Basic constitutional provisions on international law and IHRL	Specific legislation/decrees/regulations on IACtHR and domestic law	Judicial cases on implementation of IACtHR judgments	Differences between provisional measures and full judgment on the merits
		pios-rectores-de-la-Pol%C3%ADtica-Institucional-de-Derechos-Humanos.pdf	de las funciones esenciales y específicas de géstion del Ministério. Artículo 80. Son funciones del Departamento de Asesoría legal Internacional las seguintes: [...] c) Emitir opinón sobre resoluciones judiciales, sumarios, fallos y otros documentos legales que procedan del exterior, se expidan a nivel nacional o guarden relación con procesos interpuestos ante organismos internacionales y demás comisiones. [...] f) Atender y ejecutar resoluciones judiciales, sumarios, fallos y otros documentos legales que precedan de autoridades judiciales a nivel nacional o guarden relación con procesos interpuestos ante organismos internacionales y	Panamá). [...] En consecuencia, el Magistrado Sustanciador, en representación de la Sala Tercera de lo Contencioso Administrativo, administrando justicia en nombre de la República y por autoridad de la Ley, NO ADMITE el Proceso de Ejecución de Sentencia [...]'. – https://vlex.com.pa/vid/sentencia-tercera-administrativo-laboral-31666740 Corte Suprema de Justicia, Panamá, 14 Septiembre 2009, Expediente: 331–08 –	

Latin American state practice and primary sources in enforcing Inter-American Court judgments (*cont.*)

Country	Branch of government that does implementation	Basic constitutional provisions on international law and IHRL	Specific legislation/decrees/regulations on IACtHR and domestic law	Judicial cases on implementation of IACtHR judgments	Differences between provisional measures and full judgment on the merits
			demás comisiones.' 'Artículo 85. Departamento de Derechos Humanos. Le corresponde al Departamento de Derechos Humanos cumplir y administrar los convenios y tratados internacionales en materia de Derechos Humanos suscritos por la República de Panamá, incentivando la observancia de los compromisos asumidos en este ámbito y la correcta aplicación. Artículo 86. Son funciones del Departamento de Derechos Humanos las seguientes: […] b) Articular con las instancias correspondientes, la representación del Estado ante la Comisión Interamericana de los Derechos Humanos y la Corte Interamericana de los Derechos	about exercizing conventionality control to adapt domestic law to the ACHR; makes one reference to the IACtHR's decision on preliminary exceptions on *Heliodoro Portugal vs. Panamá* – 'Así pues, a través de la presente decisión, este tribunal de legalidad dará cumplimiento a la obligación tutelar de control de convencionalidad, conforme a los extremos establecidos por la Corte Interamericana.' https://vlex.com.pa/vid/proteccion-derechos-	

Latin American state practice and primary sources in enforcing Inter-American Court judgments (*cont.*)

Country	Branch of government that does implementation	Basic constitutional provisions on international law and IHRL	Specific legislation/decrees/ regulations on IACtHR and domestic law	Judicial cases on implementation of IACtHR judgments	Differences between provisional measures and full judgment on the merits
			Humanos, respecto a denuncias presentadas por presuntar violaciones a los derechos humanos. c) Apoyar en los temas de posición país ante foros nacionales e internacionales de protección y promoción de los derechos humanos e incentivar el cumplimiento de los compromisos internacionales asumidos en dicho ámbito. [...]' 'Artículo 116. Son funciones del Departamento de Relaciones Multilaterales las seguientes: [...] b) Dar seguimiento a los compromisos multilaterales internacionales y regionales de laRepública de Panamá ante el Sistema de las Naciones Unidades, el Sistema Interamericano, los Mecanismos y Foros Regionales de	humanos-septiembre-68805711 Corte Suprema de Justicia, 3 Marzo 2015, Expediente 625-08 – also about conventionality control, also mentions *Heliodoro Portugal v Panamá* – https://vlex.com.pa/vid/primera-instancia-corte-suprema-650686469	

Latin American state practice and primary sources in enforcing Inter-American Court judgments (*cont.*)

Country	Branch of government that does implementation	Basic constitutional provisions on international law and IHRL	Specific legislation/decrees/regulations on IACtHR and domestic law	Judicial cases on implementation of IACtHR judgments	Differences between provisional measures and full judgment on the merits
			Diálogo Político y otros Organismos Internacionales [...]' https://www.gacetaoficial.gob.pa/pdfTemp/28593_A/GacetaNo_28593a_20180820.pdf Resolución No. DS-45-2016, 18 de Febrero de 2016, Ministerio Público, Procuraduría de la Administración, Art. 7. 'Artículo Séptimo: Crear la unidad administrativa denominada Departamento de Derechos Humanos, adscrita a la Dirección de Investigación y Capacitación. El Departamento de Derechos Humanos tendrá las seguientes funciones: * Planificar, coordinar y supervisar la ejecución de las actividades de formación y fortalecimiento institucional en materia de derechos humanos y derecho internacional		

Latin American state practice and primary sources in enforcing Inter-American Court judgments (*cont.*)

Country	Branch of government that does implementation	Basic constitutional provisions on international law and IHRL	Specific legislation/decrees/ regulations on IACtHR and domestic law	Judicial cases on implementation of IACtHR judgments	Differences between provisional measures and full judgment on the merits
			humanitario. * Desarrollar Planes, Programas y Registros de capacitación a los servidore4s públicos en cuanto a la temática de derechos humanos.' —https://www.gacetaoficial.gob.pa/pdfTemp/27986/GacetaNo_27986_20160310.pdf (p. 26). Resolución N° 63, 4 Diciembre 2017. 'Que establece la estructura funcional de La Secretaria de Derechos Humanos, Acceso a la Justicia y Género, se le asignan funciones y modifica la Resolución N° 25 de 19 de marzo de 2013'. 'Segundo: Serán funciones de la Secretaría de Derechos Humanos, Acceso a la Justicia y Género del Ministerio Público: [...] 2. Evaluar, monitorear y dar seguimiento a la		

Latin American state practice and primary sources in enforcing Inter-American Court judgments (*cont.*)

Country	Branch of government that does implementation	Basic constitutional provisions on international law and IHRL	Specific legislation/decrees/ regulations on IACtHR and domestic law	Judicial cases on implementation of IACtHR judgments	Differences between provisional measures and full judgment on the merits
			política institucional de derechos humanos, acceso a la justicia y género, con el fin de promover el cumplimiento de las normas jurídicas que constituyen el marco normativo que fundamenta la creación de la secrataría, así como crear los mecanismos que sean necesarios para lograr la coordinación entre los diferentes ámbitos del Ministerio Púbilco, responsables de su aplicación.' https://ministeriopublico.gob.pa/wp-content/uploads/2018/02/Res.-63-4-12-2017-Establece-la-estructura-funcional-de-la-Secretar%C3%ADa-de-Derechos-Humanos.pdf		
Paraguay	Executive – The Interinstitutional Executive	Constitución Nacional, 1992, Arts. 142, 143(5).	Decreto N° 4367, 2015, Arts. 3–5, 8. 'Por cual se reestructura da Comisión Interinstitucional	No cases found concerning implementation of an	Decree N° 4367 does not distinguish between 'judgments,

Latin American state practice and primary sources in enforcing Inter-American Court judgments (*cont.*)

Country	Branch of government that does implementation	Basic constitutional provisions on international law and IHRL	Specific legislation/decrees/ regulations on IACtHR and domestic law	Judicial cases on implementation of IACtHR judgments	Differences between provisional measures and full judgment on the merits
	Commission, presided by the vice-president of Paraguay, is the organ responsible for the execution of the necessary actions for the implementation of the IACtHR's judgments.[u]	'Artículo 142 – DE LA DENUNCIA DE LOS TRATADOS Los tratados internacionales relativos a los derechos humanos no podrán ser denunciados sino por los procedimientos que rigen para la enmienda de esta Constitución.' 'Artículo 143 – DE LAS RELACIONES INTERNACIONALES	responsable de la ejecución de la acciones necesarias para el cumplimiento de las sentencias internacionales (CICSI): [...]' 'Art. 3°.- La Comisión Interinstitucional Ejecutiva tiene como objetivos establecer el cronograma de acciones y la implementación del mismo, para el cumplimiento efoctivo de las Sentencias, Recomendaciones, Solicitudes y otros compromisos internacionales en materia de derechos humanos, emanados tanto del Sistema Interamericano de Derechos Humanos, de los diferentes órganos de tratados,	IACtHR judgment by searching for every judgment against Paraguay in the IACtHR using the Supreme Court of Justice's search mechanism: https://www.csj.gov.py/jurisprudencia/# Corte Suprema de Justicia, Resolución N° 677, 2007. Case broadly discussing the IACtHR jurisprudence on pre-trial detention: https://www.csj.gov.py/jurispru	recommendations, and requests',[v] and does not mention provisional measures specifically. Decree N° 1730 also does not make a distinction.

u Decreto n. 4367, 2015, Art. 3.

v 'Sentencias, recomendaciones y solicitudes.'

Latin American state practice and primary sources in enforcing Inter-American Court judgments (*cont.*)

Country	Branch of government that does implementation	Basic constitutional provisions on international law and IHRL	Specific legislation/decrees/ regulations on IACtHR and domestic law	Judicial cases on implementation of IACtHR judgments	Differences between provisional measures and full judgment on the merits
		La República del Paraguay, en sus relaciones internacionales, acepta el derecho internacional y se ajusta a los siguientes principios: […] 5. la protección internacional de los derechos humanos.' https://www.oas.org/juridico/spanish/par_res3.htm	mecanismos y relatorías del Sistema de Naciones Unidas.' 'Art. 4°.- La Presidencia de la Comisión estará a cargo de la Vicepresidencia de la República.' 'Art. 5°.- La Coordinación General de la Comisión estará a cargo del Ministerio de Relaciones Exteriores, que actuará, además, como soporte técnico y documental de la misma.' 'Art. 8°.- El Consejo Consultivo se reunirá en pleno o con las instituciones que resulten efectivamente competentes para las Sentencias, Solicitudes, Recomendaciones y otros compromisos internacionales en materia de Derechos Humanos, a convocatoria de la Coordinación General. Las instituciones que resulten competentes para las	dencia/home/DocumentoJurisprudencia?codigo=13879 On the same topic, see also: https://www.csj.gov.py/jurisprudencia/home/DocumentoJurisprudencia?codigo=14608	

Latin American state practice and primary sources in enforcing Inter-American Court judgments (*cont.*)

Country	Branch of government that does implementation	Basic constitutional provisions on international law and IHRL	Specific legislation/decrees/ regulations on IACtHR and domestic law	Judicial cases on implementation of IACtHR judgments	Differences between provisional measures and full judgment on the merits
			mismas, deberán presentar un biforme sobre los planes y acciones a desarrollar para su cumplimiento en cada reunión a la cual son convocadas.' —https://www.presidencia.gov.py/url-sistema-visor-decretos/index.php/ver_decreto/18280 Decreto N° 1730, 27 Marzo 2009, Art. 8. 'Por el cual se establecen la organización y atribuciones del Viceministério de Justicia y Derechos Humanos, dependiente del Ministerio de Justicia y Trabajo.' 'Art. 8 – Dirección General de Derechos Humanos. La Dirección General de Derechos Humanos está encargada de coordinar, articular, formular u ejecutar acciones que posibiliten dotar de		

Latin American state practice and primary sources in enforcing Inter-American Court judgments (*cont.*)

Country	Branch of government that does implementation	Basic constitutional provisions on international law and IHRL	Specific legislation/decrees/ regulations on IACtHR and domestic law	Judicial cases on implementation of IACtHR judgments	Differences between provisional measures and full judgment on the merits
			institucionalidad permanente a la promoción, defensa y realización de los derechos humanos a través del compromiso de las autoridades, otros funcionarios públicos y de la organizaciones no gibernamentales. La Dirección General de Derechos Humanos tine las seguientes funciones: a) Efectuar el seguimiento y monitoreo de la obligaciones asumidas por el Estado Paraguayo ante los organismos regionales e internacionales procurando la adecuación del accionar del Estado Paraguayo a las exigencias del ordenamiento internacional de Derechos Humanos.' Resolución N° 584, 04 julio 2016, Anexo 1, Reglamento Interno de la		

Latin American state practice and primary sources in enforcing Inter-American Court judgments (*cont.*)

Country	Branch of government that does implementation	Basic constitutional provisions on international law and IHRL	Specific legislation/decrees/regulations on IACtHR and domestic law	Judicial cases on implementation of IACtHR judgments	Differences between provisional measures and full judgment on the merits
			Red de Derechos Humanos del Poder Ejecutivo, Art. 9. 'Art. 9 Funciones: La Red tendrá las seguientes funciones: [...] 6) Velar por la vigencia y la aplicación de los Tratados y Convenios Internacionales de Derechos Humanos, adecuando el accionar del Estado paraguayo a las exigencias del ordenamiento internacional.' —https://www.derechoshumanos.gov.py/application/files/4614/7309/9770/Reglamento_Red.pdf		
			JUDICIARY-LED		
Brazil	Judiciary (scholarly view) – Superior Court of Justice implements foreign judgments via homologation (part	Constituição Federal, 1988, Arts. 84, 105, 109. 'Art. 84. Compete privativamente ao Presidente da	Portaria Nº 412, de 19 de Julho de 2023, Art. 1. 'Art. 1º Instituir, no âmbito do Ministério dos Direitos Humanos e da Cidadania – MDHC, a Rede Nacional de Implementação de	Tribunal Regional Federal, 1ª Região, Acórdão 1023279-03.2018.4.01.0000: https://pje2g.trf1.jus.br/consultapublica/Consul	Decreto N. 9673 and Portaria Nº 412, de 19 de Julho de 2023 make no distinction. Código de Processo Civil, 2015, Art. 962.

Latin American state practice and primary sources in enforcing Inter-American Court judgments (*cont.*)

Country	Branch of government that does implementation	Basic constitutional provisions on international law and IHRL	Specific legislation/decrees/regulations on IACtHR and domestic law	Judicial cases on implementation of IACtHR judgments	Differences between provisional measures and full judgment on the merits
	of the scholarship argues that international courts' judgments are equivalent to foreign judgments and could be implemented the same way); Federal judges responsible to enforce decisions in cases in which the state is part, or in reference to cases founded on a treaty or relative to human rights. Or the Attorney-General is responsible, by asking the Superior	República [...] VII – manter relações com Estados estrangeiros e acreditar seus representantes diplomáticos; VIII – celebrar tratados, convenções e atos internacionais, sujeitos a referendo do Congresso Nacional.' 'Art. 105. Compete ao Superior Tribunal de Justiça: I – processar e julgar, originariamente: i) a homologação de sentenças estrangeiras e a	Decisões dos Sistemas Internacionais de Direitos Humanos – RNID/SIDH, com a finalidade de assegurar o cumprimento das decisões proferidas pelos órgãos internacionais de direitos humanos previstos nos tratados aos quais a República Federativa do Brasil se encontra juridicamente vinculada. §1º Dentre as finalidades da RNID/SIDH, inclui-se a implementação de medidas provisórias e de sentenças proferidas pela Corte Interamericana de Direitos Humanos. §2º A RNID/SIDH também tem como objetivo implementar as medidas cautelares e afins, assim como as recomendações proferidas pela Comissão	taPublica/DetalheProcessoConsultaPublica/listView.seam?ca=ce4c42463e75b1af70580d5894ffbf9836a79047b9387b97 or https://pje2g.trf1.jus.br/consultapublica/ConsultaPublica/listView.seam Supremo Tribunal Federal, HC 115539 / RO – refers to IACtHR's Resolution concerning the case of the *Urso Branco Prison*. —https://redir.stf.jus.br/paginadorpub/paginador.jsp?docTP=TP&docID=4531406	'Art. 962. É passível de execução a decisão estrangeira concessiva de medida de urgência. § 1º A execução no Brasil de decisão interlocutória estrangeira concessiva de medida de urgência dar-se-á por carta rogatória. § 2º A medida de urgência concedida sem audiência do réu poderá ser executada, desde que garantido o contraditório em momento posterior. § 3º O juízo sobre a urgência da medida compete

Latin American state practice and primary sources in enforcing Inter-American Court judgments (*cont.*)

Country	Branch of government that does implementation	Basic constitutional provisions on international law and IHRL	Specific legislation/decrees/regulations on IACtHR and domestic law	Judicial cases on implementation of IACtHR judgments	Differences between provisional measures and full judgment on the merits
	Court of Justice to send the case to Federal Courts. Executive – the Ministry of Human Rights and Citizenship, and its organs, is responsible to take actions toward the implementation of IACtHR decisions; other entities are also engaged as needed.[w]	concessão de exequatur às cartas rogatórias; […] Art. 109. Aos juízes federais compete processar e julgar: I – as causas em que a União, entidade autárquica ou empresa pública federal forem interessadas na condição de autoras, rés, assistentes ou oponentes, exceto as de falência, as de acidentes de trabalho e as sujeitas	Interamericana de Direitos Humanos e pelos órgãos de tratados do Sistema de Direitos Humanos da Organização das Nações Unidas (ONU), bem como cumprir os acordos celebrados pela República Federativa do Brasil e homologados pela Comissão Interamericana de Direitos Humanos.' DECRETO Nº 11.341, DE 1º DE JANEIRO DE 2023, Anexo I, Art. 6. ANEXO I – ESTRUTURA REGIMENTAL DO MINISTÉRIO DOS DIREITOS HUMANOS E DA CIDADANIA 'Art. 6º À Assessoria Especial de Assuntos Internacionais compete:		exclusivamente à autoridade jurisdicional prolatora da decisão estrangeira. § 4º Quando dispensada a homologação para que a sentença estrangeira produza efeitos no Brasil, a decisão concessiva de medida de urgência dependerá, para produzir efeitos, de ter sua validade expressamente reconhecida pelo juiz

w Decree No. 11.341, 1 January 2023; Portaria Nº 412, DE 19 DE JULHO DE 2023.

Latin American state practice and primary sources in enforcing Inter-American Court judgments (*cont.*)

Country	Branch of government that does implementation	Basic constitutional provisions on international law and IHRL	Specific legislation/decrees/ regulations on IACtHR and domestic law	Judicial cases on implementation of IACtHR judgments	Differences between provisional measures and full judgment on the merits
		à Justiça Eleitoral e à Justiça do Trabalho; [...] III – as causas fundadas em tratado ou contrato da União com Estado estrangeiro ou organismo internacional; [...] V-A as causas relativas a direitos humanos a que se refere o § 5º deste artigo; (Incluído pela Emenda Constitucional nº 45, de 2004) [...] § 5º Nas hipóteses de grave violação de direitos humanos, o	I – articular a implementação de atos necessários ao cumprimento de decisões de organismos internacionais motivadas por violação dos direitos humanos; [...] III – coordenar e articular o cumprimento dos compromissos decorrentes da assinatura de tratados de direitos humanos pelo Estado brasileiro; IV – coordenar, em articulação com o Ministério das Relações Exteriores, a elaboração de relatórios sobre o cumprimento de compromissos decorrentes de tratados de direitos humanos de que o Estado brasileiro faça parte e de relatórios do Estado brasileiro ao Mecanismo de Revisão Periódica Universal da ONU, aos		competente para dar-lhe cumprimento, dispensada a homologação pelo Superior Tribunal de Justiça.'

Latin American state practice and primary sources in enforcing Inter-American Court judgments (*cont.*)

Country	Branch of government that does implementation	Basic constitutional provisions on international law and IHRL	Specific legislation/decrees/regulations on IACtHR and domestic law	Judicial cases on implementation of IACtHR judgments	Differences between provisional measures and full judgment on the merits
		Procurador-Geral da República, com a finalidade de assegurar o cumprimento de obrigações decorrentes de tratados internacionais de direitos humanos dos quais o Brasil seja parte, poderá suscitar, perante o Superior Tribunal de Justiça, em qualquer fase do inquérito ou processo, incidente de deslocamento de competência para a Justiça Federal.' http://www.planalto.gov.br/ccivil	órgãos de tratados ou procedimentos especiais da ONU ou da OEA, às relatorias temáticas da Comissão Interamericana de Direitos Humanos – CIDH e aos demais órgãos de tratados ou procedimentos internacionais de direitos humanos.' On entities specifically created to monitor implementation of IACtHR decisions, see Resolução Nº 364 de 12/01/2021, arts. 1–2. https://atos.cnj.jus.br/atos/detalhar/3659 Legislation referring to the scholarly view of the Judiciary's role in enforcing IACtHR judgments as foreign decisions: Código de Processo Civil, 2015, Arts. 515, 960. 'Art. 515. São títulos executivos judiciais, cujo cumprimento dar-		

Latin American state practice and primary sources in enforcing Inter-American Court judgments (*cont.*)

Country	Branch of government that does implementation	Basic constitutional provisions on international law and IHRL	Specific legislation/decrees/regulations on IACtHR and domestic law	Judicial cases on implementation of IACtHR judgments	Differences between provisional measures and full judgment on the merits
		_03/Constituicao/Constituicao.htm#art105I	se-á de acordo com os artigos previstos neste Título: [...] VIII – a sentença estrangeira homologada pelo Superior Tribunal de Justiça; [...] Art. 960. A homologação de decisão estrangeira será requerida por ação de homologação de decisão estrangeira, salvo disposição especial em sentido contrário prevista em tratado.' http://www.planalto.gov.br/ccivil_03/_ato2015-2018/2015/lei/l13105.htm#art960 Regimento Interno do STJ, Arts. 216(A),(N). 'Art. 216-A. É atribuição do Presidente do Tribunal homologar sentença estrangeira, ressalvado o disposto no art. 216-K. [...] Art. 216-N. A sentença estrangeira		

Latin American state practice and primary sources in enforcing Inter-American Court judgments (*cont.*)

Country	Branch of government that does implementation	Basic constitutional provisions on international law and IHRL	Specific legislation/decrees/ regulations on IACtHR and domestic law	Judicial cases on implementation of IACtHR judgments	Differences between provisional measures and full judgment on the merits
			homologada será executada por carta de sentença no Juízo Federal competente.' https://www.stj.jus.br/publicacaoinstitucional/index.php/Regimento/article/view/3115/3839		
Dominican Republic	Judiciary-led – the Constitutional Tribunal is responsible for regulating the execution of IACtHR's decisions.[x]	Constitución de la República Dominicana, 2015, Arts. 26, 74, 185. 'Artículo 26.- Relaciones internacionales y derecho internacional. La República	Ley No. 137-11, 11 Junio 2011, Ley Orgánica del Tribunal Constitucional y de los procedimientos constitucionales. 'CONSIDERANDO DECIMOTERCERO: Que dentro de los procedimientos constitucionales a ser regulados se encuentra el control preventivo de los tratados internacionales y la	Constitutional Tribunal, Decision TC/0256/14, 2014. Direct Action of Unconstitutionality against the Dominican instrument of acceptance of the IACtHR's competence: 'DECLARAR la inconstitucionalidad	No indication of different treatment found in legislation or case law, although Law N° 137-11 only mentions as a constitutional procedure under the responsibility of the Constitutional

x Ley No. 137–11, 11 Junio 2011, Considerando 13°. See also Ley Orgánica del Tribunal Constitucional y de los procedimientos constitucionales. G. O. No. 10622 del 15 de junio de 2011.

Latin American state practice and primary sources in enforcing Inter-American Court judgments (*cont.*)

Country	Branch of government that does implementation	Basic constitutional provisions on international law and IHRL	Specific legislation/decrees/ regulations on IACtHR and domestic law	Judicial cases on implementation of IACtHR judgments	Differences between provisional measures and full judgment on the merits
		Dominicana es un Estado miembro de la comunidad internacional, abierto a la cooperación y apegado a las normas del derecho internacional, en consecuencia: 1) Reconoce y aplica las normas del derecho internacional, general y americano, en la medida en que sus poderes públicos las hayan adoptado;	regulación de la ejecución de las sentencias de la Corte Interamericana de Derechos Humanos.' 'Artículo 2.- Objeto y Alcance. Esta ley tiene por finalidad regular la organización del Tribunal Constitucional y el ejercicio de la justicia constitucional para garantizar la supremacía y defensa de las normas y principios constitucionales y del Derecho Internacional vigente en la República, su uniforme interpretación y aplicación, así como los derechos y libertades fundamentales consagrados en la Constitución o en los	del instrumento de aceptación de la competencia de la Corte IDH suscrito por el presidente de la República Dominicana el diecinueve (19) de febrero de mil novecientos noventa y nueve (1999), por los motivos que figuran en el cuerpo de esta sentencia' (p 49). https://tribunalsitestorage.blob.core.windows.net/media/15760/sentencia-tc-0256-14-c.pdf Constitutional Tribunal,	Tribunal the regulation of execution of '*judgments*'[y] of the IACtHR.

y 'Sentencias.'

Latin American state practice and primary sources in enforcing Inter-American Court judgments (*cont.*)

Country	Branch of government that does implementation	Basic constitutional provisions on international law and IHRL	Specific legislation/decrees/ regulations on IACtHR and domestic law	Judicial cases on implementation of IACtHR judgments	Differences between provisional measures and full judgment on the merits
		2) Las normas vigentes de convenios internacionales ratificados regirán en el ámbito interno, una vez publicados de manera oficial; 3) Las relaciones internacionales de la República Dominicana se fundamentan y rigen por la afirmación y promoción de sus valores e intereses nacionales, el respeto a los derechos humanos y al derecho	instrumentos internacionales de derechos humanos aplicables. [...]' 'Artículo 6.- Infracciones Constitucionales. Se tendrá por infringida la Constitución cuando haya contradicción del texto de la norma, acto u omisión cuestionado, de sus efectos o de su interpretación o aplicación con los valores, principios y reglas contenidos en la Constitución y en los tratados internacionales sobre derechos humanos suscritos y ratificados por la República Dominicana o cuando los mismos tengan como consecuencia restar efectividad a los principios y mandatos contenidos en los mismos' 'Artículo 7.- Principios Rectores. El sistema de justicia constitucional se rige por los siguientes	Decision TC/0168/13, 2013 – refers to the IACtHR's judgment on the *Case of the Girls Yean and Bosico v Dominican Republic*. (pp. 68–75) The Constitutional Tribunal relies on discretion and on 'margin of appreciation' ([2.5]–[2.6], [2.7]–[2.12]). —https://tribunalsitestorage.blob.core.windows.net/media/7592/sentencia-tc-0168-13-c.pdf	

Latin American state practice and primary sources in enforcing Inter-American Court judgments (*cont.*)

Country	Branch of government that does implementation	Basic constitutional provisions on international law and IHRL	Specific legislation/decrees/ regulations on IACtHR and domestic law	Judicial cases on implementation of IACtHR judgments	Differences between provisional measures and full judgment on the merits
		internacional; 4) En igualdad de condiciones con otros Estados, la República Dominicana acepta un ordenamiento jurídico internacional que garantice el respeto de los derechos fundamentales, la paz, la justicia, y el desarrollo político, social, económico y cultural de las naciones. Se compromete a actuar en el plano internacional, regional y nacional de modo compatible	principios rectores: [...] 10) Interdependencia. Los valores, principios y reglas contenidos en la Constitución y en los tratados internacionales sobre derechos humanos adoptados por los poderes públicos de la República Dominicana, conjuntamente con los derechos y garantías fundamentales de igual naturaleza a los expresamente contenidos en aquéllos, integran el bloque de constitucionalidad que sirve de parámetro al control de la constitucionalidad y al cual está sujeto la validez formal y material de las normas infraconstitucionales. [...] 13) Vinculatoriedad. Las decisiones del Tribunal Constitucional y las interpretaciones que adoptan o hagan los tribunales		

Latin American state practice and primary sources in enforcing Inter-American Court judgments (*cont.*)

Country	Branch of government that does implementation	Basic constitutional provisions on international law and IHRL	Specific legislation/decrees/ regulations on IACtHR and domestic law	Judicial cases on implementation of IACtHR judgments	Differences between provisional measures and full judgment on the merits
		con los intereses nacionales, la convivencia pacífica entre los pueblos y los deberes de solidaridad con todas las naciones; […]' 'Artículo 74.- Principios de reglamentación e interpretación. La interpretación y reglamentación de los derechos y garantías fundamentales, reconocidos en la presente Constitución, se rigen por los principios	internacionales en materia de derechos humanos, constituyen precedentes vinculantes para los poderes públicos y todos los órganos del Estado. […]' https://poderjudicial.gob.do/wp-content/uploads/2021/06/LEY_137_11.pdf Regulamento No 142-17 de la Ley Orgánica del Ministerio de Relaciones Exteriores y del Servicio Exterior, 2017, Arts. 9, 18 'Artículo 9. De la Cancillería. La Cancillería es el órgano central y la sede oficial del Ministerio de Relaciones Exteriores. Estará conformada de acuerdo con la siguiente estructura: […] 3) Viceministerio de Política Exterior Multilateral, con las siguientes dependencias: […] d) Dirección de Derechos		

Latin American state practice and primary sources in enforcing Inter-American Court judgments (*cont.*)

Country	Branch of government that does implementation	Basic constitutional provisions on international law and IHRL	Specific legislation/decrees/ regulations on IACtHR and domestic law	Judicial cases on implementation of IACtHR judgments	Differences between provisional measures and full judgment on the merits
		siguientes: […] 3) Los tratados, pactos y convenciones relativos a derechos humanos, suscritos y ratificados por el Estado dominicano, tienen jerarquía constitucional y son de aplicación directa e inmediata por los tribunales y demás órganos del Estado; […]'; 'Artículo 185.- Atribuciones. El Tribunal Constitucional será competente para conocer en única instancia: […] 2) El	Humanos […]' 'Artículo 18. Del propósito y funciones de las Direcciones del Viceministerio de Política Exterior Multilateral. El propósito y funciones de las dependencias de este Viceministerio son las siguientes: […] 18.4. Dirección de Derechos Humanos. Propósito: Apoyar los esfuerzos del Estado dominicano y la comunidad internacional en la promoción y defensa de los derechos humanos dentro del marco del derecho interno y las normas del Derecho Internacional y presentar la posición del país ante los organismos internacionales en esa materia. Funciones: […] b) Participar en la elaboración, conjuntamente con las lemas jpstanciás cpppetentes,		

Latin American state practice and primary sources in enforcing Inter-American Court judgments (*cont.*)

Country	Branch of government that does implementation	Basic constitutional provisions on international law and IHRL	Specific legislation/decrees/ regulations on IACtHR and domestic law	Judicial cases on implementation of IACtHR judgments	Differences between provisional measures and full judgment on the merits
		control preventivo de los tratados internacionales antes de su ratificación por el órgano legislativo; […]'. —http://extwprlegs1.fao.org/docs/pdf/dom187716.pdf	de los informes periódicos o cualquier otro que en materia de derechos humanos deba presentar la República Dominicana ante, los organismos internacionales. […] d) Analizar e interpretar, conjuntamente con las instituciones nacionales competentes, los informes o documentos que recibe el país por parte de las entidades internacionales del sistema universal y regional de derechos humanos sobre temas migratorios, laborales, mujer, envejecientes, discapacitados, niños y niñas, derechos civiles y políticos, así como derechos económicos, sociales y culturales. e) Canalizar las convocatorias a seminarios, paneles, asambleas y demás mecanismos de seguimiento o		

Latin American state practice and primary sources in enforcing Inter-American Court judgments (*cont.*)

Country	Branch of government that does implementation	Basic constitutional provisions on international law and IHRL	Specific legislation/decrees/regulations on IACtHR and domestic law	Judicial cases on implementation of IACtHR judgments	Differences between provisional measures and full judgment on the merits
			implementación de programas sobre derechos humanos en los cuales el país participa, en coordinación con las diferentes entid vinculadas al tema.' —https://www.mirex.gob.do/transparencia/media/base-legal/base-legal-leyes/Reglamento_no_142_17.pdf Dec. No 408-04 que integra la Comision Interinstitucional para los Derechos Humanos adscrita a la Secretaria de Estado de Relaciones Exteriores, Art. 5. 'ARTICULO 5.- La Comision tendra como proposito asistir y apoyar a1 Estado en todos los asuntos relativos a los derechos humanos a traves de las recomendaciones que estime de lugar elevar al Poder Ejecutivo para su decision, y muy		

Latin American state practice and primary sources in enforcing Inter-American Court judgments (*cont.*)

Country	Branch of government that does implementation	Basic constitutional provisions on international law and IHRL	Specific legislation/decrees/regulations on IACtHR and domestic law	Judicial cases on implementation of IACtHR judgments	Differences between provisional measures and full judgment on the merits
			especialmente en la preparacion y presentacion de los informes periodicos a las instancias correspondientes dispuestas por los instrumentos internacionales pertinentes.' https://egdhdih.mil.do/wp-content/uploads/Decreto-408-04.pdf		
Peru	Judiciary – The Ministry of Foreign Affairs communicates the decision to the President of the Supreme Court, who sends it to the chamber where internal remedies were exhausted for the execution by a specialized or mixed	Código Procesal Constitucional, Art. 115. 'Artículo 115.- Ejecución de resoluciones Las resoluciones de los organismos jurisdiccionales a cuya competencia se haya sometido expresamente el Estado peruano no requieren, para su	Ley Nº 27775, Ley que regula el procedimiento de ejecución de sentencias emitidas por tribunales supranacionales, Art. 2. 'Artículo 2. – a) Competencia.- La sentencia emitida por el Tribunal Internacional será transcrita por el Ministerio de Relaciones Exteriores al Presidente de la Corte Suprema, quien la remitirá a la Sala en que se agotó la jurisdicción interna, disponiendo su ejecución por el Juez	Casación N° 00277, 2012 (Devolución de Pago en Exceso) – refers to the case of the *'Five Pensioners' v Peru.* https://www.corteidh.or.cr/docs/casos/articulos/seriec_98_ing.pdf Recurso de Nulidad N° 2014, 2013 – refers to the *Case of Baldeón-García v Perú.* https://www.corteidh.or.cr/	Ley N° 27775, Art. 2 (b)–(e). Provisional measures: immediate compliance; the specialized or mixed judge must order execution within 24 hours after receiving communication of the decision. Full judgment on the merits: depends on

Latin American state practice and primary sources in enforcing Inter-American Court judgments (*cont.*)

Country	Branch of government that does implementation	Basic constitutional provisions on international law and IHRL	Specific legislation/decrees/ regulations on IACtHR and domestic law	Judicial cases on implementation of IACtHR judgments	Differences between provisional measures and full judgment on the merits
	judge.[z] Where the amount of compensation needs to be established, the Ministry of Justice (now 'Ministry of Justice and Human Rights') can contradict the amount intended by the executor, but the process is still in the hands of the specialized or mixed judge.	validez y eficacia, de reconocimiento, revisión, ni examen previo alguno. Dichas resoluciones son comunicadas por el Ministerio de Relaciones Exteriores al Presidente del Poder Judicial, quien a su vez, las remite al tribunal donde se agotó la jurisdicción interna y dispone su ejecución por el juez competente, de conformidad con lo	Especializado o Mixto que conoció el proceso previo. En el caso de no existir proceso interno previo, dispondrá que el Juez Especializado o Mixto competente conozca de la ejecución de la resolución.' Decreto Legislativo N° 1068, Art. 7. 'Artículo 7°.- De las Atribuciones y Obligaciones del Consejo de Defensa Jurídica del Estado El Consejo de Defensa Jurídica del Estado tiene las siguientes atribuciones y obligaciones: [...] m) Realizar todas las acciones que permitan cumplir las sentencias recaídas en los procesos o procedimientos donde el Estado	docs/casos/articulos/seriec_147_ing.pdf Sala Penal Permanente, Recurso de Nulidad N.° 2752–2017, Lima – addresses *Ivcher Bronstein v Peru.* https://jurisprudencia.pj.gob.pe/jurisprudenciaweb/faces/page/resultado.xhtml#no-back-button	whether the decision a) asks for a determined financial reparation, or b) a financial reparation that still needs to be determined, or c) if it still requires fixation of patrimonial responsibility and of the monetary amount of reparation. If a): The specialized or mixed judge must notify the Ministry of Justice and Human Rights so that it pays the amount

z Ley N° 27775, artículo 2(a).

Latin American state practice and primary sources in enforcing Inter-American Court judgments (*cont.*)

Country	Branch of government that does implementation	Basic constitutional provisions on international law and IHRL	Specific legislation/decrees/ regulations on IACtHR and domestic law	Judicial cases on implementation of IACtHR judgments	Differences between provisional measures and full judgment on the merits
		previsto por la Ley Nº 27775, que regula el procedimiento de ejecución de sentencias emitidas por tribunales supranacionales.' Constitución Política del Peru, 1993, Art. 44, 55–57. 'Artículo 44.- Deberes del Estado Son deberes primordiales del Estado: defender la soberanía nacional; garantizar la plena vigencia de los derechos humanos; proteger a la población de las amenazas contra su	es parte.' DS. Nº 017-2008 – JUS Reglamento del Sistema de Defensa Jurídica del Estado, 2008, Art. 28. 'Artículo 28.- Del procedimiento en la atención de las denuncias o demandas presentadas contra el Estado en materia de Derechos Humanos – La atención de denuncias o demandas internacionales contra el Estado en materia de derechos humanos seguirá el siguiente trámite: 1. El Ministerio de Relaciones Exteriores, por intermedio de la Dirección General de Derechos Humanos, informará y remitirá al Consejo toda denuncia o demanda que se formule contra el Estado peruano ante los diferentes órganos o mecanismos de protección de Derechos Humanos.		established in the decision within 10 days; If b): The specialized or mixed judge will transfer the request of the executor with the available evidence to the Ministry of Justice within 10 days; the Ministry of Justice and Human Rights may offer contradiction on the amount intended; regardless of contradiction, the judge will order the evidence to be produced in a conciliation hearing in no more than 30 days, and will decide

Latin American state practice and primary sources in enforcing Inter-American Court judgments (*cont.*)

Country	Branch of government that does implementation	Basic constitutional provisions on international law and IHRL	Specific legislation/decrees/regulations on IACtHR and domestic law	Judicial cases on implementation of IACtHR judgments	Differences between provisional measures and full judgment on the merits
		seguridad; y promover el bienestar general que se fundamenta en la justicia y en el desarrollo integral y equilibrado de la Nación.' 'Artículo 55.- Tratados Los tratados celebrados por el Estado y en vigor forman parte del derecho nacional.' 'Artículo 56.- Aprobación de tratados Los tratados deben ser aprobados por el Congreso antes de su ratificación por el	Asimismo, el Consejo remitirá copia de la denuncia o demanda a la Entidad que haya generado el precedente, con el respectivo informe, a fin que tome conocimiento de los hechos y, de ser el caso, adopte las medidas pertinentes de acuerdo a lo dispuesto en el artículo 70 inciso 70.3 de la Ley Nº 28411 – Ley General del Sistema Nacional de Presupuesto. 2. El Consejo remitirá al Procurador Público Supranacional la denuncia o la demanda y sus anexos, enviados por la Comisión o por la Corte, según sea el caso, así como toda la documentación posterior que se genere en el caso, informando asimismo a la Alta Dirección del Ministerio de Justicia. […]		within 15 days; an appeal will have suspensive effect and will be decided by the Chamber of the corresponding Superior Court within the same deadline; If c): If the judgment declares that the party suffered damages and has established that the party's right should be guaranteed according to the domestic jurisdiction, the party must file the corresponding suit according to the abbreviated/abridged procedure according to Title II of the Fifth

Latin American state practice and primary sources in enforcing Inter-American Court judgments (*cont.*)

Country	Branch of government that does implementation	Basic constitutional provisions on international law and IHRL	Specific legislation/decrees/regulations on IACtHR and domestic law	Judicial cases on implementation of IACtHR judgments	Differences between provisional measures and full judgment on the merits
		Presidente de la República, siempre que versen sobre las siguientes materias: 1. Derechos Humanos. 2. Soberanía, dominio o integridad del Estado. 3. Defensa Nacional. 4. Obligaciones financieras del Estado. (...)' 'Artículo 57.- Tratados Ejecutivos El Presidente de la República puede celebrar o ratificar	4. Toda documentación desde y hacia los diversos órganos y mecanismos internacionales de protección de derechos humanos se remitirá por la vía oficial a través de la Dirección General de Derechos Humanos del Ministerio de Relaciones Exteriores.' —https://www.oas.org/juridico/PDFs/mesicic4_per_ds017_08.pdf		Section of the Code of Civil Process.[aa]

aa See Ley N° 27775, Artículo 2(b)–(e).

Latin American state practice and primary sources in enforcing Inter-American Court judgments (*cont.*)

Country	Branch of government that does implementation	Basic constitutional provisions on international law and IHRL	Specific legislation/decrees/ regulations on IACtHR and domestic law	Judicial cases on implementation of IACtHR judgments	Differences between provisional measures and full judgment on the merits
		tratados o adherir a éstos sin el requisito de la aprobación previa del Congreso en materias no contempladas en el artículo precedente. En todos esos casos, debe dar cuenta al Congreso. Cuando el tratado afecte disposiciones constitucionales debe ser aprobado por el mismo procedimiento que rige la reforma de la Constitución, antes de ser ratificado por el Presidente de la República.			

Latin American state practice and primary sources in enforcing Inter-American Court judgments (*cont.*)

Country	Branch of government that does implementation	Basic constitutional provisions on international law and IHRL	Specific legislation/decrees/regulations on IACtHR and domestic law	Judicial cases on implementation of IACtHR judgments	Differences between provisional measures and full judgment on the merits
		La denuncia de los tratados es potestad del Presidente de la República, con cargo de dar cuenta al Congreso. En el caso de los tratados sujetos a aprobación del Congreso, la denuncia requiere aprobación previa de éste.'			
LEGISLATIVE-LED (OR INDEPENDENT ENTITY CREATED/HARBORED BY THE LEGISLATIVE)					
Barbados	Unclear, likely Legislative-led. Considering the Explanatory Memorandum of the *Offences Against the Person (Amendment) Act,*	Constitution, 1966, Preamble. 'Now, therefore, the people of Barbados (a) proclaim that they are a sovereign nation founded upon principles that	No legislation found concerning the relationship between the IACtHR and domestic law. The *Offences Against the Person (Amendment) Act, 2018,* and the *Offences Against the Person (Amendment) Act, 2019,* were passed to substitute a section of	Caribbean Court of Justice, *Jabari Sensimania Nervais v. The Queen* and *Dwayne Omar Severin v. The Queen* [2018] IACtHR's 19 (AJ) – addresses the IACtHR's *Boyce et al. v*	No information found.

Latin American state practice and primary sources in enforcing Inter-American Court judgments (*cont.*)

Country	Branch of government that does implementation	Basic constitutional provisions on international law and IHRL	Specific legislation/decrees/regulations on IACtHR and domestic law	Judicial cases on implementation of IACtHR judgments	Differences between provisional measures and full judgment on the merits
	2018 which acknowledges the IACtHR's *Tyrone Dacosta Cadagon v. Barbados* decision, it may be assumed that the Legislative is responsible for implementation; however, given the type of reparation required by the IACtHR in this case, perhaps only the Legislative would be able to implement this part of the decision.	acknowledge the supremacy of God, the dignity of the human person, their unshakeable faith in fundamental human rights and freedoms and the position of the family in a society of free men and free institutions.' —https://www.oas.org/dil/The_Constitution_of_Barbados.pdf	the Constitution that established death penalty. Both IACtHR judgements against Barbados refer to this situation and call on the state to pass legislation changing the Constitution's provision on death penalty. Yet, from the IACtHR's order monitoring compliance with the *Boyce et al v Barbados* judgment, the new legislation seems to have been more in response to a Caribbean Court of Justice decision than the 2007 and 2009 IACtHR judgements. Yet, the Explanatory Memorandum of the *Offences Against the Person (Amendment) Act, 2018* acknowledges the role of the IACtHR judgment on *Tyrone DaCosta Cadagan v Barbados* in the change of legislation:	*Barbados* and *Dacosta Cadogan v Barbados* judgments and whether Barbados had already accepted the need to abolish death penalty following the two judgments. —http://www.ccj.org/wp-content/uploads/2021/02/2018-CCJ-19-AJ-1.pdf	

Latin American state practice and primary sources in enforcing Inter-American Court judgments (*cont.*)

Country	Branch of government that does implementation	Basic constitutional provisions on international law and IHRL	Specific legislation/decrees/ regulations on IACtHR and domestic law	Judicial cases on implementation of IACtHR judgments	Differences between provisional measures and full judgment on the merits
			'Section 2A (1) (a) seeks to address persons who have already been sentenced under the current Offences Against the Persons Act, Cap. 141. The persons who were sentenced already must be re-sentenced because the original sentences have been deemed to be unconstitutional by the Inter-American Court of Human Rights in Case 12.645: *Tyrone Dacosta Cadagon v. Barbados*.'[ab] IACtHR's Order monitoring compliance: https://www.corteidh.or.cr/docs/supervisiones/boyce_09_03_20_ing.pdf [8-] Domestic Acts: 2018 (with Explanatory		

ab Explanatory Memorandum of the Offences Against the Person (Amendment) Act, 2018, iii.

Latin American state practice and primary sources in enforcing Inter-American Court judgments (*cont.*)

Country	Branch of government that does implementation	Basic constitutional provisions on international law and IHRL	Specific legislation/decrees/ regulations on IACtHR and domestic law	Judicial cases on implementation of IACtHR judgments	Differences between provisional measures and full judgment on the merits
			Memorandum) – https://www.barbadosparliament.com/uploads/bill_resolution/194e20f4c24596f073bf72414faae7d5.pdf 2019 – https://www.barbadosparliament.com/uploads/bill_resolution/d61fd3e167b37b6bc6b734fd4d3af2df.pdf		
El Salvador	Independent organ – 'Office of Procurator for the Protection of Human Rights'[ac] is the organ responsible for safeguarding human	Constitución de la República de El Salvador, 1983, Arts. 144, 194(4). 'Art. 144.- Los tratados internacionales celebrados por El	Ley de la Procuraduria para la Defensa de los Derechos Humanos, Decreto Legislativo Nº 183, 20 de febrero de 1992, Arts. 11(2, 4), 12(5–6), 30. 'Artículo 11.- Son atribuciones del Procurador: […] 2°) Investigar, de oficio o por	Sala de lo Constitucional de la Corte Suprema de Justicia, 142-2015Ac, Habeas Corpus – Brief reference to the IACtHR regarding the states' duty to	No information found.

ac 'Procuraduria para la Defensa de los Derechos Humanos.'

Latin American state practice and primary sources in enforcing Inter-American Court judgments (*cont.*)

Country	Branch of government that does implementation	Basic constitutional provisions on international law and IHRL	Specific legislation/decrees/ regulations on IACtHR and domestic law	Judicial cases on implementation of IACtHR judgments	Differences between provisional measures and full judgment on the merits
	rights domestically, but in its organic law there is no reference to enforcement of decisions by international human rights bodies. See IACtHR, 'El Salvador: Caso Masacres de El Mozote y lugares aledaños Vs. El Salvador. Solicitud de Medidas Provisionales y Supervisión de Cumplimiento de Sentencia' – footnote 11 – seems to confirm the role of the Procurator in	Salvador con otros Estados o con organismos internacionales, constituyen leyes de la República al entrar en vigencia, conforme a las disposiciones del mismo tratado y de esta Constitución.' 'Art. 194.- el procurador para la defensa de los derechos humanos y el procurador general de la republica, tendran las siguientes funciones: [...] 4º- promover recursos judiciales o	denuncia que hubiere recibido, casos de violaciones a los Derechos Humanos; [...] 4º) Promover recursos judiciales o administrativos para la protección de los Derechos Humanos; [...]' 'Artículo 12.- Además de las atribuciones contempladas en el artículo anterior, el Procurador tendrá las siguientes: 5º) Promover la firma, ratificación o adhesión a tratados internacionales sobre derechos humanos; 6º) Emitir resoluciones de censura pública contra los responsables materiales o intelectuales de violaciones a los derechos humanos;' '8º) Crear, fomentar y desarrollar nexos de comunicación y cooperación con organismos de	investigate cases of violation of the human rights of the American Convention on Human Rights. —https://tinyurl.com/mcd7u4a3 Cámara de lo Penal de la Primera Sección de Occidente, 99-2020, 13 Mayo 2020 – Discusses the prevalence of the IACtHR's jurisprudence over domestic jurisprudence; does not refer to any case against El Salvador. —https://tinyurl.com/2rravfpf Sala de lo Constitucional de la Corte Suprema de Justicia, 119-2016, 06	

Latin American state practice and primary sources in enforcing Inter-American Court judgments (*cont.*)

Country	Branch of government that does implementation	Basic constitutional provisions on international law and IHRL	Specific legislation/decrees/ regulations on IACtHR and domestic law	Judicial cases on implementation of IACtHR judgments	Differences between provisional measures and full judgment on the merits
	implementing IACtHR decisions – https://www.refworld.org.es/publisher, iacrthr,, slv,5d9cd6fa4,0.html	administrativos para la protección de los derechos humanos.'	promoción y defensa de los derechos humanos, gubernamentales, intergubernamentales y no gubernamentales, tanto nacionales como internacionales y con los diversos sectores de la vida nacional;' 'Artículo 30.- Al reunirse suficientes elementos y considerar establecida la violación a los derechos humanos; la Procuraduría preparará un informe, en el que se expondrán los hechos, sus conclusiones y además: 1º) Promoverá el cese inmediato de la violación y la restitución de los derechos violados, si fuese posible e interpondrá los recursos	diciembre 2017 – explores the IACtHR's jurisprudence on forced disappearances and its importance domestically. —https://tinyurl.com/3zcc5vyp On the same topic, see also: Sala de lo Constitucional de la Corte Suprema de Justicia, 145-2015, 23/01/2017. https://tinyurl.com/2wwh8bxr Sala de lo Constitucional de la Corte Suprema de Justicia, 197-2007 – 26/06/2009 – briefly addresses the Human Rights General Attorney's efforts in	

Latin American state practice and primary sources in enforcing Inter-American Court judgments (*cont.*)

Country	Branch of government that does implementation	Basic constitutional provisions on international law and IHRL	Specific legislation/decrees/ regulations on IACtHR and domestic law	Judicial cases on implementation of IACtHR judgments	Differences between provisional measures and full judgment on the merits
			judiciales y administrativos pertinentes; 2º) Si lo considera conveniente, hará las recomendaciones pertinentes para cambiar las prácticas o reformar las políticas, leyes, reglamentos o disposiciones normativas que propicien la violación; 3º) Podrá solicitar la aplicación del debido procedimiento legal respectivo contra el responsable, inclusive su destitución o la imposición de cualquier otra sanción prevista en otras leyes y reglamentos; 4º) Recomendará la indemnización a la víctima y si ésta hubiese muerto a sus familiares; y 5º) Adoptará cualquier otra medida que considere necesaria	implementing the IACtHR's decision on the case of *Hermanas Serrano Cruz*. —https://tinyurl.com/paxszp6s Sala de lo Constitucional de la Corte Suprema de Justicia, 44–2013/145–2013 – refers to the Court's jurisprudence on amnesty. —https://tinyurl.com/35m97ez6	

Latin American state practice and primary sources in enforcing Inter-American Court judgments (*cont.*)

Country	Branch of government that does implementation	Basic constitutional provisions on international law and IHRL	Specific legislation/decrees/regulations on IACtHR and domestic law	Judicial cases on implementation of IACtHR judgments	Differences between provisional measures and full judgment on the merits
			para el cumplimiento de sus atribuciones y la garantía de los derechos humanos en general.' https://www.refworld.org/docid/3e5100074.html Informe de Labores de la Procuradora para la Defensa de los Derechos Humanos 2016–2017 – document indicates actions taken by the Office of Procurator for the Protection of Human Rights in implementing or assisting in the implementation of the IACtHR's decisions (pp. 35 (1.2.14), 38 (1.4.5)). https://www.pddh.gob.sv/portal/wp-content/uploads/2018/02/memoria-de-labores-2016-2017.pdf		
Guatemala	Seemingly Legislative-led; lack of clarity – The	Constitución Política de la República de	Decreto Numero 54–86, Ley de la Comisión de Derechos Humanos del Congreso de la República de	Corte de Constitucionalidad, en Calidad de Tribunal	No information found in legislation or case

Latin American state practice and primary sources in enforcing Inter-American Court judgments (*cont.*)

Country	Branch of government that does implementation	Basic constitutional provisions on international law and IHRL	Specific legislation/decrees/ regulations on IACtHR and domestic law	Judicial cases on implementation of IACtHR judgments	Differences between provisional measures and full judgment on the merits
	Congress's Commission of Human Rights and the 'Human Rights Ombudsman'[ad] seem to be, at least formally, responsible for the implementation of IACtHR's decisions.	Guatemala (1985 con reformas de 1993), Arts. 46, 171 (k), 274. 'ARTICULO 46. Preeminencia del Derecho Internacional. Se establece el principio general de que en materia de derechos humanos, los tratados y convenciones aceptados y ratificados por Guatemala, tienen preeminencia sobre el derecho interno.'	Guatemala y del Procurador de los Derechos Humanos, Arts. 4, 13–14. 'ARTICULO 4. Reformado por el Artículo 1 del Decreto Número 32–87 del Congreso de la República, publicado en el Diario de Centro América el 16 de junio de 1987. Atribuciones: Son atribuciones de la Comisión [de los Derechos Humanos]:' 'f. Formular recomendaciones a los Organismos del Estado para que adopten medidas en favor de los derechos humanos y solicitarles los informes respectivos.	Extraordinario de Amparo, Expediente 548-2010 – refers to case *Bámaca Velásquez v Guatemala*, and questions the self-execution of IACtHR judgments domestically. —http://138.94.255.164/Sentencias/814343.548-2010.pdf Corte Suprema de Justicia, Cámara Penal, Casación No. 6-2009, Sentencia del 22/07/2010 – relies on *Raxcacó Reyes v. Guatemala*, not about its	law expressly differentiating both.

ad 'Procurador de los Derechos Humanos.'

Latin American state practice and primary sources in enforcing Inter-American Court judgments (*cont.*)

Country	Branch of government that does implementation	Basic constitutional provisions on international law and IHRL	Specific legislation/decrees/ regulations on IACtHR and domestic law	Judicial cases on implementation of IACtHR judgments	Differences between provisional measures and full judgment on the merits
		'ARTICULO 171. Otras atribuciones del Congreso. Corresponde también al Congreso: […] k. Decretar, a solicitud del Organismo Ejecutivo, reparaciones o indemnizaciones en caso de reclamación internacional, cuando no se haya recurrido a arbitraje o a juicio internacional;' 'ARTICULO 274. Procurador de los Derechos Humanos. El procurador de los	g. Mantener comunicación constante con los Organismos Nacionales o Internacionales de Defensa de los Derechos Humanos para consulta e intercambio de información. […] i. Recibir y trasladar al Procurador de los Derechos Humanos las comunicaciones y quejas provenientes del exterior del país, que dirijan personas o instituciones al Congreso de la República, denunciando violaciones de los Derechos Humanos en Guatemala. j. Examinar las comunicaciones y quejas provenientes del exterior del país, que dirijan personas o instituciones al Congreso de la República, denunciando violaciones de los Derechos Humanos en Guatemala.'	implementation but more generally about the enforceability of IACtHR's decisions in Guatemala.	

Latin American state practice and primary sources in enforcing Inter-American Court judgments (*cont.*)

Country	Branch of government that does implementation	Basic constitutional provisions on international law and IHRL	Specific legislation/decrees/regulations on IACtHR and domestic law	Judicial cases on implementation of IACtHR judgments	Differences between provisional measures and full judgment on the merits
		Derechos Humanos es un comisionado del Congreso de la República para la defensa de los Derechos Humanos que la Constitución garantiza. Tendrá facultades de supervisar la administración; ejercerá su cargo por un período de cinco años, y rendirá informe anual al pleno del Congreso, con el que se relacionará a través de la Comisión de Derechos Humanos.'	ARTICULO 13. 'Reformado por el Artículo 5 del Decreto Número 32–87 del Congreso de la República, publicado en el Diario de Centro América el 16 de junio de 1987. Atribuciones. Son atribuciones esenciales del Procurador: a. Promover el buen funcionamiento y la agilización de la gestión administrativa gubernamental, en materia de Derechos Humanos; […] c. Investigar toda clase de denuncias que le sean planteadas por cualquier persona, sobre violaciones a los Derechos Humanos; […] f. Promover acciones o recursos, judiciales o administrativos, en los casos en que sea procedente;' 'ARTICULO 14. Reformado por el Artículo 6 del Decreto Número		

Latin American state practice and primary sources in enforcing Inter-American Court judgments (*cont.*)

Country	Branch of government that does implementation	Basic constitutional provisions on international law and IHRL	Specific legislation/decrees/ regulations on IACtHR and domestic law	Judicial cases on implementation of IACtHR judgments	Differences between provisional measures and full judgment on the merits
			32–87 del Congreso de la República, publicado en el Diario de Centro América el 16 de junio de 1987. Otras atribuciones. Corresponde también al Procurador: [...] g. Iniciar de oficio las investigaciones que considere necesarias en los casos que tenga conocimiento sobre violaciones de los Derechos Humanos; h. Investigar en cualquier local o instalación, sobre indicios racionales que constituyan violación sobre cualesquiera de los Derechos Humanos, previa orden de juez competente. La inspección no requiere la notificación previa a los funcionarios o encargados de quien, directa o indirectamente, dependen los locales o instalaciones; [...] j. Emitir resolución de censura		

Latin American state practice and primary sources in enforcing Inter-American Court judgments (*cont.*)

Country	Branch of government that does implementation	Basic constitutional provisions on international law and IHRL	Specific legislation/decrees/regulations on IACtHR and domestic law	Judicial cases on implementation of IACtHR judgments	Differences between provisional measures and full judgment on the merits
			pública en contra de los responsables materiales y/o intelectuales de la violación de los Derechos Humanos, cuando el resultado de la investigación arribe a esa conclusión;' – https://www.pdh.org.gt/files/Ley_Procurador_Derechos%20Humanos.pdf Decreto del Congreso N° 512, 1948, Ley Organica del Ministerio Público. 'CAPITULO II – DE LA PROCURADURIA [...] ARTICULO 13. El ejercicio de la personería de la Nación comprende las siguientes funciones: 1. Representar y sostener los derechos de Nación en todos los juicios en que fuere parte, de acuerdo con las instrucciones del		

Latin American state practice and primary sources in enforcing Inter-American Court judgments (*cont.*)

Country	Branch of government that does implementation	Basic constitutional provisions on international law and IHRL	Specific legislation/decrees/regulations on IACtHR and domestic law	Judicial cases on implementation of IACtHR judgments	Differences between provisional measures and full judgment on the merits
			Ejecutivo, y promover la oportuna ejecución de las sentencias que se dicten en ellos; 2. Intervenir, si así lo dispusiere el Ejecutivo y conforme a las instrucciones de éste, en los negocios en que estuviere interesada la Nación, formalizar los actos y suscribir los contratos que sean necesarios a tal fin; y 3. Cumplir los deberes que, en relación con esta materia, señalen otras leyes al Ministerio Público o al Procurador General de la Nación.'		
Uruguay	Autonomous Organ (within Legislative) – The National Human Rights Institute seems to be in charge of	Constitución de la Republica, 1967, Arts. 6, 239. 'Artículo 6º.- En los tratados internacionales que celebre la República	Ley Nº 18446, 2008, Creación Institución Nacional de Derechos Humanos (INDDHH), Arts. 1–4. 'Artículo 1 (Creación).- Créase la Institución Nacional de Derechos Humanos y Defensoría del Pueblo,	Supreme Court of Justice, Judgment 506/2013 – addresses the unconstitutionality of provisions that enable the prosecution of	Case law and legislation make no distinction.

Latin American state practice and primary sources in enforcing Inter-American Court judgments (*cont.*)

Country	Branch of government that does implementation	Basic constitutional provisions on international law and IHRL	Specific legislation/decrees/ regulations on IACtHR and domestic law	Judicial cases on implementation of IACtHR judgments	Differences between provisional measures and full judgment on the merits
	promoting the adoption of measures to implement IACtHR decisions, although Law No. 18446 does not expressly say so. The Executive may also have a role to play working with the Institute. Legislative – Several laws were passed by Congress in efforts to implement IACtHR decisions.	propondrá la cláusula de que todas las diferencias que surjan entre las partes contratantes, serán decididas por el arbitraje u otros medios pacíficos. La República procurará la integración social y económica de los Estados Latinoamericanos, especialmente en lo que se refiere a la defensa común de sus productos y materias primas. Asimismo, propenderá a la efectiva complementación	como una institución del Poder Legislativo, la que tendrá por cometido, en el ámbito de competencias definido por esta ley, la defensa, promoción y protección en toda su extensión, de los derechos humanos reconocidos por la Constitución de la República y el Derecho Internacional. Artículo 2 (Autonomía).- La INDDHH no se hallará sujeta a jerarquía y tendrá un funcionamiento autónomo no pudiendo recibir instrucciones ni órdenes de ninguna autoridad. Artículo 3 (Efectos de las resoluciones).- Las resoluciones de la INDDHH tendrán el carácter de recomendaciones y, consecuentemente, no podrán modificar ni anular actos	perpetrators from the dictatorship and goes against the IACtHR decision in *Gelman v Uruguay*; 'En relación a las disposiciones internacionales los Sres. Ministros que integran la mayoría expresan, que no existe un deber de Derecho Internacional de seguir la jurisprudencia de los órganos del sistema interamericano. La intérprete última de la Convención Americana de Derechos Humanos es la Corte Interamericana de Derechos Humanos y la	

Latin American state practice and primary sources in enforcing Inter-American Court judgments (*cont.*)

Country	Branch of government that does implementation	Basic constitutional provisions on international law and IHRL	Specific legislation/decrees/ regulations on IACtHR and domestic law	Judicial cases on implementation of IACtHR judgments	Differences between provisional measures and full judgment on the merits
		de sus servicios públicos.' 'Artículo 239.- A la Suprema Corte de Justicia corresponde: 1º) Juzgar a todos los infractores de la Constitución, sin excepción alguna; sobre delitos contra Derecho de Gentes y causas de Almirantazgo; en las cuestiones relativas a tratados, pactos y convenciones con otros Estados; conocer en las causas de los diplomáticos acreditados en la	administrativos o jurisdiccionales. Artículo 4 (Competencia).- La INDDHH será competente para: A) Proponer la suscripción, aprobación, ratificación, adhesión e implementación de tratados internacionales relacionados con derechos humanos. [...] C) Promover la adopción de las medidas que considere adecuadas para que el ordenamiento jurídico y las prácticas administrativas e institucionales se armonicen con los instrumentos internacionales relacionados con derechos humanos en los que el Estado sea parte. D) Emitir opiniones y recomendaciones sobre los informes que el Estado se proponga presentar o que hubiere presentado a los órganos	intérprete última de la Constitución es la Suprema Corte de Justicia.' —https://justis.vlex.com/#vid/578162522 Supreme Court of Justice, Judgment 4.492/2011 – refers to *Gelman v Uruguay* and addresses the Supreme Court's lack of competence to implement the IACtHR decision in *Gelman*, according to art. 239 of the Constitution. —http://bjn.poderjudicial.gub.uy/BJNPUBLICA/hojaInsumo2.seam?cid=124898 Supreme Court of Justice, Judgment 899/	

Latin American state practice and primary sources in enforcing Inter-American Court judgments (*cont.*)

Country	Branch of government that does implementation	Basic constitutional provisions on international law and IHRL	Specific legislation/decrees/ regulations on IACtHR and domestic law	Judicial cases on implementation of IACtHR judgments	Differences between provisional measures and full judgment on the merits
		República, en los casos previstos por el Derecho Internacional.'	encargados del contralor internacional de las obligaciones contraídas por el Estado, en virtud de tratados internacionales relacionados con derechos humanos y sobre las observaciones que dichos órganos internacionales de contralor hubieran emitido respecto de los informes del Estado. […] M) Cooperar, para la promoción y protección de los derechos humanos, con los órganos internacionales encargados del contralor internacional de las obligaciones contraídas por el Estado, con instituciones u organizaciones internacionales regionales o instituciones nacionales, que sean competentes en la promoción y protección de los derechos	2012 – discusses the applicability of the IACtHR decision on *Gelman v Uruguay* in the case at hand, considering the state's position before the Court: 'Asimismo, cabe agregar que, con relación a la incidencia de la citada sentencia de la Corte Interamericana de Derechos Humanos ('caso XX'), este Colegiado coincide con el Sr. Fiscal de Corte en punto a que es preciso destacar que el procedimiento ante la Corte Interamericana no debe confundirse	

Latin American state practice and primary sources in enforcing Inter-American Court judgments (*cont.*)

Country	Branch of government that does implementation	Basic constitutional provisions on international law and IHRL	Specific legislation/decrees/ regulations on IACtHR and domestic law	Judicial cases on implementation of IACtHR judgments	Differences between provisional measures and full judgment on the merits
			humanos.' —https://www.impo.com.uy/bases/leyes/18446-2008 Ley 19.149 (2013) – Aprobacion de Rendicion de Cuentas y Balance De Ejecucion Presupuestal – Ejercicio 2012: 'Artículo 165 Encomiéndase al Ministerio de Relaciones Exteriores, a través del Instituto Artigas del Servicio Exterior, la creación de un programa permanente de formación en materia de Derechos Humanos, para dar cumplimiento a la sentencia de la Corte Interamericana de Derechos Humanos.' —https://legislativo.parlamento.gub.uy/temporales/leytemp3255129.htm Ley Nº 19.085 – Barbani Duarte y Otros Versus Uruguay, 2013. 'Artículo único.- Autorízase al Poder Ejecutivo a crear una	con un proceso penal internacional, ya que los Estados no comparecen ante ella como sujetos pasivos de la acción penal y, además, porque el proceso no tiene por objeto imponer penas a personas responsables de violaciones a los derechos humanos, sino que se endereza a amparar a las víctimas y a disponer la reparación de los daños causados (fs. 2.379 vto.).' —http://bjn.poderjudicial.gub.uy/BJNPUBLICA/hojaInsumo2.seam?cid=124898	

Latin American state practice and primary sources in enforcing Inter-American Court judgments (*cont.*)

Country	Branch of government that does implementation	Basic constitutional provisions on international law and IHRL	Specific legislation/decrees/ regulations on IACtHR and domestic law	Judicial cases on implementation of IACtHR judgments	Differences between provisional measures and full judgment on the merits
			Comisión de tres miembros a los únicos efectos de recibir e instruir las peticiones que pudiesen presentarse al amparo del numeral segundo de la Sentencia definitiva dictada por la Corte Interamericana de Derechos Humanos en el caso 12.587 'Barbani Duarte y otros versus Uruguay', así como a asesorar al Poder Ejecutivo en relación a la decisión a tomar con respecto a cada una de esas peticiones, en el marco de lo dispuesto por el artículo 31 de la Ley Nº 17.613, de 27 de diciembre de 2002. […] La Comisión, al analizar cada caso, y el Poder Ejecutivo, al resolverlo, tendrá las más amplias facultades para analizar si se verificaron los requisitos establecidos en el artículo 31 de la Ley Nº 17.613, de		

Latin American state practice and primary sources in enforcing Inter-American Court judgments (*cont.*)

Country	Branch of government that does implementation	Basic constitutional provisions on international law and IHRL	Specific legislation/decrees/ regulations on IACtHR and domestic law	Judicial cases on implementation of IACtHR judgments	Differences between provisional measures and full judgment on the merits
			27 de diciembre de 2002, a la luz de los criterios de valoración de la prueba dispuestos por la normativa vigente y los establecidos en la Sentencia referida en el inciso primero del presente artículo.' —https://legislativo.parlamento.gub.uy/temporales/leytemp6224104.htm Ley Nº 17.613, 2002, Fortalecimiento del Sistema Bancario Intermediación Financiera, Protección del Ahorro Bancario y Subsidio por Desempleo para Afiliados a la Caja De Jubilaciones y Pensiones Bancarias, Art. 31. 'Artículo 31.- Facúltase al Banco Central del Uruguay a otorgar a los ahorristas de los Bancos de Montevideo y La Caja Obrera, cuyos depósitos hayan sido		

Latin American state practice and primary sources in enforcing Inter-American Court judgments (*cont.*)

Country	Branch of government that does implementation	Basic constitutional provisions on international law and IHRL	Specific legislation/decrees/ regulations on IACtHR and domestic law	Judicial cases on implementation of IACtHR judgments	Differences between provisional measures and full judgment on the merits
			transferidos a otras instituciones sin mediar su consentimiento, los mismos derechos que correspondan a los demás ahorristas de dichos Bancos. A dichos efectos y por acto fundado, el Banco Central del Uruguay conformará una Comisión que se expedirá en un plazo máximo prorrogable de 60 (sesenta) días.' —https://www.impo.com.uy/bases/leyes/17613-2002 Resolución N° 450/011, 2011, Creacion de Comision Interministerial Tendiente a Esclarecer el Destino de los Desaparecidos Entre los Años 1973 y 1985. 'VISTO: la sentencia dictada por la Corte Interamericana de Derechos Humanos de fecha 24 de febrero		

Latin American state practice and primary sources in enforcing Inter-American Court judgments (*cont.*)

Country	Branch of government that does implementation	Basic constitutional provisions on international law and IHRL	Specific legislation/decrees/ regulations on IACtHR and domestic law	Judicial cases on implementation of IACtHR judgments	Differences between provisional measures and full judgment on the merits
			de de 2011, caso 'Gelman vs. Uruguay'; RESULTANDO: I) que en el numeral 274 de dicha sentencia se valora la medida ofrecida por el Estado Uruguayo para crear una Comisión Interministerial que se encargue de dar impulso a las investigaciones tendientes a esclarecer el destino de los desaparecidos entre los años 1973 y 1985 señalándose las características de composición y modo de actuación de la misma; [...] ATENTO: a lo dispuesto por la sentencia de la Corte Interamericana de Derechos Humanos de fecha 24 de febrero de 2011, la Declaración Universal de los Derechos Humanos, el Pacto Internacional de Derechos Civiles y		

Latin American state practice and primary sources in enforcing Inter-American Court judgments (*cont.*)

Country	Branch of government that does implementation	Basic constitutional provisions on international law and IHRL	Specific legislation/decrees/ regulations on IACtHR and domestic law	Judicial cases on implementation of IACtHR judgments	Differences between provisional measures and full judgment on the merits
			Políticos, la Convención sobre los Derechos del Niño, la Convención Internacional para la Protección de todas las Personas contra las Desapariciones Forzadas, el Estatuto de la Corte Penal Internacional, la Convención Interamericana de Derechos Humanos, la Convención Interamericana sobre Desaparición Forzada de Personas y demás normas referidas en esta resolución;' 'EL PRESIDENTE DE LA REPÚBLICA actuando en Consejo de Ministros RESUELVE: 1 Créase una Comisión Interministerial que dependerá directamente de la Presidencia de la República a través de la Secretaría de la Presidencia de la República que la presidirá,		

Latin American state practice and primary sources in enforcing Inter-American Court judgments (*cont.*)

Country	Branch of government that does implementation	Basic constitutional provisions on international law and IHRL	Specific legislation/decrees/ regulations on IACtHR and domestic law	Judicial cases on implementation of IACtHR judgments	Differences between provisional measures and full judgment on the merits
			integrada por los titulares de los Ministerios de Educación y Cultura, Relaciones Exteriores, Defensa Nacional e Interior, además de la Coordinadora Ejecutiva de la Secretaría de Seguimiento de la Comisión para la Paz. [...] 2 Serán cometidos de dicha Comisión Interministerial: a) supervisar elcumplimiento por parte del Estado de la sentencia de la Corte Interamericana referida en el 'Visto'; b) (*); c) coordinar con los diferentes organismos nacionales e internacionales a los efectos de dar cumplimiento a los cometidos anteriores; y d) (*)'. https://www.impo.com.uy/bases/resoluciones/450-2011 Ley N° 19.307, 2014, Ley de Medios;		

Latin American state practice and primary sources in enforcing Inter-American Court judgments (*cont.*)

Country	Branch of government that does implementation	Basic constitutional provisions on international law and IHRL	Specific legislation/decrees/ regulations on IACtHR and domestic law	Judicial cases on implementation of IACtHR judgments	Differences between provisional measures and full judgment on the merits
			Regulacion de la Prestacion de Servicios de Radio, Television y Otros Servicios de Comunicacion Audiovisual, Arts. 2, 5. 'Artículo 2 (Interpretación de la ley).- Constituyen principios rectores para la interpretación y aplicación de la presente ley las disposiciones consagradas en la Declaración Universal de Derechos Humanos, en la Convención Americana sobre Derechos Humanos y en el Pacto Internacional de Derechos Civiles y Políticos. Asimismo, se tomarán en cuenta muy especialmente los criterios recogidos en las sentencias y opiniones consultivas de la Corte Interamericana de Derechos Humanos y en las resoluciones e informes de la Comisión		

Latin American state practice and primary sources in enforcing Inter-American Court judgments (*cont.*)

Country	Branch of government that does implementation	Basic constitutional provisions on international law and IHRL	Specific legislation/decrees/regulations on IACtHR and domestic law	Judicial cases on implementation of IACtHR judgments	Differences between provisional measures and full judgment on the merits
			Interamericana de Derechos Humanos, siempre que ello no implique disminuir los estándares de protección establecidos en la Constitución de la República, en la legislación nacional o reconocidos por la jurisprudencia nacional.' 'Artículo 5 – [...]Les son aplicables la Constitución de la República, los instrumentos internacionales referidos tanto a la protección y promoción de la libertad de expresión y de la diversidad de expresiones culturales tales como la Convención sobre la Protección y Promoción de la Diversidad de las Expresiones Culturales de la Unesco, así como los emanados de los organismos del Sistema Interamericano de Derechos Humanos, entre otros.' —https://		

Latin American state practice and primary sources in enforcing Inter-American Court judgments (*cont.*)

Country	Branch of government that does implementation	Basic constitutional provisions on international law and IHRL	Specific legislation/decrees/ regulations on IACtHR and domestic law	Judicial cases on implementation of IACtHR judgments	Differences between provisional measures and full judgment on the merits
			www.impo.com.uy/bases/leyes/19307-2014 Ley No. 19.822, 2019, Cometese al Instituto Nacional de Derechos Humanos y Defensoria del Pueblo la Busqueda de las Personas Detenidas y Desaparecidas, Art. 14. 'Artículo 14 Cométese al Ministerio de Educación y Cultura a través de la Dirección de Asuntos Constitucionales, Legales y Registrales el seguimiento del estado de cumplimiento de las sentencias pasadas en autoridad de cosa juzgada, de carácter nacional o internacional, así como de las recomendaciones dictadas por los organismos de supervisión en la materia, así como del estado de situación de causas, juicios y denuncias a nivel nacional, sin		

Latin American state practice and primary sources in enforcing Inter-American Court judgments (*cont.*)

Country	Branch of government that does implementation	Basic constitutional provisions on international law and IHRL	Specific legislation/decrees/ regulations on IACtHR and domestic law	Judicial cases on implementation of IACtHR judgments	Differences between provisional measures and full judgment on the merits
			perjuicio de los cometidos de la INDDHH y de la Fiscalía Especializada en Crímenes de Lesa Humanidad.' —https://www.impo.com.uy/bases/leyes/19822-2019		

Index

www.ingramcontent.com/pod-product-compliance
Lightning Source LLC
Chambersburg PA
CBHW031322230926
51848CB00001B/50
* 9 7 8 9 0 0 4 7 3 8 0 6 5 *